MW00426935

FINANCIAL ECONOMICS OF INSURANCE

Financial Economics
of Insurance

RALPH S. J. KOIJEN
MOTOHIRO YOGO

PRINCETON UNIVERSITY PRESS
PRINCETON & OXFORD

Published by Princeton University Press
41 William Street, Princeton, New Jersey 08540
99 Banbury Road, Oxford OX2 6JX

press.princeton.edu

All Rights Reserved
ISBN 978-0-691-19326-7
ISBN (e-book) 978-0-691-24597-3

British Library Cataloging-in-Publication Data is available

Editorial: Joe Jackson and Whitney Rauenhorst
Production Editorial: Jenny Wolkowicki
Jacket design: Karl Spurzem
Production: Lauren Reese
Publicity: Kate Hensley and Charlotte Coyne
Copyeditor: Bhisham Bherwani

Jacket images: matsabe / Shutterstock

This book has been composed in Arno Pro

10 9 8 7 6 5 4 3 2 1

CONTENTS

Preface   xv

1	Introduction to Modern Insurance	1
1.1	*Overview of the Insurance Sector*	1
	1.1.1 Liabilities	2
	1.1.2 Assets	4
	1.1.3 Leverage	5
	1.1.4 Ownership Structure	7
1.2	*Insurance Products*	9
	1.2.1 Life Insurance	10
	1.2.2 Fixed Annuities	10
	1.2.3 Variable Annuities	11
1.3	*Insurance Data*	14
	1.3.1 Financial Statements	14
	1.3.2 Insurance Prices	17
1.4	*Institutional Background*	19
	1.4.1 State Guaranty Associations	19
	1.4.2 Risk-Based Capital Regulation	20
	1.4.3 Accounting Standards	21
1.5	*A Baseline Model of Insurance Pricing*	25
	1.5.1 Insurance Market	25
	1.5.2 Balance Sheet Dynamics	25
	1.5.3 Financial Frictions	26

	1.5.4	Optimal Pricing	27
	1.5.5	Empirical Implications	28
2	**Risks in the Insurance Sector**		**30**
2.1	*Variable Annuities*		31
2.2	*Derivatives*		33
2.3	*Evidence on Risk Mismatch*		34
	2.3.1	Interest Risk Mismatch	34
	2.3.2	SRISK	37
	2.3.3	Stock Returns during the COVID-19 Crisis	38
2.4	*Shadow Insurance*		38
	2.4.1	A Case Study of MetLife	40
	2.4.2	Aggregate Facts	42
2.5	*Securities Lending*		45
2.6	*Potential Transmission Mechanisms*		47
	2.6.1	Corporate Bond Market	48
	2.6.2	Households	49
	2.6.3	Firms	49
	2.6.4	Banks	49
3	**Insurance Pricing**		**51**
3.1	*Annuity and Life Insurance Prices*		52
	3.1.1	Summary Statistics	52
	3.1.2	Pricing during the Global Financial Crisis	54
	3.1.3	Evidence against Default Risk	57
3.2	*Statutory Reserve Regulation*		59
	3.2.1	Term Annuities	61
	3.2.2	Life Annuities	62
	3.2.3	Life Insurance	64
3.3	*Insurance Pricing Model*		65
	3.3.1	Insurance Market	65
	3.3.2	Balance Sheet Dynamics	66

	3.3.3	Financial Frictions	66
	3.3.4	Optimal Pricing	67
	3.3.5	Empirical Implications	68
3.4		*Estimating the Insurance Pricing Model*	69
	3.4.1	Empirical Specification	69
	3.4.2	Identifying Assumptions	70
	3.4.3	Marginal Cost of Capital	71
3.5		*Evidence for Financial Frictions*	76
	3.5.1	Frictions in External Capital Markets	76
	3.5.2	Frictions in Internal Capital Markets	77
4		**Modeling Supply and Demand**	**81**
4.1		*Aggregate Facts about the Variable Annuity Market*	82
4.2		*A Model of Variable Annuity Supply*	86
	4.2.1	Variable Annuity Market	86
	4.2.2	Balance Sheet Dynamics	88
	4.2.3	Financial Frictions	90
	4.2.4	Optimal Fee and Rollup Rate	90
	4.2.5	Evidence from the Cross Section of Insurers	93
4.3		*Estimating Variable Annuity Demand*	94
	4.3.1	A Model of Variable Annuity Demand	96
	4.3.2	Identifying Assumptions	98
	4.3.3	Estimation Methodology	99
	4.3.4	Estimated Model of Variable Annuity Demand	100
	4.3.5	Consumer Surplus	103
4.4		*Estimating Variable Annuity Supply*	103
	4.4.1	Empirical Specification	103
	4.4.2	Estimation Methodology	107
	4.4.3	Estimated Model of Variable Annuity Supply	108

5   Reinsurance   114

  5.1 Risk of Shadow Insurance   115

       5.1.1 Relation between Ratings and Shadow Insurance   115

       5.1.2 Estimating Risk   117

       5.1.3 Estimating Expected Loss   120

  5.2 A Model of Insurance Pricing and Reinsurance   121

       5.2.1 Insurance Holding Company   122

       5.2.2 Balance Sheet Dynamics   122

       5.2.3 Financial Frictions   124

       5.2.4 Optimal Pricing and Reinsurance   124

       5.2.5 Holding Company's Risk-Based Capital   126

  5.3 Modeling the Life Insurance Market   127

       5.3.1 A Model of Life Insurance Demand   127

       5.3.2 Empirical Specification for Marginal Cost   128

       5.3.3 Identifying Assumptions   129

       5.3.4 Estimated Model of the Life Insurance Market   130

       5.3.5 Retail Market in the Absence of Shadow Insurance   131

6   Portfolio Choice and Asset Pricing   133

  6.1 Insurers' Bond Portfolios   134

       6.1.1 Portfolio Composition   134

       6.1.2 Duration   137

       6.1.3 Credit Risk   139

  6.2 A Portfolio Puzzle for Insurers   140

  6.3 Asset Pricing with an Insurance Sector   141

       6.3.1 Financial Assets   142

       6.3.2 Insurers   143

       6.3.3 Portfolio-Choice Problem   144

       6.3.4 Optimal Portfolio Choice   146

       6.3.5 Asset Prices   147

       6.3.6 Insurers' Optimal Portfolio   149

6.4   *Empirical Implications*   150

  6.4.1   Demand for Low-Beta Assets   150

  6.4.2   Sensitivity to Risk-Based Capital   150

  6.4.3   Trend in Relative Credit Risk   152

6.5   *Potential Extensions*   153

  6.5.1   Interest Risk Mismatch   153

  6.5.2   Capital Structure   154

  6.5.3   Insurance Pricing   154

  6.5.4   Agency Problems   154

7   Research Topics and Policy Implications   155

7.1   *Research Topics*   155

  7.1.1   Insurance of New Risks   155

  7.1.2   Microfoundations of Insurance Demand   156

  7.1.3   Regulatory Gaps   157

  7.1.4   Political Economy of Insurance Regulation 157

  7.1.5   Optimal Insurance Regulation   158

7.2   *Policy Implications*   159

  7.2.1   Financial Disclosure   159

  7.2.2   Stress Tests   160

  7.2.3   Regulatory Oversight   160

A   Data Appendix   162

A.1   *Variables Based on the Financial Accounts
of the United States*   162

A.2   *Insurer Characteristics*   163

A.3   *Portfolio of US Life Insurers*   165

B   Optimality Conditions for a Multiproduct Insurer   166

Bibliography   169

Index   177

LIST OF FIGURES

1.1 Insurance and Pension Liabilities   3

1.2 Composition of Life Insurers' Liabilities   5

1.3 Composition of General Account Assets   6

1.4 Institutional Ownership of Corporate Bonds   6

1.5 Leverage of Financial Institutions   7

1.6 Life Insurers' Liabilities by Ownership Structure   8

1.7 Composition of Life Insurers' Liabilities by Ownership Structure   9

1.8 An Example of a Guaranteed Living Withdrawal Benefit   12

2.1 Impact of Derivatives on the Equity Growth Rate   35

2.2 Equity Drawdowns during the COVID-19 Crisis   39

2.3 Comparison of Equity Drawdowns across Crises   40

2.4 Reinsurance Ceded by Reinsurer Type   43

2.5 Life versus Annuity Reinsurance Ceded to Shadow Reinsurers   44

2.6 Capital Gain for Insurers with Securities Lending Agreements   48

3.1 Average Markup on Term Annuities   55

3.2 Average Markup on Life Annuities   56

3.3 Average Markup on Life Insurance   57

3.4 Relation between Price Changes and Balance Sheet Shocks   58

3.5 Discount Rates for Annuities and Life Insurance   62

3.6 Reserve to Actuarial Value for Annuities and Life Insurance   63

3.7 Marginal Cost of Capital   73

4.1 Variable Annuity Sales   83

4.2 Number of Insurers and Contracts with Minimum Return
Guarantees   84

4.3 Fees and Rollup Rates on Minimum Return Guarantees   85

4.4 Cross Section of Insurers during the Global Financial Crisis   95

4.5 Consumer Surplus from Variable Annuities   104

4.6 Interior versus Corner Solution for the Rollup Rate   105

4.7 Decomposition of Fees   111

4.8 Decomposition of Rollup Rates   112

6.1 Portfolio Composition   135

6.2 Corporate Bond Portfolio Composition   136

6.3 Average Duration of Bond Portfolios   138

6.4 Credit Risk of Bond Portfolios   139

LIST OF TABLES

1.1 Liabilities of Financial Institutions in 2017   2
1.2 Composition of Life Insurers' Liabilities in 2017   4
2.1 Summary of the Variable Annuity Market   31
2.2 Top Insurers by Variable Annuity Liabilities   32
2.3 Risk Exposure of Variable Annuity Insurers   36
2.4 SRISK of US Financial Institutions   37
2.5 Affiliated Reinsurance within MetLife   41
2.6 Top Insurers by Shadow Insurance   42
2.7 Equity of Iowa Captives   45
2.8 Top Insurers by Securities Lending Agreements   47
3.1 Summary of Annuity and Life Insurance Prices   53
3.2 Default Probabilities Implied by Term Annuities versus Credit
     Default Swaps   60
3.3 Estimated Insurance Pricing Model   72
3.4 Marginal Cost of Capital in November 2008   74
3.5 Recapitalization Activity by the Holding Companies   78
4.1 Estimated Model of Variable Annuity Demand   101
4.2 Estimated Model of Variable Annuity Supply   109
5.1 Relation between Ratings and Shadow Insurance   116
5.2 Risk Measures Adjusted for Shadow Insurance   119
5.3 Expected Loss Adjusted for Shadow Insurance   121
5.4 Estimated Model of the Life Insurance Market   131
A.1 Publicly Traded US Life Insurers   164

PREFACE

THE TRADITIONAL role of insurers is to insure idiosyncratic risk through products such as life annuities, life insurance, and health insurance. A large insurance literature has identified adverse selection and moral hazard as key frictions that affect insurance pricing, contract design, and market completeness. With the secular decline of private defined benefit plans and government pension plans around the world, insurers are increasingly taking on the role of insuring market risk through minimum return guarantees. In addition, insurers have started to use more complex capital management tools such as derivatives, off-balance-sheet reinsurance, and securities lending. Combined with the concentrated nature of the industry, the modern insurance sector calls for a new framework to understand the role of financial and regulatory frictions in imperfectly competitive markets.

In this book, we develop a unified framework to study the impact of financial and regulatory frictions on all decisions of insurers, including insurance pricing, contract design, reinsurance, portfolio choice, and risk management. We also apply empirical methods from industrial organization to model market power and estimate structural models to provide quantitative answers to questions. This book represents our understanding of the subject based on a decade of our own research and exciting contributions by other researchers. The intended audience is anyone interested in doing their own research on insurance. This book is at the level of graduate students in economics, finance, and insurance, who have completed their first-year coursework. Instructors could teach the material as part of a course on asset pricing, corporate finance, industrial organization, or public economics. The teaching slides are available at insurance.princeton.edu.

A secondary audience is researchers and policymakers at central banks and other policy institutions that regulate insurers. Chapters 1 and 2 provide a nontechnical overview of the modern insurance sector and its main sources of risk. The next four chapters provide policy-relevant descriptions of insurance pricing, variable annuities, shadow insurance, and portfolio choice. The first two sections of Chapter 3 describe the consequences of statutory reserve regulation for insurance pricing. The first section of Chapter 4 describes the consequences of risk-based capital regulation for the variable annuity market. The first section of Chapter 5 quantifies the potential risk of shadow insurance, which is a type of off-balance-sheet reinsurance that relaxes regulatory constraints. The first section of Chapter 6 summarizes important facts about insurers' bond portfolios in relation to risk-based capital regulation. Chapter 7 concludes with policy implications of the research presented in this book. Thus, large parts of this book are accessible and relevant to policymakers.

The pioneering work of Gron (1990), Froot (2007), and others has firmly established the view that financial frictions and market power are important for understanding property and casualty insurers. We have a similar view but focus on life insurers, which are a much larger part of the financial sector. The earlier literature shows that economic risk constraints are important for property and casualty insurers, which we also view as important for products such as variable annuities that insure tail risk. Our novel view of life insurers is that capital regulation and accounting rules are just as important and could interact with financial frictions to explain insurance pricing, contract design, reinsurance, portfolio choice, and risk management.

We focus on frictions on the supply side of insurance markets. We do not cover the large literature on informational frictions on the demand side that followed Rothschild and Stiglitz (1976), for which there are excellent surveys (Einav, Finkelstein, and Levin, 2010; Einav and Finkelstein, 2011; Dione, 2013). The limited scope of this book reflects our view that the research agenda on supply-side frictions is still emerging and not yet mainstream, while the research agenda on informational frictions is already successful across many insurance markets (e.g., health insurance, life annuities, and property and casualty insurance). Of course, a study of supply-side frictions still requires a model of insurance demand. Since our data are prices and market shares by contract or insurer, we model insurance demand as a differentiated product demand system, following a standard empirical strategy in industrial organization.

We take an empirically oriented approach. We typically start with aggregate facts about the insurance sector and highlight cross-sectional heterogeneity across insurers. We then develop a model that explains the evidence and estimate the model to quantify the relative importance of the various economic forces. The facts may become obsolete as the world changes. Nevertheless, we hope that this book will have more longevity than the facts as a systematic approach to understanding all functions of the insurance sector. The modeling and estimation techniques that we develop should also be relevant to the study of other types of regulated and leveraged financial institutions such as banks and pension funds.

OVERVIEW OF THE CHAPTERS

In Chapter 1, we provide an overview of the insurance sector in the context of financial markets and financial intermediation more broadly. We summarize data sources for research on insurance and the relevant institutional background. We also present a baseline model of insurance pricing with financial frictions and market power. The same model explains underwriting cycles in catastrophe insurance (Gron, 1994; Froot and O'Connell, 1999).

In Chapter 2, we describe the main sources of risk for life insurers, including variable annuities, derivatives, shadow insurance, and securities lending. We present evidence of risk mismatch based on life insurers' stock returns during the global financial crisis, the subsequent low interest rate environment, and the COVID-19 crisis. We discuss how these sources of risk could affect the stability of the insurance sector and could be transmitted to the rest of the economy through the corporate bond market, households, firms, and banks. This chapter primarily draws upon material from Koijen and Yogo (2017, 2022b).

In Chapter 3, we extend the insurance pricing model to multiple types of policies with different statutory reserve requirements. The model explains the extraordinary pricing of fixed annuities and life insurance during the global financial crisis. In the cross section of policies, the model predicts lower pricing for policies with looser statutory reserve requirements. In the cross section of insurers, the model predicts lower pricing for insurers that are more constrained. We identify the cost of financial frictions from the cross-sectional relation between pricing and statutory reserve requirements. This chapter primarily draws upon material from Koijen and Yogo (2015).

In Chapter 4, we extend the insurance pricing model to contract design with an application to the variable annuity market. Thus, we present a complete model of insurance markets in which financial frictions and market power are important determinants of pricing, contract characteristics, and the degree of market completeness. We model variable annuity demand through a differentiated product demand system. We use the estimated model of the variable annuity market to explain why insurers increased fees and made minimum return guarantees less generous or stopped offering guarantees after the global financial crisis. This chapter primarily draws upon material from Koijen and Yogo (2022a).

In Chapter 5, we extend the insurance pricing model to study a trade-off posed by shadow insurance. On the one hand, shadow insurance could increase leverage and risk for the insurance group because shadow reinsurers could hold less equity than the operating companies that sell policies. On the other hand, shadow insurance could reduce the cost of regulatory frictions and thereby improve retail market efficiency. We model life insurance demand through a differentiated product demand system. We use the estimated model of the life insurance market to quantify the impact of shadow insurance on the retail market. This chapter primarily draws upon material from Koijen and Yogo (2016).

In Chapter 6, we extend the insurance pricing model to explain portfolio choice. We develop an equilibrium asset pricing model with insurers that are subject to risk-based capital regulation and households and institutional investors who are subject to leverage constraints. The model explains why insurers, who have relatively cheap access to leverage through their underwriting activity, hold low-beta assets such as investment-grade corporate bonds instead of riskless government bonds. The model provides a unifying explanation of recent empirical findings on insurers' portfolio choice and its impact on asset prices. This chapter primarily draws upon material from Koijen and Yogo (2023).

In Chapter 7, we conclude with a discussion of promising directions for future research and policy implications. Our view is that insurance is still under-researched in finance relative to banking, mutual funds, hedge funds, and other financial intermediaries. We hope that this book will facilitate more research on insurance.

NOTATION

We have made an effort to make the notation as consistent as possible throughout the book. We denote scalars with regular letters and vectors and matrices with bold letters. We use $\mathbf{0}$ for a vector of 0s and $\mathbf{1}$ for a vector of 1s. We use $\mathbf{1}_n$ for a vector, where the nth element is 1 and the other elements are 0s. We denote a diagonal matrix as $\mathrm{diag}(\cdot)$. For example, $\mathrm{diag}(\mathbf{1})$ is the identity matrix. We use $\mathbb{E}[\cdot]$ for the expectations operator, $\mathrm{Var}(\cdot)$ for the variance, and $\mathrm{Cov}(\cdot,\cdot)$ for the covariance. We denote a standard normal distribution with mean μ and variance σ^2 as $\mathbb{N}(\mu,\sigma^2)$.

ACKNOWLEDGEMENTS

The National Science Foundation (under grant 1727049) and the Julis-Rabinowitz Center for Public Policy and Finance at Princeton University supported the research in Chapters 4 and 6. The National Science Foundation and the Bendheim Center for Finance at Princeton University supported the Workshop on the Financial Economics of Insurance in 2018 and 2019, where we taught some of the material in this book. Koijen received financial support from the European Research Council (under grant 338082), the Center for Research in Security Prices at the University of Chicago, and the Fama Research Fund at the University of Chicago Booth School of Business while working on some of the material in this book.

We thank Don Noh, Jihong Song, and Haiyue Yu for assistance on the empirical work in Chapter 6. We thank Adam Xu and Zhen Ye for assistance on the data construction in Chapter 4. We thank Don Noh, Simon Oh, Jihong Song, and the anonymous reviewers for helpful comments on earlier drafts of the manuscript. We thank the following people for helpful comments on the research in this book in their capacity as journal editors and conference discussants: Tobias Adrian, Daniel Bergstresser, Philip Bond, Itamar Drechsler, Liran Einav, Andrew Ellul, Mark Flannery, Kenneth Froot, Scott Harrington, Victoria Ivashina, Pab Jotikasthira, Arvind Krishnamurthy, Robert McDonald, Alexander Michaelides, Emanuel Mönch, Alan Morrison, Adair Morse, Borghan Narajabad, Gregory Niehaus, Anna Paulson, Luigi Pistaferri, Michael Roberts, David Scharfstein, and Annette Vissing-Jørgensen.

We thank Joe Jackson and the staff at the Princeton University Press for their encouragement and support throughout this project. Finally, we thank our respective families for their constant love and support.

FINANCIAL ECONOMICS OF INSURANCE

1

Introduction to Modern Insurance

IN SECTION 1.1, we start with an overview of the insurance sector in the context of financial markets and, more broadly, financial intermediation. In Section 1.2, we describe the insurance products that we cover in the empirical work throughout the book. In Section 1.3, we summarize the data sources for research on insurance. In Section 1.4, we summarize the relevant institutional background, including state guaranty associations, risk-based capital regulation, and accounting standards. In Section 1.5, we present a baseline model of insurance pricing with financial frictions and market power.

1.1 Overview of the Insurance Sector

We start with an overview of the insurance sector through historical data on the balance sheets of both life insurers and property and casualty insurers. Since the 1980s, life insurers have grown significantly, and the composition of their liabilities has shifted from life insurance to variable annuities. Along with the changing nature of their business, life insurers' leverage has become more volatile because of greater risk mismatch since the 1990s. Thus, the primary function of life insurers has changed from traditional insurance to financial engineering. The presence of high leverage and risk mismatch makes life insurers similar to pension funds. However, the minimum return guarantees make life insurers unique because they are engineering complex payoffs for policyholders over long horizons that are difficult to hedge with traded options. In terms of portfolio choice, life insurers have shifted from loans to corporate bonds since the 1960s.

TABLE 1.1. Liabilities of Financial Institutions in 2017

Sector	Trillion $
Life insurance	6.5
Property and casualty insurance	1.2
Banks	16.9
Private defined contribution	6.2
Private defined benefit	3.2

Authors' tabulation based on the *Financial Accounts of the United States* (Board of Governors of the Federal Reserve System, 2017). See Appendix A.1 for variable definitions.

1.1.1 Liabilities

Insurers are among the largest of financial institutions. Table 1.1 reports the liabilities of US financial institutions in 2017. Life insurers had $6.5 trillion of liabilities, and property and casualty insurers had $1.2 trillion of liabilities. Life insurers are larger than private defined contribution plans and private defined benefit plans but smaller than banks. However, size does not tell the whole story because these financial institutions serve distinct and important functions.

The large size of the banking sector reflects its importance for payments and short-term liquid savings. Of the $16.9 trillion in liabilities, $11.7 trillion are in savings deposits, which is a rough estimate of the short-term liquid savings function of the banking sector. In contrast, defined contribution plans are long-term retirement savings in tax-advantaged accounts. Defined benefit plans are also long-term retirement savings but typically offer guaranteed income during retirement. Annuities sold by life insurers have a similar function to defined contribution plans because they are long-term savings products with a tax advantage. Fixed annuities have a similar function to defined benefit plans because they offer guaranteed income during retirement. In addition to guaranteed income, variable annuities offer and an upside potential if investment returns are high.

Figure 1.1 shows the shares of US household net worth that are intermediated by insurers and pension funds. In 2017, life insurers accounted for 10.0% of household savings, which is higher than 9.6% for private defined contribution plans and 5.0% for private defined benefit plans. Property and casualty insurers accounted for 1.9% of household savings. Although property and casualty insurance is important for insuring idiosyncratic risk, it is

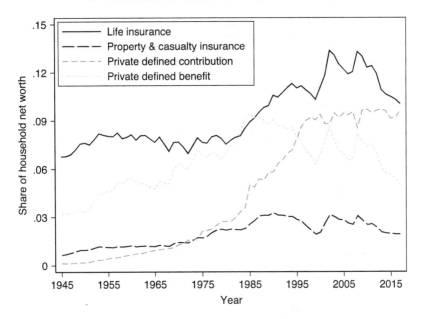

FIGURE 1.1. Insurance and Pension Liabilities. Authors' tabulation based on the *Financial Accounts of the United States* for 1945 to 2017 (Board of Governors of the Federal Reserve System, 2017). See Appendix A.1 for variable definitions.

not a large share of household savings because the policies typically have short maturities.

Private defined benefit plans peaked at 9.4% of household net worth in 1985 and fell thereafter. The fall of defined benefit plans is offset by the rise of life insurers and defined contribution plans. Private employers are shifting from defined benefit plans to defined contribution plans to avoid the risk of underfunded pensions. However, not all employers offer defined contribution plans, and some employees may not be eligible for pension benefits. In contrast, life insurers could play an important role in retirement savings, even for households without access to defined contribution plans. Households can hold annuities in defined contribution plans, individual retirement accounts, and non-retirement accounts.

Table 1.2 reports the composition of US life insurers' liabilities in 2017. Life insurance and annuities in the general account each accounted for $1.2 trillion of liabilities. Life insurers manage some private pension funds, and these liabilities accounted for $0.7 trillion. Other liabilities, including accident and health insurance, accounted for $0.8 trillion.

TABLE 1.2. Composition of Life Insurers' Liabilities in 2017

Liability	Trillion $
General account	
Life insurance	1.2
Annuities	1.2
Pension funds	0.7
Other (including accident & health)	0.8
Separate account (variable annuities)	2.7

Authors' tabulation based on the *Financial Accounts of the United States* (Board of Governors of the Federal Reserve System, 2017). See Appendix A.1 for variable definitions.

Separate account liabilities, which are primarily variable annuities, accounted for $2.7 trillion in 2017. The mutual fund underlying a variable annuity is held in a separate account on behalf of policyholders, which is not subject to the insurer's default risk. The minimum return guarantee on the mutual fund is part of annuity liabilities in the general account. General account liabilities are subject to default risk because of risk mismatch with general account assets.

Figure 1.2 shows the composition of US life insurers' liabilities, which are in shares of household net worth for comparison with Figure 1.1. In the early part of the sample before the 1980s, life insurance was larger than annuities. Since the 1990s, variable annuities have grown rapidly and are now the largest liability. In 2017, fixed and variable annuities together accounted for 4.9% of household net worth, which is about twice the size of 2.4% for life insurance. The label "life insurance companies" was appropriate back in 1945, but they should perhaps be relabeled "annuity and life insurance companies" in modern times. However, even the latter label does not do justice to the fact that the majority of the annuity business involves financial engineering of complex payoffs.

1.1.2 Assets

Figure 1.3 shows the composition of US life insurers' general account assets. Loans (primarily mortgages) were a major share of assets in the early part of the sample. Loans were 44% of assets in 1967 but were only 15% of assets by 2017. Instead, 58% of assets are in corporate and foreign bonds, and 15% are in government bonds in 2017.

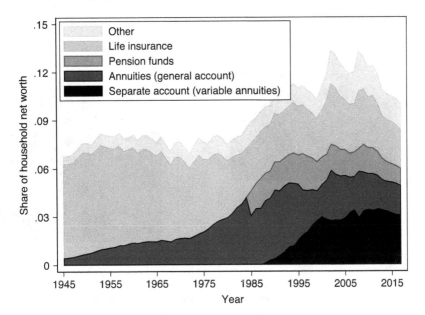

FIGURE 1.2. Composition of Life Insurers' Liabilities. Authors' tabulation based on the *Financial Accounts of the United States* for 1945 to 2017 (Board of Governors of the Federal Reserve System, 2017). General account annuities include pension liabilities before 1985. See Appendix A.1 for variable definitions.

Figure 1.3 also shows the composition of US property and casualty insurers' assets. Government bonds have always been the largest asset class in their portfolio. Property and casualty insurers have a more conservative portfolio than life insurers because of the less predictable nature of their liabilities with tail risk. Nevertheless, property and casualty insurers have gradually shifted their portfolio from government bonds to corporate bonds since the 1960s.

Figure 1.4 shows the institutional ownership of US corporate bonds. Insurers have always been the largest institutional investors of corporate bonds and thus play a central role in corporate funding and investment. In 2017, insurers owned 38% of corporate bonds, which is higher than 16% for pension funds, 10% for banks, and 30% for mutual funds.

1.1.3 Leverage

Figure 1.5 shows the leverage (i.e., ratio of liabilities to assets) of US financial institutions. Property and casualty insurers have always had lower and more volatile leverage than life insurers because of the less predictable nature

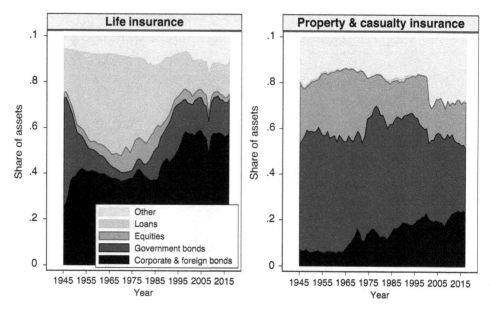

FIGURE 1.3. Composition of General Account Assets. Authors' tabulation based on the *Financial Accounts of the United States* for 1945 to 2017 (Board of Governors of the Federal Reserve System, 2017). Government bonds include Treasury, agency, and municipal bonds. Equities include mutual funds. See Appendix A.1 for variable definitions.

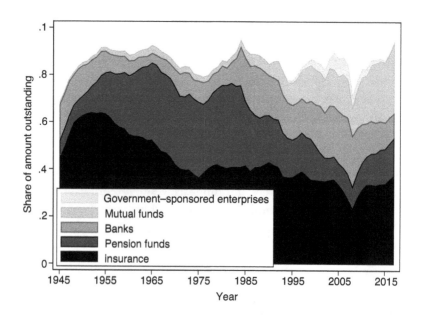

FIGURE 1.4. Institutional Ownership of Corporate Bonds. Authors' tabulation based on the *Financial Accounts of the United States* for 1945 to 2017 (Board of Governors of the Federal Reserve System, 2017). See Appendix A.1 for variable definitions.

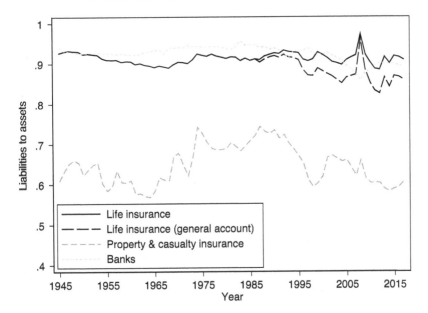

FIGURE 1.5. Leverage of Financial Institutions. Authors' tabulation based on the *Financial Accounts of the United States* for 1945 to 2017 (Board of Governors of the Federal Reserve System, 2017). See Appendix A.1 for variable definitions.

of their liabilities. Life insurers have a nearly constant leverage ratio of just above 90% from 1945 through the 1990s. However, the shift from life insurance to variable annuities since the 1990s means that life insurers now have less predictable liabilities subject to risk mismatch. Along with the changing nature of their business, life insurers' leverage has become more volatile since the 1990s.

Life insurers and banks have similar levels of leverage, but they moved in opposite directions during the global financial crisis. In 2008, life insurers' leverage spiked up to 97%, while banks' leverage spiked down to 86%. Life insurers can afford to let leverage increase in response to a transitory shock to asset values because of the long-term and less runnable nature of their liabilities.

1.1.4 Ownership Structure

An insurance company could be either a stock or a mutual company. The shareholders receive the dividends in a stock company, whereas the policyholders receive the dividends in a mutual company. A stock company need

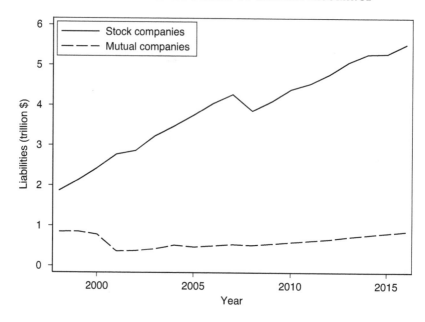

FIGURE 1.6. Life Insurers' Liabilities by Ownership Structure. Authors' tabulation based on the *Best's Statement File* for 1998 to 2016 (A.M. Best Company, 1999–2017).

not be publicly traded because it could be privately held. An advantage of a stock company is access to external capital markets, which facilitates faster growth. A disadvantage is that the stockholders' incentives are not necessarily aligned with the policyholders' incentives, so there is greater scope for agency problems (Mayers and Smith, 1981).

Figure 1.6 shows US life insurers' liabilities by ownership structure. Stock companies have accounted for all of the growth since the late 1990s. On the extensive margin, there was a higher than average rate of demutualization from 1997 to 2001 (Erhemjamts and Phillips, 2012). On the intensive margin, access to external capital markets partly explains the faster growth of stock companies. In addition, stock companies specialize in insurance products that have experienced the fastest growth since the 2000s. Figure 1.7 shows that variable annuities are the largest liability for stock companies, while life insurance is the largest liability for mutual companies.

Another recent trend in ownership structure is the acquisition of life insurers by private equity firms. Kirti and Sarin (2020) find that private equity investment in life insurers grew from $23 billion in 2009 to $250 billion in 2014. When acquired by private equity firms, life insurers increase leverage

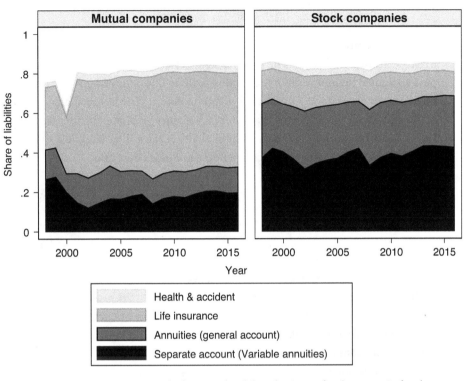

FIGURE 1.7. Composition of Life Insurers' Liabilities by Ownership Structure. Authors' tabulation based on the *Best's Statement File* for 1998 to 2016 (A.M. Best Company, 1999–2017).

and portfolio risk by holding non-agency mortgage-backed securities (MBSs) instead of highly rated corporate bonds.

1.2 Insurance Products

We describe the insurance products that we cover in the empirical work throughout the book. We also define the actuarial value of life insurance and fixed annuities. An insurer that issues life insurance or a fixed annuity must buy a portfolio of Treasury bonds to replicate its future cash flows. A portfolio of corporate bonds, for example, does not replicate the cash flows because of credit risk. Therefore, the law of one price implies that the Treasury yield curve is the appropriate cost of capital for the valuation of life insurance and fixed annuities.

1.2.1   Life Insurance

Term life insurance pays a death benefit upon the death of the insured during a fixed maturity of M years. The policy is in effect as long as the policyholder pays an annual premium while the insured is alive. The policy is lapsed if the policyholder stops paying the annual premium before maturity or the death of the insured. Let $y_t(m)$ be the zero-coupon Treasury yield at maturity m and time t. Let π_n be the one-year survival probability at age n. The actuarial value of M-year term life insurance at age n per dollar of death benefit is

$$V_t(n, M) = \left(1 + \sum_{m=1}^{M-1} \frac{\prod_{l=0}^{m-1} \pi_{n+l}}{(1 + y_t(m))^m}\right)^{-1} \left(\sum_{m=1}^{M} \frac{\prod_{l=0}^{m-2} \pi_{n+l}(1 - \pi_{n+m-1})}{(1 + y_t(m))^m}\right).$$

(1.1)

The first term in parentheses is the present value of the premiums divided by the annual premium. The second term in parentheses is the present value of the death benefits. This formula does not account for the potential lapsation of policies. There is currently no agreed-upon standard for lapsation pricing, partly because lapsations are difficult to model and predict.

Guaranteed universal life insurance provides lifetime coverage at a constant guaranteed premium and accumulates no cash value. Thus, guaranteed universal life insurance is essentially term life insurance without a fixed maturity. The actuarial value of guaranteed universal life insurance is a special case of equation (1.1) when $M = N - n$, where N is the maximum attainable age according to the appropriate mortality table.

We briefly mention other types of life insurance that are not a focus of this book. Universal life insurance without a constant guaranteed premium as well as whole life insurance provide lifetime coverage and accumulate cash value. These types of policies can be thought of as a combination of life insurance and a savings account. Variable life insurance also provides lifetime coverage and accumulates cash value in a subaccount that is essentially an equity or bond mutual fund.

1.2.2   Fixed Annuities

A term annuity pays an annual income for a fixed maturity of M years. Since term annuities have a fixed income stream that is independent of survival, they are straight bonds rather than longevity insurance. The actuarial value of an

M-year term annuity per dollar of income is

$$V_t(M) = \sum_{m=1}^{M} \frac{1}{(1+y_t(m))^m}. \tag{1.2}$$

A life annuity with an M-year guarantee pays an annual income for the first M years regardless of survival, then continues paying income thereafter until the death of the insured. Let π_n be the one-year survival probability at age n, and let N be the maximum attainable age according to the appropriate mortality table. The actuarial value of a life annuity with an M-year guarantee at age n per dollar income is

$$V_t(n,M) = \sum_{m=1}^{M} \frac{1}{(1+y_t(m))^m} + \sum_{m=M+1}^{N-n} \frac{\prod_{l=0}^{m-1}\pi_{n+l}}{(1+y_t(m))^m}. \tag{1.3}$$

A life annuity without a guarantee is a special case when $M = 0$.

1.2.3   Variable Annuities

A variable annuity is a mutual fund with longevity insurance and a potential tax advantage that is sold through an insurer. For an additional fee, the insurer offers an optional minimum return guarantee on the mutual fund. Thus, a variable annuity with a minimum return guarantee is a retail financial product that packages a mutual fund with a long-maturity put option on the mutual fund. To illustrate how variable annuities work, we start with an example of an actual product.

MetLife Investors USA Insurance Company (2008) offers a variable annuity called MetLife Series VA, which comes with various investment options and guaranteed living benefits. In 2008:3, one of the investment options was the American Funds Growth Allocation Portfolio, which is a mutual fund with a target equity allocation of 70% to 85% and an annual portfolio expense of 1.01%. One of the guaranteed living benefits was a Guaranteed Lifetime Withdrawal Benefit (GLWB). MetLife Series VA has an annual base contract expense of 1.3% of account value, and a GLWB has an annual fee of 0.5% of account value. Thus, the total annual fee for the variable annuity with a GLWB is 1.8%, which is on top of the annual portfolio expense on the mutual fund.

To understand the GLWB, we first describe a standalone investment in the mutual fund and the withdrawals that it would enable for retirement income. Suppose that a policyholder were to invest in the American Funds Growth

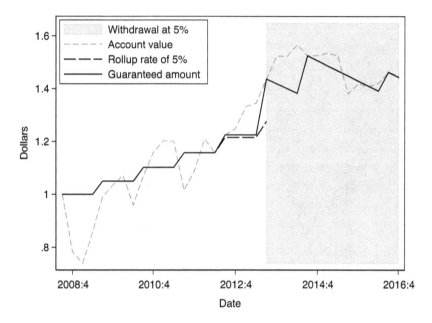

FIGURE 1.8. An Example of a Guaranteed Living Withdrawal Benefit. This example shows the evolution of account value and the guaranteed amount for MetLife Series VA with a GLWB from 2008:3 to 2016:4. The investment option is the American Funds Growth Allocation Portfolio. The policyholder is assumed to annually withdraw 5% of the highest guaranteed amount after 2013:3. For simplicity, this example abstracts from the impact of fees on account value and the guaranteed amount.

Allocation Portfolio in 2008:3. After 2013:3, the policyholder withdraws a constant dollar amount each year that is 5% of the highest account value ever reached. This behavior describes a policyholder who invests in a mutual fund five years before retirement and subsequently spends down her wealth by consuming a constant dollar amount each year. Figure 1.8 shows the path of account value per $1 of initial investment with the shaded region covering the withdrawal period after 2013:3. The account value fluctuates over time because of uncertainty in investment returns.

The same policyholder could purchase a GLWB from MetLife and guarantee her investment returns. A GLWB has an annual rollup rate of 5% before the first withdrawal, which means that at each contract anniversary, the guaranteed amount steps up to the greater of the account value and the previous guaranteed amount accumulated at 5%. Thus, a GLWB is a put option on the mutual fund that locks in each year to a strike price that accumulates at an annual rate of 5%. Figure 1.8 shows that the guaranteed amount can only increase during the five-year accumulation period, protecting the policyholder from downside market risk.

When the policyholder enters the withdrawal period, she can annually withdraw up to 5% of the highest guaranteed amount ever reached. In our example, the guaranteed amount in 2013:3 is $1.44, which means that the policyholder can withdraw up to $1.44 \times 0.05 = 0.072 per year. Each withdrawal gets deducted from both the account value and the guaranteed amount. A GLWB is a lifetime guarantee in that the policyholder receives income (i.e., $0.072 per year) as long as she lives, even after the account is depleted to zero. During the withdrawal period, the guaranteed amount steps up to the account value at each contract anniversary. In Figure 1.8, these step-ups occur in 2014:3 and 2016:3 because of high investment returns.

Because the annual rollup rate is 5% and the annual fee is 0.5%, one may be tempted to conclude that the guaranteed return on the variable annuity is 4.5% during the accumulation period. This logic turns out to be incorrect because the guaranteed amount of $1.44 in 2013:3 is only payable as an annual income of $0.072 over 20 years (or until the policyholder's death). Because of the time value of money, the present value of $0.072 per year over 20 years is worth substantially less than $1.44. Koijen and Yogo (2022a, appendix A) show the empirical relevance of this contract feature based on the historical term structure of interest rates.

A GLWB is the most common type of guaranteed living benefit. The three other types of guaranteed living benefits are a Guaranteed Minimum Withdrawal Benefit (GMWB), a Guaranteed Minimum Income Benefit (GMIB), and a Guaranteed Minimum Accumulation Benefit (GMAB). A GMWB is similar to a GLWB, except that the policyholder does not receive income after the account is depleted to zero. A GMIB is similar to a GLWB, except that the guaranteed amount at the beginning of the withdrawal period converts to a life annuity (i.e., fixed income for life). A GMAB provides a minimum return guarantee much like the accumulation period of a GLWB, but it does not have a withdrawal period with a guaranteed income.

If a policyholder were to die while the contract is in effect, her estate would receive a standard death benefit that is equal to the remaining account value. For an additional fee, the insurer offers four types of guaranteed death benefits (highest anniversary value, rising floor, earnings enhancement benefit, and return of premium) that enhance the death benefit during the accumulation period.

Even without minimum return guarantees, variable annuities may be attractive to policyholders because of a potential tax advantage in nonqualified accounts. Earnings on variable annuities can be deferred and accumulate tax free if the first withdrawal occurs after age 59.5. However, all earnings, including the capital gains, are taxed at the ordinary income tax rate, which is higher than the capital gains tax rate. Therefore, the tax advantage can justify the variable annuity fees only if the accumulation period is sufficiently long. In an illustrative example, Brown and Poterba (2006, table 5.2) show that the accumulation period must be longer than 40 years to justify an annual fee of 0.25% under the 2003 tax rates and an 8% pre-tax return (with 2% from dividends and 6% from capital gains).

1.3   Insurance Data

We describe the data on financial statements and insurance prices, much of which we use throughout the book.

1.3.1   Financial Statements

US insurers prepare annual financial statements according to the statutory accounting principles and file them with the National Association of Insurance Commissioners (NAIC). In addition to the balance sheets and the income statements, these data contain variable annuities in General Interrogatories Part 2 Table 9.2, portfolio holdings in Schedule D, derivatives in Schedule DB, and reinsurance in Schedule S. The National Association of Insurance Commissioners (1994–2019) sells the financial statements to academic researchers at a discounted price. The A.M. Best Company and SNL Financial also sell the same financial statements in a processed and cleaned format that may be easier to use.

The A.M. Best Company offers two products that contain the financial statements and rating information. *Best's Insurance Reports* contain highlights from the financial statements that are the most relevant to ratings and are available since 1992 (A.M. Best Company, 1993–2012). *Best's Statement File* contains the complete financial statements and is available since 1999 (A.M. Best Company, 1999–2017).

Based on the financial statements, we construct insurer characteristics that we use throughout the book. They are log assets, log liabilities, asset growth, leverage, and net equity flow. We also use insurer characteristics that the

A.M. Best Company constructs as part of the rating process. They are the A.M. Best rating, risk-based capital, current liquidity, return on equity, and the A.M. Best financial size category. We provide a complete definition of these insurer characteristics in Appendix A.2.

GENERAL INTERROGATORIES

General Interrogatories Part 2 Table 9.2 reports the total related account value, the gross amount of variable annuity reserves, and the reinsurance reserve credit on variable annuities. The total related account value is the market value of the mutual funds. The gross amount of variable annuity reserves is the accounting value of the minimum return guarantees net of hedging programs.

We define *variable annuity liabilities* as the total related account value plus the gross amount of variable annuity reserves minus the reinsurance reserve credit on variable annuities. For each insurer, we define its *reserve valuation* as the ratio of the gross amount of variable annuity reserves to the total related account value. The reserve valuation measures the value of the minimum return guarantees per dollar of underlying mutual funds. In the cross section, the reserve valuation is higher for insurers that have sold more generous guarantees. In the time series, the reserve valuation increases when the stock market falls, interest rates fall, or volatility rises. We define the *reinsurance share of variable annuities* as the ratio of the reinsurance reserve credit on variable annuities to the gross amount of variable annuity reserves.

SCHEDULE D

Schedule D reports all fixed income and equity holdings at the CUSIP level. Other than insurers, mutual funds and exchange-traded funds (ETF) are the only other US institutional investors who report fixed income holdings. The importance of insurers in the corporate bond market and the availability of holdings data create an opportunity to study the impact of institutional investors on corporate bond prices, following the demand system approach in Koijen and Yogo (2019). In fact, recent research takes the corporate bond literature in this direction (Bretscher et al., 2021; Yu, 2021; Siani, 2022).

SCHEDULE DB

Schedule DB reports all derivatives, including futures, options, and swaps, at the contract level. Such detailed data are not available for US banks. The data are ideal for studying the hedging and risk-shifting motives of insurers (e.g., Cummins, Phillips, and Smith, 2001; Sen, 2022).

SCHEDULE S

Our data on life and annuity reinsurance agreements are from Schedule S for 2002 to 2013 (A.M. Best Company, 2003–2014). The relevant parts of Schedule S are Part 1.1 (Reinsurance Assumed), Part 3.1 (Reinsurance Ceded), and Part 4 (Reinsurance Ceded to Unauthorized Companies). The data contain all reinsurance agreements (both ceded and assumed) at each fiscal year-end for any operating company or authorized reinsurer. An authorized reinsurer is subject to the same reporting and capital requirements as an operating company in its state of domicile, whereas an unauthorized reinsurer is not. In particular, the data contain reinsurance ceded by an operating company to an unauthorized reinsurer, such as a domestic captive or a foreign reinsurer. However, we do not observe reinsurance ceded by unauthorized reinsurers that do not report to the NAIC.

For each reinsurance agreement, we observe the identity of the reinsurer, the type of reinsurance, the effective date, the reserve credit taken (or reserves held), and the modified coinsurance reserve. The sum of the reserve credit taken and modified coinsurance reserve is the total amount of reinsurance ceded. We know the identity of the reinsurer up to its name, domicile, whether it is affiliated with the ceding company, whether it is authorized in the ceding company's domicile, and whether it is rated by the A.M. Best Company. We define *shadow reinsurers* as affiliated and unauthorized reinsurers without an A.M. Best rating. Our definition is stricter than "captives" because some captives are actually authorized.

CONSOLIDATED FINANCIAL STATEMENTS

Compustat contains the consolidated financial statements under the generally accepted accounting principles (GAAP) for publicly held holding companies. These financial statements are not as detailed as the financial statements for the subsidiaries under the statutory accounting principles. Reconciling the financial statements of the holding company and its subsidiaries is a daunting task because of differences in accounting standards, captive reinsurance, and non-insurance subsidiaries without public financial statements. However, Compustat data may suffice for some empirical applications in which only information at the holding company level is necessary.

INTERNATIONAL FINANCIAL STATEMENTS

The A.M. Best Company offers separate products that contain the financial statements for global insurers, European insurers reporting under Solvency II, and Canadian insurers. The Securities Holding Statistics of the European Central Bank contain all fixed income and equity holdings of European insurers at the ISIN level (Koijen et al., 2021).

1.3.2   Insurance Prices

LIFE INSURANCE

Our data on life insurance premiums are from Compulife Software (2002–2012), which is a computer-based quotation system for insurance agents. In Chapter 4, we focus on guaranteed universal life insurance for males and females aged 30 to 80 (every 10 years in between). We pull monthly quotes from January 2005 to July 2011 for all states at the regular health category and a face amount of $250K.

In Chapter 5, we focus on 10-year guaranteed level term life insurance for males aged 30 as representative of the life insurance market. However, we have also examined 20-year policies and older age groups for robustness. We pull quotes at the end of June of each year from 2002 to 2012 for all states at the regular health category and a face amount of $1 million.

We calculate the actuarial value of life insurance based on equation (1.1), the appropriate mortality table from the American Society of Actuaries, and the zero-coupon Treasury yield curve (Gürkaynak, Sack, and Wright, 2007). We use the 2001 Valuation Basic Table before January 2008 and the 2008 Valuation Basic Table since January 2008. These mortality tables are derived from the actual mortality experience of insured pools, based on data provided by various insurers. Thus, they account for adverse selection such that an insured pool has a lower life expectancy than the overall population. We smooth the transition between the two vintages of the mortality tables by geometric averaging.

FIXED ANNUITIES

Our data on term and life annuity prices are from the WebAnnuities Insurance Agency, which has published quotes from the leading insurers at a semiannual frequency since January 1989 (Stern, 1989–2011) and at a monthly frequency from January 2007 to August 2009 (Stern, 2007–2009). We focus on single premium immediate annuities in nonqualified accounts, for which only the interest is taxable. These policies cannot be lapsed because the premium is paid up front as a lump sum. For term annuities, we have quotes for 5- to 30-year maturities (every five years in between). For life annuities, we have quotes for "life only" policies without guarantees as well as those with 10- or 20-year guarantees. These quotes are available for both males and females aged 50 to 85 (every five years in between).

We calculate the actuarial value of term annuities based on equation (1.2) and the zero-coupon Treasury yield curve. We calculate the actuarial value of life annuities based on equation (1.3), the appropriate mortality table from the American Society of Actuaries, and the zero-coupon Treasury yield curve. We use the 1983 Annuity Mortality Basic Table before January 1999 and the 2000 Annuity Mortality Basic Table since January 1999. These mortality tables are derived from the actual mortality experience of insured pools, based on data provided by various insurers. Thus, they account for adverse selection such that an insured pool has a higher life expectancy than the overall population. We smooth the transition between the two vintages of the mortality tables by geometric averaging.

VARIABLE ANNUITIES

Based on Morningstar (2016a), we construct a comprehensive panel data set on the variable annuity market at the contract level since 1999. The data contain quarterly sales and a textual summary of the prospectus for each contract, from which we extract the history of fees and contract characteristics. The key contract characteristics are the base contract expense, the number of investment options, and the types of guaranteed living and death benefits that are offered.[1] For each guaranteed living benefit, the key characteristics are the type (i.e., GLWB, GMWB, GMIB, or GMAB), the fee, the rollup rate, and the withdrawal rate. Morningstar provides the open and close dates for each contract and guaranteed living benefit, from which we construct the history of when different benefits were offered.

Sales are available at the contract level but not at the benefit level. Therefore, we must aggregate fees and rollup rates over all guaranteed living benefits

---

1. We use assets under management by subaccount from Morningstar (2016b) to compute a measure of investment options that adjusts for the nonuniform distribution of assets across subaccounts within a contract. Our measure is the inverse of the Herfindahl index over the subaccount shares within each contract, which equals the number of investment options when the subaccounts are uniformly distributed.

that a contract offers to construct a panel data set on sales, fees, and characteristics at the contract level. For each date and contract, we first average the fees and the rollup rates by the type of guaranteed living benefit. We then use the average fee and rollup rate in the order of GLWB, GMWB, GMIB, and GMAB, based on availability. For example, if a contract does not offer a GLWB but offers a GMWB, we use the average fee and rollup rate on the GMWB. Because a GLWB is the most common type of guaranteed living benefit and a GMWB is the closest substitute for a GLWB, our procedure yields a representative set of fees and rollup rates that are comparable across contracts.

We merge the Morningstar data and the annual financial statements by company name. The annual financial statements are from the *Best's Statement File*, which is merged with NAIC's General Interrogatories Part 2 Table 9.2 by the NAIC company code. The final data set is a quarterly panel on the variable annuity market from 2005:1 to 2015:4, where the start date is dictated by the availability of the NAIC data. For the summary statistics that only require the Morningstar data, we use a longer sample that starts in 1999:1.

1.4 Institutional Background

Since the McCarran Ferguson Act of 1945, states have regulated US insurers, and there is no national insurance regulator. States regulate many aspects of the insurance business, including the coverage requirements for policies, the premiums for some types of insurance such as health, revisions in the premiums of existing policies, the accounting standards for financial reporting, and the capital requirements to ensure solvency. Although the regulation can vary across states, most states adopt the model regulation established by a coordinating organization known as the NAIC.

1.4.1 State Guaranty Associations

Since the Life and Health Insurance Guaranty Association Model Act in 1970, all states have established guaranty associations to cover insurance claims in case of default. The maximum coverage varies across states and types of policies. For example, California covers up to $250K for annuities and $300K for life insurance. Guaranty associations assess the surviving companies to pay off the defaulted insurance claims. All states cap annual guaranty association assessments, typically at 2% of recent life insurance and annuity premiums.

State taxpayers indirectly bear the cost of defaulted insurance claims because the assessments are tax deductible.

On the one hand, guaranty associations protect policyholders, who may not be informed or coordinated enough to monitor their insurer. On the other hand, guaranty associations create a risk-shifting motive for managers and shareholders (Lee, Mayers, and Smith, 1997). Therefore, state regulators must set and enforce capital requirements to limit excessive risk taking. As we have seen, the insurance sector was already large and functioning as a relatively unregulated system before 1970. It is unclear whether the insurance sector is better off in the current system of capital regulation protecting guaranty associations.

Although the US government does not explicitly guarantee insurers, it did bail out AIG, Hartford, and Lincoln Financial through the Troubled Asset Relief Program (TARP) during the global financial crisis. Other insurers such as Allstate, Genworth Financial, and Prudential Financial applied for TARP but were ultimately rejected or withdrew their application. In the aftermath of the global financial crisis, the Financial Stability Oversight Council designated AIG, Prudential Financial, and MetLife as systemically important financial institutions to enforce higher capital requirements that would prevent future bailouts. However, all three insurers have successfully challenged this decision and are no longer designated systemically important as of October 2018.

1.4.2   Risk-Based Capital Regulation

Since the Risk-Based Capital for Insurers Model Act in 1993, insurance regulators have used risk-based capital as an important metric of an insurer's financial strength. Rating agencies also use risk-based capital as an important metric for assigning credit ratings. Risk-based capital is the ratio of accounting equity to required capital:

$$\text{RBC} = \frac{\text{Assets} - \text{Reserves}}{\text{Required capital}}. \tag{1.4}$$

Reserves in the numerator are an accounting measure of liabilities that may not coincide with the market value. Required capital in the denominator is a measure of how much equity could be lost in an adverse scenario. Although the exact formula for computing the required capital is complex, it is helpful to think of it as proportional to reserves and increasing in the riskiness of the liabilities, as we discuss below. For a sufficiently high risk-based capital ratio, insurance regulators view equity capital as adequate to meet the insurer's existing liabilities, even in an adverse scenario.

To avoid a rating downgrade or regulatory action, an insurer may behave as if there were a risk-based capital constraint. There are four levels of risk-based capital that trigger regulatory action. When the risk-based capital ratio falls below the "company action level" of 2, the insurer must submit a plan of corrective actions. When the risk-based capital ratio falls below the "regulatory action level" of 1.5, the insurance regulator examines the insurer and orders corrective actions. When the risk-based capital ratio falls below the "authorized control level" of 1, the insurance regulator has the authority to place the insurer under regulatory control. When the risk-based capital ratio falls below the "mandatory control level" of 0.7, the insurance regulator places the insurer under regulatory control.

An economic risk constraint works similarly to a risk-based capital constraint. For example, let ϵ be a multiplicative shock to the leverage ratio with a cumulative distribution function $F(\epsilon)$, which arises from a risk mismatch between assets and liabilities. Consider a value-at-risk constraint under which the probability that assets cover liabilities must exceed a threshold:

$$\Pr\left(\frac{\text{Liabilities}}{\text{Assets}}\epsilon \le 1\right) = F\left(\frac{\text{Assets}}{\text{Liabilities}}\right) \ge \kappa. \qquad (1.5)$$

We can rewrite this constraint as

$$\frac{\text{Assets} - \text{Liabilities}}{(F^{-1}(\kappa) - 1)\text{Liabilities}} \ge 1. \qquad (1.6)$$

Comparing the left side of this equation with risk-based capital (1.4), required capital must be a fraction $F^{-1}(\kappa) - 1$ of reserves for the two equations to be equivalent. An insurer with more conservative risk management has a higher $F^{-1}(\kappa)$ due to a higher κ or lower risk reflected in the cumulative distribution function. The horizon over which a value-at-risk constraint matters for life insurers is presumably much longer than that for banks and property and casualty insurers, given the long-term and less runnable nature of their liabilities.

1.4.3 Accounting Standards

An insurance holding company consists of operating companies that sell insurance and reinsurers that specialize in reinsurance. An operating company reports financial statements according to the statutory accounting principles, based on the NAIC's model regulation. A reinsurer that is not licensed to sell insurance reports financial statements under GAAP. The holding company reports consolidated financial statements under GAAP. European insurers report under Solvency II, which is different from GAAP. However, the European Union allows insurers to operate outside of the European Union under the home country's solvency regime under Solvency II equivalence.

Reserve valuation is the valuation of an insurance liability under an accounting standard for the purposes of financial reporting, and it is important because higher reserves reduce risk-based capital (see equation (1.4)). The reserve valuation of life insurance differs substantially between the statutory accounting principles and GAAP. This difference in accounting standards creates an incentive for life insurers to use shadow insurance, which we discuss in Chapters 2 and 5. We also discuss the statutory accounting principles for variable annuities, which is important for Chapter 4.

LIFE INSURANCE

In January 2000, the NAIC adopted Model Regulation 830 (commonly known as Regulation XXX) for the reserve valuation of term life insurance. In January 2003, the NAIC adopted Actuarial Guideline 38 (commonly known as Regulation AXXX) for the reserve valuation of universal life insurance with secondary guarantees. By increasing the reserve valuation, the new regulation forced insurers to hold more capital on newly issued life insurance policies.

The new regulation was a matter of the statutory accounting principles and does not apply to GAAP. The reserve valuation under GAAP is much lower and closer to the actuarial value. Therefore, an operating company that reports under the statutory accounting principles could cede reinsurance to either an affiliated or unaffiliated reinsurer that reports under GAAP to reduce overall reserves. In practice, unaffiliated reinsurance can be expensive because of capital market frictions and market power (Froot, 2001).

CAPTIVE LAWS

South Carolina introduced new laws in 2002 that allow insurers to establish captives, whose primary function is to assume reinsurance from affiliated companies for the purpose of reducing overall reserves. States compete for captive business to increase employment and tax revenue (Cole and McCullough, 2008). Furthermore, the captive's state of domicile does not directly bear risk because the liabilities go back to the operating company (and ultimately the guaranty associations of states in which the policies were sold) when a captive fails. A captive structure that has proven especially successful is the special purpose financial captive, which is a type of special purpose vehicle that was introduced by South Carolina in 2004 and Vermont in 2007. Twenty-six states have adopted a version of the captive laws, eight of which have defined special purpose financial captives (Captives and Special Purpose Vehicle Use Subgroup, 2013).

Captives differ from traditional reinsurers in several important ways. First, captive reinsurance can be less expensive than unaffiliated reinsurance, especially after the fixed costs of entry have been paid. Second, captives can operate with less equity because they report under GAAP and are not subject to risk-based capital regulation. For example, captives in Vermont are required to have only $250K in equity and could count letters of credit as admitted assets (Captives and Special Purpose Vehicle Use Subgroup, 2013). Third, captives have a more flexible financial structure that allows them to fund reinsurance transactions through letters of credit or securitization. Finally, their financial statements are confidential to the public, rating agencies, and even regulators outside their state of domicile.

US tax laws disallow reinsurance for the primary purpose of reducing tax liabilities. However, it can be an important side benefit of captive reinsurance that motivates where an insurer establishes its captives. Life insurance premiums are taxable at the state level, and the tax rates on premiums vary across states (Cole and McCullough, 2008). In addition, profits are taxable at the federal level, so an operating company can reduce the overall tax liabilities by ceding reinsurance to an offshore captive. Bermuda, Barbados, and the Cayman Islands are important captive domiciles for this purpose.

Operating companies are ultimately responsible for all liabilities that they issue, even those that they cede to reinsurers. Moreover, captives typically do not transfer risk to outside investors through securitization (Stern et al., 2007). These facts together imply that captives do not transfer risk outside the insurance group and exist only for the purpose of capital and tax management. Thus, captives have a function similar to asset-backed commercial paper conduits with explicit guarantees from the sponsoring bank (Acharya, Schnabl, and Suarez, 2013), before the regulatory reform of shadow banking (Adrian and Ashcraft, 2012).

VARIABLE ANNUITIES

Variable annuity liabilities enter both reserves and required capital in risk-based capital (1.4). As summarized by Junus and Motiwalla (2009), Actuarial Guideline 43 has determined the reserve value of variable annuities since December 2009, and the C-3 Phase II regulatory standard has determined the contribution of variable annuities to required capital since December 2005. Actuarial Guideline 43 is a higher reserve requirement than its precursor Actuarial Guideline 39, so insurers were given a phase-in period through December 2012 to fully comply with the new requirement.

To compute reserves and required capital, insurance regulators provide various scenarios for the joint path of Treasury, corporate bond, and equity prices. Insurers simulate the path of equity deficiency for their variable annuity business (net of hedging programs and reinsurance) under each scenario and keep the highest present value of equity deficiency along each path. Insurers then compute reserves as a conditional mean over the upper 30% of equity deficiencies (called CTE 70). This conditional tail expectation builds in a degree of conservatism that is conceptually similar to a correction for risk premia, but reserves do not coincide with the market value of liabilities. Insurers use the same methodology for required capital, except that they compute a conditional mean over the upper 10% of equity deficiencies (called CTE 90).

More generous guarantees with higher rollup rates or better coverage of downside market risk relative to fees require higher reserves and more capital. Moreover, minimum return guarantees are long-maturity put options on mutual funds, whose value increases when the stock market falls, interest rates fall, or volatility rises. Therefore, both reserves and required capital increase in an adverse scenario like the global financial crisis, which puts downward pressure on risk-based capital.

In contrast to the conditional tail expectation under Actuarial Guideline 43, GAAP allows insurers to record variable annuity reserves at market value. As a result, variable annuity reserves under the statutory accounting principles could increase relative to those under GAAP after a period of high volatility (Credit Suisse, 2012). Moreover, an insurer that implements a hedging program under GAAP could actually increase the volatility of accounting equity under the statutory accounting principles. For these reasons, insurers have an incentive for captive reinsurance of variable annuities either to increase risk-based capital or to implement a hedging program under GAAP.

1.5   A Baseline Model of Insurance Pricing

Traditional theories of insurance markets assume that insurers operate in an efficient capital market and supply policies at actuarially fair prices. Consequently, the market equilibrium is primarily determined by the demand side, either by life-cycle demand (Yaari, 1965) or informational frictions (Rothschild and Stiglitz, 1976). In contrast, we present a baseline model in which financial frictions and market power are the primary determinants of insurance prices.

We build on the baseline model in the subsequent chapters. In Chapter 3, we extend the insurance pricing model to multiple types of policies to explain pricing across policies with different statutory reserve requirements. In Chapter 4, we extend the insurance pricing model to contract design with an application to the variable annuity market. In Chapter 5, we extend the insurance pricing model to reinsurance to explain shadow insurance and its impact on the retail market. In Chapter 6, we extend the insurance pricing model to portfolio choice to explain why insurers are the largest institutional investors of corporate bonds.

1.5.1   Insurance Market

For simplicity, we assume that an insurer sells just one type of policy (e.g., annuities or life insurance). Insurers compete in an oligopolistic market and have market power because of product differentiation along policy characteristics other than the price, which we parameterize through a differentiated product demand system in Section 4.3.1. For now, we assume that the insurer faces a demand function that depends on its own price and the prices of its competitors. The demand function is continuously differentiable and strictly decreasing in its own price.

In period t, the insurer chooses the price P_t per policy and sells Q_t policies. The actuarial value per policy is V_t. The reserve value per policy is $\widehat{V}_t$. As we discuss in Section 1.4.3, the reserve value depends on the statutory accounting principles and could be greater or less than the actuarial value.

1.5.2   Balance Sheet Dynamics

We describe how the sale of policies affects the balance sheet. Let A_{t-1} be the assets at the beginning of period t, and let $R_{A,t}$ be an exogenous gross asset return in period t. The assets at the end of period t, after the sale of policies, are

$$A_t = R_{A,t}A_{t-1} + P_tQ_t. \tag{1.7}$$

The insurer must also record reserves on the liability side of its balance sheet. Let L_{t-1} be the reserves at the beginning of period t, and let $R_{L,t}$ be an exogenous gross return on reserves in period t. The reserves at the end of period t, after the sale of policies, are

$$L_t = R_{L,t}L_{t-1} + \widehat{V}_tQ_t. \tag{1.8}$$

We define statutory capital as equity minus required capital, which is proportional to reserves:

$$K_t = \underbrace{A_t - L_t}_{\text{equity}} - \underbrace{\phi L_t}_{\text{required capital}}, \tag{1.9}$$

where $\phi > 0$ is a risk charge on liabilities under risk-based capital regulation. In comparison to equation (1.4), we specify statutory capital as a difference (rather than a ratio) of equity and required capital to simplify the derivation of the optimal insurance price. However, we could scale statutory capital by lagged liabilities without substantively altering the results. Substituting equations (1.7) and (1.8) into equation (1.9), the law of motion for statutory capital is

$$K_t = R_{K,t}K_{t-1} + \left(P_t - (1+\phi)\widehat{V}_t\right)Q_t, \tag{1.10}$$

where

$$R_{K,t} = \frac{A_{t-1}}{K_{t-1}}R_{A,t} - \frac{(1+\phi)L_{t-1}}{K_{t-1}}R_{L,t} \tag{1.11}$$

is the return on statutory capital.

1.5.3 Financial Frictions

Following the discussion in Section 1.4.2, low statutory capital could lead to a rating downgrade or regulatory action, which have adverse consequences in both retail and capital markets. Moreover, financial frictions make equity issuance costly. We model the cost of financial frictions through a cost function:

$$C_t = C(K_t). \tag{1.12}$$

This cost function is continuous, twice continuously differentiable, strictly decreasing, and strictly convex. The cost function is decreasing because higher statutory capital reduces the likelihood of a rating downgrade or regulatory action. The cost function is convex because these benefits of higher statutory capital have diminishing returns. An alternative interpretation of the cost function is that the insurer has an economic risk constraint, such as the value-at-risk constraint in Section 1.4.2.

1.5.4 Optimal Pricing

The insurer's profit from selling policies is

$$D_t = (P_t - V_t)Q_t. \tag{1.13}$$

A simple interpretation of this profit function is that for each policy that the insurer sells for P_t, it can buy a portfolio of Treasury bonds that replicates its expected claims for V_t. For term annuities, this interpretation is exact because the future claims are deterministic. For life annuities and life insurance, we assume that the mortality risk is idiosyncratic and that the insured pool is sufficiently large for the law of large numbers to apply.[2] The insurer chooses the price P_t to maximize firm value, which is the profit minus the cost of financial frictions:

$$J_t = D_t - C_t. \tag{1.14}$$

We could specify firm value as the present value of profits, but we opt for the simpler presentation because the key insights do not depend on dynamics.

To simplify the exposition, we present the optimality condition for a single insurer with the understanding that all insurers have the same optimality conditions in a Nash equilibrium. To simplify the notation, we define the demand elasticity as $\epsilon_t = -\partial \log(Q_t)/\partial \log(P_t)$. We also define the marginal cost of capital as

$$c_t = -\frac{\partial C_t}{\partial K_t} > 0. \tag{1.15}$$

The marginal cost of capital represents the importance of financial frictions, which decreases in statutory capital by the convexity of the cost function.

---

2. For life insurance, we also assume that the policy is annually renewable or that the lapsation risk is idiosyncratic.

The first-order condition for the price is

$$\frac{\partial J_t}{\partial P_t} = \frac{\partial D_t}{\partial P_t} + c_t \frac{\partial K_t}{\partial P_t}$$

$$= Q_t + \frac{\partial Q_t}{\partial P_t}(P_t - V_t) + c_t \left(Q_t + \frac{\partial Q_t}{\partial P_t}\left(P_t - (1+\phi)\widehat{V}_t\right)\right)$$

$$= (1+c_t)Q_t + \frac{\partial Q_t}{\partial P_t}\left((1+c_t)P_t - V_t - c_t(1+\phi)\widehat{V}_t\right) = 0. \quad (1.16)$$

We rearrange this equation to solve for the optimal price:

$$P_t = \left(1 - \frac{1}{\epsilon_t}\right)^{-1} \frac{1 + c_t(1+\phi)\frac{\widehat{V}_t}{V_t}}{1 + c_t} V_t. \quad (1.17)$$

The optimal price is the product of three terms. The first term is the markup that is inversely related to the demand elasticity. This term decreases to one as demand becomes perfectly elastic (i.e., $\epsilon_t \to \infty$). The second term arises from financial frictions. This term approaches one as the marginal cost of capital decreases to zero. The third term is the actuarial value or the frictionless marginal cost.

1.5.5   Empirical Implications

Because $c_t > 0$, the optimal price (1.17) satisfies an inequality:

$$P_t \gtrless \left(1 - \frac{1}{\epsilon_t}\right)^{-1} V_t \text{ if } \frac{(1+\phi)\widehat{V}_t}{V_t} \gtrless 1. \quad (1.18)$$

When $(1+\phi)\widehat{V}_t/V_t$ is high, the capital regulation is conservative through a high risk charge ϕ on liabilities or a high reserve valuation $\widehat{V}_t$ relative to the actuarial value V_t. In this case, statutory capital decreases when the insurer sells more policies. Thus, the optimal price is higher than the frictionless price if the insurer is financially constrained (i.e., high $c_t > 0$).

This case describes property and casualty insurance. The capital regulation for property and casualty insurers is conservative to ensure an adequate capital buffer against tail risk. Thus, the supply contracts and prices increase when property and casualty insurers are financially constrained after a severe weather event that causes operating losses (Gron, 1994; Froot and O'Connell, 1999). This case also describes variable annuities, as we discuss in Chapter 4. It is also related to the banking literature, which shows that the loan supply contracts when banks are financially constrained (e.g., Peek and Rosengren, 1997).

When $(1 + \phi)\widehat{V}_t / V_t$ is low, the capital regulation is aggressive through a low risk charge on liabilities or a low reserve valuation relative to the actuarial value. In this case, statutory capital increases when the insurer sells more policies. Thus, the optimal price is lower than the frictionless price if the insurer is financially constrained (i.e., high $c_t > 0$). When the reserve value is less than the actuarial value, the insurer can raise accounting equity as long as the price is above the reserve value, even if the economic profit is negative because the price is below the actuarial value. Although this case is less common, it describes fixed annuities and life insurance during the global financial crisis, as we discuss in Chapter 3.

2

Risks in the Insurance Sector

THE TRADITIONAL sources of risk for life insurers are uncertainty in interest rates, aggregate longevity or mortality, and policyholder behavior. A nearly constant leverage ratio from 1945 through the 1990s in Figure 1.5 suggests that life insurers managed these risks well for decades when fixed annuities and life insurance were their primary liabilities. Life insurers manage interest rate risk by investing a significant share of their assets in long-term bonds. They manage longevity or mortality risk by offsetting annuities with life insurance. Uncertainty in policyholder behavior may be more difficult to hedge, but life insurers have decades of experience to assess the policyholder risk of fixed annuities and life insurance. Finally, life insurers diversify these risks through unaffiliated reinsurance.

Since the 2000s, life insurers have had greater equity and interest risk mismatch as variable annuities have become their primary liability. Variable annuities expose life insurers to long-run volatility risk, which is difficult to hedge with traded options that have short maturities. Life insurers have not sufficiently increased the duration of their bond portfolios or used derivatives to offset the negative duration and the negative convexity from variable annuities. Therefore, life insurers are vulnerable to a low interest rate environment, such as the decade after the global financial crisis.

At the same time, life insurers' balance sheets have become more complex and opaque because of complex capital management tools such as shadow insurance and securities lending. Variable annuities, shadow insurance, and securities lending are all activities that are highly concentrated among the top insurance groups. We describe these sources of risk in Sections 2.1 to 2.5. In Section 2.6, we discuss how these sources of risk could affect the stability of the insurance sector and be transmitted to the rest of the economy through banks, households, and the corporate bond market.

TABLE 2.1. Summary of the Variable Annuity Market

	VA liabilities		Number	Reserve
Year	Billion $	% of total liabilities	of insurers	valuation (%)
2005	1,071	35	45	0.9
2006	1,276	38	47	0.8
2007	1,435	41	46	0.8
2008	1,068	34	44	4.1
2009	1,195	35	43	3.4
2010	1,344	36	43	2.5
2011	1,358	35	42	4.9
2012	1,434	36	39	3.9
2013	1,606	37	40	1.8
2014	1,599	37	38	2.3
2015	1,499	35	38	2.9

Copyright American Finance Association; reprint of Koijen and Yogo (2022a, table 2) with permission. Variable annuity liabilities are the total related account value plus the gross amount of variable annuity reserves minus the reinsurance reserve credit on variable annuities. The reserve valuation is the ratio of the gross amount of variable annuity reserves to the total related account value.

2.1 Variable Annuities

Table 2.1 summarizes the variable annuity market. In 2005, variable annuity liabilities across all insurers were $1.071 trillion or 35% of total liabilities. Variable annuity liabilities varied between 34% and 41% of total liabilities as their value fluctuates with the market value of the underlying mutual funds. In 2015, variable annuity liabilities were $1.499 trillion or 35% of total liabilities. The variable annuity market is fairly concentrated as measured by the number of insurers. The total number of insurers decreased from 44 in 2008 to 38 in 2015.

The reserve valuation (i.e., ratio of the gross amount of variable annuity reserves to the total related account value) measures the value of the minimum return guarantees per dollar of the underlying mutual funds. Table 2.1 shows that the reserve valuation aggregated across all insurers increased sharply from 0.8% in 2007 to 4.1% in 2008. Since 2008, the reserve valuation has been volatile and remains high relative to the level before the global financial crisis.

Table 2.2 lists the top insurers ranked by their variable annuity liabilities in 2007. Eight of these insurers (Aegon, Allianz, AXA, Delaware Life, Hartford, Jackson National, Metropolitan Life, and Voya) suffered large increases in the reserve valuation ranging from 2.9 to 7.6 percentage points. These increases

TABLE 2.2. Top Insurers by Variable Annuity Liabilities

Insurer	VA liabilities in 2007 (billion $)	Change from 2007 to 2008	
		Reserve valuation (%)	Reserves (% of equity)
AXA	140	7.6	125
Metropolitan Life	129	2.9	6
Prudential	122	1.4	13
Voya	121	4.2	42
Hartford	120	2.9	13
AIG	99	0.8	2
Lincoln	97	1.3	15
John Hancock	95	1.8	27
Ameriprise	81	1.0	13
Aegon	63	7.3	29
Pacific Life	56	1.5	13
Nationwide	46	1.7	18
Jackson National	33	3.6	13
Delaware Life	24	3.7	44
Allianz	23	5.3	35
New York Life	19	2.2	2
Genworth	17	0.5	1
Northwestern	12	0.2	0
Ohio National Life	11	2.2	22
Fidelity Investments	10	1.0	8
Security Benefit	10	1.3	12
MassMutual	6	1.7	0
Thrivent Financial	3	0.4	0

Copyright American Finance Association; reprint of Koijen and Yogo (2022a, table 3) with permission. Variable annuity liabilities are the total related account value plus the gross amount of variable annuity reserves minus the reinsurance reserve credit on variable annuities. The reserve valuation is the ratio of the gross amount of variable annuity reserves to the total related account value. The change in the gross amount of variable annuity reserves is reported as a share of total equity in 2007. The sample includes all insurers with at least $1 billion of variable annuity sales in 2007.

in the reserve valuation are significant shocks because these insurers have high leverage (i.e., ratio of total liabilities to total assets) that ranges from 92% to 97%. For five of the eight insurers, the increases in variable annuity reserves are a significant share of total equity, ranging from 29% to 125%.

The risks associated with minimum return guarantees are not limited to the United States. For example, Equitable Life in the United Kingdom failed partly because of guarantees that were too generous (Roberts, 2012). Perhaps more relevant to the low interest rate environment, many Japanese life insurers experienced significant losses because of overly generous guarantees in the early 2000s (Kashyap, 2002). Minimum return guarantees are important globally and represent a major share of life insurer liabilities in Austria, Denmark, France, Germany, the Netherlands, and Sweden (European Systemic Risk Board, 2015; Hombert and Lyonnet, 2022; Koijen and Yogo, 2022b). In these countries, the average duration of liabilities exceeds that of assets by 5 to 10 years (European Insurance and Occupational Pensions Authority, 2014), which implies significant losses if interest rates remain unexpectedly low, as they were since the European sovereign debt crisis through 2021.

2.2 Derivatives

Insurers could use derivatives to hedge equity and interest risk mismatch between their general account assets and liabilities, including the minimum return guarantees on variable annuities. US life insurers held $1.1 trillion in notional amount of over-the-counter derivatives in 2014 (Berends and King, 2015). Although this amount is a nontrivial share of their liabilities, insurers do not fully hedge for various economic and institutional reasons.

Insurers may not be able to fully hedge because the minimum return guarantees have longer maturities than traded options. Insurers are exposed to unexpected changes in implied volatility if they attempt to hedge the minimum return guarantees by rolling over shorter-maturity options. A dynamic hedging program would be subject to basis risk because of model uncertainty, especially regarding long-run volatility (Sun, 2009; Sun et al., 2009). In addition to basis risk, derivatives could expose insurers to counterparty risk. Although collateral could reduce counterparty risk, it would increase the cost of the hedging programs (Berends and King, 2015). A deeper economic question is why the market for long-maturity options is incomplete if insurers would want to hedge such risks. A potential reason is that someone must bear aggregate risk by market clearing, and insurers may have a comparative advantage over other types of institutions because their liabilities have a longer maturity and are less vulnerable to runs (Paulson et al., 2012).

Insurers, especially stock rather than mutual companies, may not want to hedge because of risk-shifting motives that arise from limited liability and state guaranty associations (Lee, Mayers, and Smith, 1997). Another reason that insurers may not want to hedge is that existing regulation does not properly reward hedging of fluctuations in market value. Insurers report accounting equity under the statutory accounting principles at the operating company level and under GAAP at the holding company level. Therefore, hedge positions differ depending on whether the insurer targets economic, statutory, or GAAP capital. A hedging program that smooths market equity could actually increase the volatility of accounting equity under the statutory accounting principles or GAAP (Credit Suisse, 2012).

Whether insurers target market or accounting equity depends on whether economic frictions (e.g., value-at-risk constraint) or regulatory frictions (i.e., risk-based capital constraint) are more important. Shadow insurance is more efficient than hedging for the purposes of reducing regulatory frictions. Section 2.4 shows that shadow insurance of annuities increased during the global financial crisis, suggesting a role for regulatory frictions.

Sen (2022) uses a difference-in-difference identification strategy around the adoption of Actuarial Guideline 43 to show that insurers target accounting equity. Under the new regulation, the statutory accounting values of GMWB and GMAB became more sensitive to interest rates, while the statutory accounting value of GMIB remained insensitive. Insurers that primarily sold risk-sensitive products increased hedging under the new regulation. In contrast, insurers that primarily sold risk-insensitive products did not increase hedging and instead used shadow insurance to reduce the cost of regulatory frictions.

A basic question in understanding the role of derivatives is whether they indeed hedge, rather than amplify, balance sheet fluctuations. For banks, Begenau, Piazzesi, and Schneider (2015) find that interest rate derivatives actually amplify fluctuations in the overall balance sheet. Figure 2.1 shows the impact of derivatives for the equity growth rate of US life insurers. Derivatives have consistently reduced the volatility of equity. In 2008, equity fell by 6%, which would have been 15% without offsetting gains on derivatives.

2.3   Evidence on Risk Mismatch

2.3.1   Interest Risk Mismatch

If the minimum return guarantees have higher duration and higher convexity than the general account assets, the overall balance sheet is potentially exposed to interest rate risk. The market value of equity decreases with unexpected decreases in interest rates, especially when interest rates are low. Consistent with this view, Hartley, Paulson, and Rosen (2017) find that US life insurers' stock returns have significantly negative exposure to long-term bond

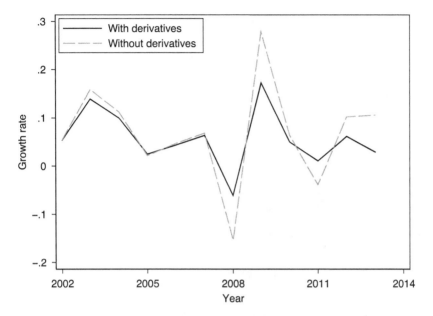

FIGURE 2.1. Impact of Derivatives on the Equity Growth Rate. Copyright Oxford University Press; reprint of Koijen and Yogo (2017, figure 5) with permission. Equity without derivatives is capital and surplus minus the sum of net investment income and total capital gain from derivatives. The sample consists of US life insurers with nonzero derivatives exposure.

returns in the low interest rate environment after the global financial crisis. Similarly, Koijen and Yogo (2022b) find that European insurers that have sold profit participation products with minimum return guarantees have significantly negative exposure to long-term bond returns in the low interest rate environment after the European sovereign debt crisis. In contrast, property and casualty insurers and UK life insurers that did not sell many products with options and high guaranteed rates (Sen and Humphry, 2020) do not have such interest risk exposure.

We update the finding in Hartley, Paulson, and Rosen (2017) with a longer sample, which provides supportive evidence that variable annuity insurers have difficulty managing interest rate risk in the low interest rate environment. We construct monthly returns on a value-weighted portfolio of publicly traded US variable annuity insurers, which are listed in Appendix A.3. We regress excess portfolio returns, relative to the one-month T-bill rate, on excess stock market returns and excess 10-year Treasury bond returns. Table 2.3 reports the betas and the monthly alpha from the factor regression.

TABLE 2.3. Risk Exposure of Variable Annuity Insurers

Factor		By subsample		
		1999–2007	2008–2009	2010–2017
Stock market return	1.36	0.56	2.56	1.11
	(0.19)	(0.15)	(0.22)	(0.08)
10-year bond return	−0.01	−0.38	1.14	−1.28
	(0.32)	(0.29)	(0.66)	(0.16)
Alpha (%)	−0.22	0.35	−1.14	0.41
	(0.46)	(0.47)	(1.70)	(0.29)
Observations	228	108	24	96

Copyright American Finance Association; reprint of Koijen and Yogo (2022a, table 1) with permission. We construct monthly returns on a value-weighted portfolio of publicly traded US variable annuity insurers, which are listed in Appendix A.3. This table reports the betas and monthly alpha from a factor regression of excess portfolio returns, relative to the one-month T-bill rate, on excess stock market returns and excess 10-year Treasury bond returns. Heteroscedasticity-robust standard errors are reported in parentheses. The sample period is January 1999 through December 2017.

Over the sample period from January 1999 to December 2017, the stock market beta is 1.36, and the 10-year bond beta is −0.01 and statistically insignificant. On average, insurers do not have significant interest risk exposure, controlling for the stock market exposure. However, the 10-year bond beta varies over time when we break the sample into three subperiods: pre-crisis (1999 to 2007), financial crisis (2008 to 2009), and post-crisis (2010 to 2017). In the post-crisis subsample, the 10-year bond beta is −1.28 with a t-statistic greater than 7. Thus, unexpected decreases in interest rates are bad news for insurers during this low interest rate environment. A coefficient near −1 implies that the negative duration gap is close to the duration of the 10-year Treasury bond.

As we discuss in Section 6.1.2, the weighted average duration of life insurers' bond portfolios is about eight years. Therefore, the duration gap would be 10 years if the minimum return guarantees have a weighted average duration of 18 years. Another possible source of interest rate risk is the franchise value, or the present value of future insurance business (Shi, 2021). For example, the franchise value could fall with interest rates if the insurer cannot offer sufficiently generous guarantees at competitive fees relative to the customers' outside investment options. Then the insurer's stock price could fall by more than what is implied by the interest risk mismatch on its current balance sheet.

Regardless of its root cause, a 10-year duration gap is surprisingly large. This raises the question of why insurers do not increase the duration of their

assets to reduce the duration gap. In Chapter 6, we argue that insurers optimally hold corporate bonds, which expose them to interest risk mismatch
because corporate bonds have a shorter maturity distribution than Treasury bonds. Thus, optimal portfolio choice actually causes insurers to leave
a negative duration gap.

2.3.2   SRISK

Acharya et al. (2017), Acharya, Philippon, and Richardson (2017), and
Brownlees and Engle (2017) propose a measure of systemic risk for leveraged
financial institutions. A financial institution's SRISK is its dollar equity shortfall in an adverse scenario when the stock market declines by 40% over six
months. Naturally, SRISK increases in market capitalization and market beta.

Table 2.4 lists the top 10 US financial institutions ranked by SRISK on January 31, 2020. Five of the institutions are insurers, which are listed in bold.
Prudential Financial has an SRISK of $36 billion, which is the highest among
insurers and represents 11.2% of the total SRISK for the US financial sector.
Other insurers that have a high SRISK are MetLife, Lincoln National, Brighthouse Financial, and AIG. Taken at face value, these estimates suggest that
insurers are just as important as banks for the stability of the financial sector.

TABLE 2.4. SRISK of US Financial Institutions

Institution	% of total SRISK	SRISK (million $)
Citigroup	19.0	61,197
Prudential Financial	11.2	36,178
Goldman Sachs Group	9.7	31,043
Morgan Stanley	9.6	30,889
Bank of America	7.5	24,096
MetLife	6.9	22,216
Wells Fargo	5.1	16,448
Lincoln National	4.0	12,913
Brighthouse Financial	3.1	9,799
AIG	2.7	8,537

Reprint of the Systemic Risk Analysis (Dynamic MES) of US financial
institutions by the V-Lab at the NYU Stern School of Business. This
table reports SRISK on January 31, 2020 for a 40% stock market decline
over six months at the default model parameters (i.e., an 8% capital
requirement and including 40% of separate accounts).

2.3.3   Stock Returns during the COVID-19 Crisis

The COVID-19 crisis has again exposed the fragility of variable annuity insurers, as we show in Panel A of Figure 2.2. From January 2 to April 2, 2020, the equity drawdown, which is the maximum decrease in the cumulative stock return, was −51% for a value-weighted portfolio of US variable annuity insurers.[1] This equity drawdown was substantially larger than −34% for the S&P 500 index and −43% for the Financial Select Sector SPDR Fund, which is the subset of financial sector stocks in the S&P 500 index. In fact, the equity drawdown on variable annuity insurers was only slightly smaller than −62% for the US Global Jets ETF, which tracks the US airline industry. Panel B of Figure 2.2 shows the equity drawdowns on individual insurers that make up the portfolio in Panel A. AIG, Brighthouse Financial, and Lincoln National suffered the largest equity drawdowns, each exceeding −65%.

The nine insurers with the largest variable annuity liabilities in Table 2.2 coincide almost perfectly with the nine insurers that suffered the largest equity drawdowns in Figure 2.2. AXA and John Hancock (part of Manulife Financial) in Table 2.2 are foreign insurers that are not part of Figure 2.2, which focuses on US insurers. Brighthouse Financial was spun off from Metropolitan Life in 2017, so it was part of Metropolitan Life at the time of Table 2.2 in 2007. Thus, Principal Financial Group is the only insurer that breaks the perfect correspondence of the top nine between Table 2.2 and Figure 2.2.

Figure 2.3 compares the equity drawdowns during the global financial crisis and the COVID-19 crisis across insurers. Insurers with large variable annuity liabilities that had low stock returns during the global financial crisis also have low stock returns during the COVID-19 crisis. The long maturity of the minimum return guarantees means that variable annuities continue to be an important source of risk and that the insurance sector remains fragile.

2.4   Shadow Insurance

We start with a case study of MetLife, which is the largest US insurance group by total assets. We then document the rapid growth of shadow insurance after

---

1. We compute the portfolio return as a buy-and-hold portfolio with fixed weights as of December 31, 2019. A continuously rebalanced portfolio would imply decreasing weights for insurers that suffered the lowest returns, even though the market value of their liabilities presumably increased.

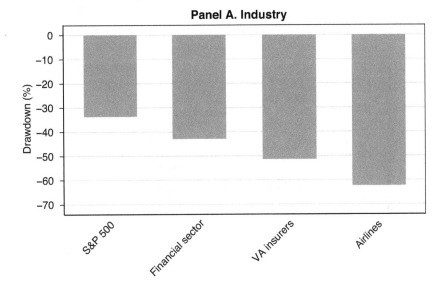

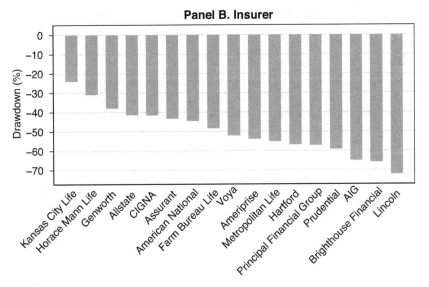

FIGURE 2.2. Equity Drawdowns during the COVID-19 Crisis. Copyright American Finance Association; reprint of Koijen and Yogo (2022a, figure 2) with permission. Panel A shows the equity drawdowns on the S&P 500 index, the Financial Select Sector SPDR Fund, a value-weighted portfolio of US variable annuity insurers, and the US Global Jets ETF. Panel B shows the equity drawdowns on individual insurers that make up the portfolio in Panel A. The equity drawdowns are based on stock returns from January 2 to April 2, 2020.

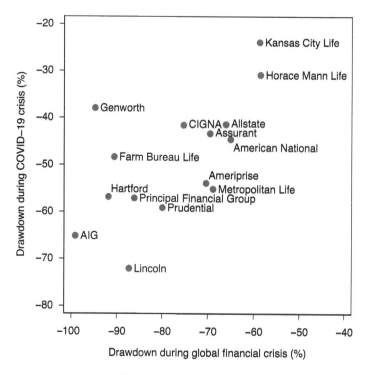

FIGURE 2.3. Comparison of Equity Drawdowns across Crises. Copyright American Economic Association; reprint of Koijen and Yogo (2022b, figure 1) with permission. The equity drawdowns during the global financial crisis are based on stock returns from January 2, 2008 to June 30, 2009. The equity drawdowns during the COVID-19 crisis are based on stock returns from January 2 to April 2, 2020.

2002, as a consequence of changes in life insurance regulation and captive laws that we summarize in Section 1.4.3.

2.4.1   A Case Study of MetLife

Table 2.5 lists the US operating companies of MetLife and their affiliated reinsurers in 2012. The operating companies all have an A.M. Best rating of A+ and cede reinsurance to the rest of the group. The reinsurers are all unrated and assume reinsurance from the rest of the group. The reinsurers are also unauthorized, except for MetLife Reinsurance of Delaware and MetLife Reinsurance of Charleston since 2009. The liabilities consistently disappear from the balance sheets of the operating companies that sell policies and end up in less regulated and unrated reinsurers.

TABLE 2.5. Affiliated Reinsurance within MetLife

Company	Domicile	A.M. Best rating	Net reinsurance ceded (billion $)
Metropolitan Life Insurance	New York	A+	39.1
MetLife Investors USA Insurance	Delaware	A+	13.3
General American Life Insurance	Missouri	A+	3.9
MetLife Insurance of Connecticut	Connecticut	A+	3.6
MetLife Investors Insurance	Missouri	A+	2.6
First MetLife Investors Insurance	New York	A+	1.6
New England Life Insurance	Massachusetts	A+	1.0
Metropolitan Tower Life Insurance	Delaware	A+	0.8
MetLife Reinsurance of Delaware	Delaware		−0.4
MetLife Reinsurance of South Carolina	South Carolina		−3.1
Exeter Reassurance	Bermuda		−5.6
MetLife Reinsurance of Vermont	Vermont		−9.9
MetLife Reinsurance of Charleston	South Carolina		−12.9
Missouri Reinsurance	Barbados		−28.4
Total for MetLife			5.7

Copyright Econometric Society; reprint of Koijen and Yogo (2016, table 3) with permission. This table lists the US operating companies of MetLife and their affiliated reinsurers, whose net reinsurance ceded is greater than $0.1 billion in absolute value in 2012. Net reinsurance ceded is the sum of reserve credit taken and modified coinsurance reserve ceded minus the sum of reserves held and modified coinsurance reserve assumed.

Net reinsurance ceded by Metropolitan Life Insurance (the flagship operating company in New York) was $39.1 billion, which was nearly three times its equity. In the same year, net reinsurance assumed by Missouri Reinsurance (a captive in Barbados) was $28.4 billion. The sum of net reinsurance ceded across all companies in Table 2.5, which is the total reinsurance ceded outside MetLife, was $5.7 billion. Thus, most of the reinsurance activity is within MetLife rather than with unaffiliated reinsurers.

As of December 2020, which is well after Brighthouse Financial was spun off in 2017, MetLife Reinsurance Company of Vermont (MRV) continues to provide $2 billion of capital relief for MetLife's term life insurance and universal life insurance reserves. This capital relief arises from differences between the statutory accounting principles and the prescribed accounting practice of Vermont. According to MetLife's 2020 annual report:

> MRV, with the explicit permission of the Commissioner of Insurance of the State of Vermont, has included, as admitted assets, the value of letters of credit serving as collateral for reinsurance credit taken by various affiliated

TABLE 2.6. Top Insurers by Shadow Insurance

Insurer	Reinsurance ceded (billion $)
John Hancock	118
MetLife	45
Athene	40
Hartford	40
Aegon	26
Great-West Life	14
Voya Financial	13
AIG	12
Global Atlantic	11
Lincoln Financial	7

Copyright Oxford University Press; reprint of Koijen and Yogo (2017, table 2) with permission. A.M. Best financial groups are ranked by life and annuity reinsurance ceded to shadow reinsurers in 2013. Reinsurance ceded is the sum of reserve credit taken and modified coinsurance reserve ceded. Shadow reinsurers are a subset of affiliated reinsurers that are unauthorized and do not have an A.M. Best rating.

cedants, in connection with reinsurance agreements entered into between MRV and the various affiliated cedants, which resulted in higher statutory capital and surplus of $2.0 billion at both December 31, 2020 and 2019. MRV's RBC would have triggered a regulatory event without the use of the state prescribed practice.

2.4.2   Aggregate Facts

Shadow insurance is highly concentrated. Table 2.6 lists the top 10 insurance groups by life and annuity reinsurance ceded to shadow reinsurers in 2013. The top 10 insurance groups ceded $331 billion of liabilities in 2013, which is a major share of $370 billion for the overall sector. These insurance groups are all stock companies and are among the largest in the sector. Stock companies are more prone to agency problems, and larger companies have a scale advantage to set up the financial and legal infrastructure necessary for shadow insurance.

Figure 2.4 shows reinsurance ceded to affiliated, shadow, and unaffiliated reinsurers. Affiliated reinsurance grew from $90 billion in 2002 to $617 billion in 2013. The part of affiliated reinsurance that was ceded to shadow

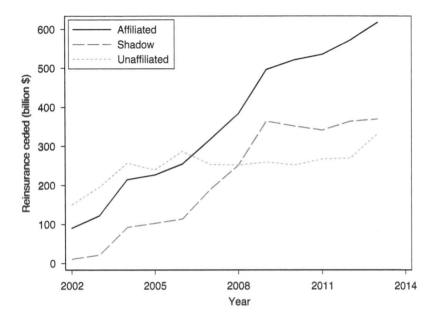

FIGURE 2.4. Reinsurance Ceded by Reinsurer Type. Copyright Oxford University Press;
reprint of Koijen and Yogo (2017, figure 2) with permission. This figure shows life and
annuity reinsurance ceded by US life insurers. Reinsurance ceded is the sum of reserve credit
taken and modified coinsurance reserve ceded. Shadow reinsurers are a subset of affiliated
reinsurers that are unauthorized and do not have an A.M. Best rating.

reinsurers grew from $11 billion to $370 billion during the same period.
The growth of shadow insurance accelerated during the global financial crisis
from 2006 to 2009. Since shadow insurance effectively reduces capital requirements, this timing supports the hypothesis that some insurers were financially
constrained during the global financial crisis.

Figure 2.5 decomposes shadow insurance in Figure 2.4 into life and annuity reinsurance. As we discuss in Section 1.4.3, shadow insurance was initially
a response to the higher capital requirements for life insurance under Regulation (A)XXX. Although these regulations do not apply to annuities, annuity
reinsurance has grown from $5 billion in 2002 to $158 billion in 2013. The
growth of annuity reinsurance was especially high from $54 billion in 2007
to $146 billion in 2009. As we discuss in Section 1.4.3, variable annuity
reserves under the statutory accounting principles could increase relative to
those under GAAP after a period of high volatility. Therefore, insurers could
increase risk-based capital through shadow insurance.

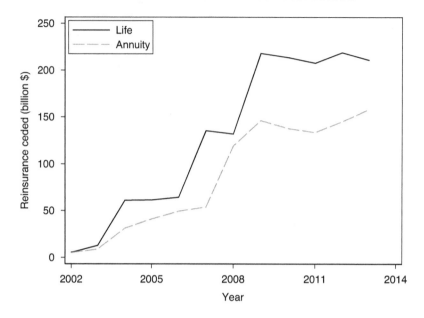

FIGURE 2.5. Life versus Annuity Reinsurance Ceded to Shadow Reinsurers. Copyright Oxford University Press; reprint of Koijen and Yogo (2017, figure 3) with permission. This figure shows life and annuity reinsurance ceded by US life insurers to shadow reinsurers. Reinsurance ceded is the sum of reserve credit taken and modified coinsurance reserve ceded. Shadow reinsurers are a subset of affiliated reinsurers that are unauthorized and do not have an A.M. Best rating.

Shadow insurance is a potential source of risk for three reasons. First, a significant share of shadow insurance is funded through letters of credit, which have a shorter maturity than the insurance liabilities. Therefore, shadow insurance exposes the insurance group to liquidity risk. Second, shadow reinsurers could take more investment risk than the operating companies, which exposes the insurance group to more risk mismatch. Finally, shadow reinsurers could hold less equity than operating companies and increase leverage for the insurance group. Of course, higher leverage amplifies any risk mismatch in the overall balance sheet.

In fact, two case studies suggest that captives have much less equity than the operating companies. First, Lawsky (2013) finds that captives that assume reinsurance from the operating companies in New York have less equity, especially in cases where letters of credit are conditional and are ultimately backed by the parent company instead of an unaffiliated bank. Moody's Investors Service shares a similar view that "because many companies' captives are

TABLE 2.7. Equity of Iowa Captives

Captive	Iowa	Statutory
Cape Verity I	27	−432
Cape Verity II	140	−548
Cape Verity III	54	−169
MNL Reinsurance	118	118
Solberg Reinsurance	207	207
Symetra Reinsurance	20	−51
TLIC Riverwood Reinsurance	817	−1,113
TLIC Oakbrook Reinsurance	114	−675
Total	1,497	−2,663

Copyright Oxford University Press; reprint of Koijen and Yogo (2017, table 3) with permission. Equity of Iowa captives in 2014 are based on the permitted accounting practices of Iowa and the statutory accounting principles. All amounts are in millions of dollars.

capitalized at lower levels compared to flagship companies, the use of captives tends to weaken capital adequacy" (Robinson and Son, 2013, p. 3).

Second, the Iowa Insurance Division (2014) released financial statements for captives in its domicile. These financial statements report equity under both the permitted accounting practices of Iowa and the statutory accounting principles. Table 2.7 summarizes these statements. Six of the eight captives would have significantly negative equity under the statutory accounting principles. The two remaining captives voluntarily report under the statutory accounting principles. When aggregated over the eight captives, total equity under the statutory accounting principles would be −$2.663 billion.

2.5   Securities Lending

In a securities lending transaction, an insurer earns a fee by lending bonds in exchange for cash collateral with an agreement to return the collateral back for the bonds at some future date. The insurer could reinvest the cash collateral to earn higher returns by taking on additional credit, interest, or liquidity risk. Liquidity risk arises when the reinvested collateral has longer duration than the maturity of the lending agreement. If borrowers are unwilling to roll over the lending agreement in bad times, the insurer may be forced to liquidate the investment at fire-sale prices. This is precisely what happened to AIG during the global financial crisis, as they had reinvested their cash collateral in MBSs and asset-backed securities. AIG lost at least $21 billion through securities lending, which is the same order of magnitude as the $34 billion that they lost through credit default swaps (McDonald and Paulson, 2015).

Before 2010, insurers were not required to report details about their security lending activity, particularly regarding how the collateral was reinvested (National Association of Insurance Commissioners, 2011b). This regulatory gap allowed securities lending to build up before the global financial crisis. The amount of admitted assets subject to securities lending agreements grew from $49 billion in 2002 to $130 billion in 2007, then suddenly collapsed to $43 billion in 2008. After important changes to the reporting requirements in 2010, securities lending further dropped to $34 billion in 2011 and remained low at $47 billion in 2013. Given the improved reporting requirements and the smaller scale of activity, securities lending no longer appears to be an important source of risk. However, the experience during the global financial crisis is a cautionary lesson that regulatory gaps could have significant consequences.

Securities lending is highly concentrated. Table 2.8 lists the top 10 insurance groups by the amount of admitted assets subject to securities lending agreements in 2007. These insurance groups accounted for $115 billion of securities lending in 2007, which is a major share of $128 billion for the overall sector. AIG alone accounted for $54 billion in securities lending.

The last column of Table 2.8 reports the total capital gain from investment activity in 2008 as a share of equity in 2007. The capital loss for AIG in 2008 was 169% of its equity in 2007. For the overall sector, life insurers with securities lending activity lost 39% of their equity, while those without securities lending activity lost 18%. To put the 2008 losses into historical perspective, Figure 2.6 shows the aggregate capital gains for life insurers with securities lending agreements in the previous year. The 2008 losses are extraordinary, both in total dollars and as a share of equity in the previous year.

Foley-Fisher, Narajabad, and Verani (2020) study a funding agreement-backed securities structure, which is subject to liquidity risk just like securities lending. Life insurers establish special purpose vehicles that issue funding agreement-backed securities to institutional investors and hold long-term assets such as corporate bonds. Liquidity risk arises because funding agreement-backed securities are puttable. If institutional investors exercise the put option in bad times, insurers may be forced to liquidate the investment at fire-sale prices. Such withdrawals amounted to $18 billion between June 2007 and December 2008.

TABLE 2.8. Top Insurers by Securities Lending Agreements

Insurer	Amount of assets (billion $)	Capital gain (share of equity)
AIG	54	−1.69
MetLife	38	−0.07
New York Life	6	−0.34
Prudential Financial	5	−0.28
Northwestern Mutual	4	−0.52
Hartford	2	−0.07
Genworth Financial	2	0.12
Allstate Financial	2	−0.48
Manulife Financial	2	−0.07
Woodmen Life	1	−0.26
Total for insurers		
with securities lending	128	−0.39
without securities lending	0	−0.18

Copyright Oxford University Press; reprint of Koijen and Yogo (2017, table 4) with permission. A.M. Best financial groups are ranked by the amount of admitted assets subject to securities lending agreements in 2007. Total capital gain from investment activity in 2008 is reported as a share of equity in 2007. The last two rows report the total for all life insurers with and without securities lending activity.

2.6   Potential Transmission Mechanisms

Insurers are interconnected through state guaranty associations. The default of one company could drag down the entire sector because the surviving companies must pay off the defaulted insurance claims through guaranty association assessments. In the aftermath of the global financial crisis, there was an active debate on whether life insurers were interconnected beyond the insurance sector and hence systemically important. Acharya and Richardson (2014) argue that life insurers are systemically important because of their equity risk exposure on both sides of the balance sheet and interconnection with the rest of the financial sector. However, other authors make the counterargument that the risks are relatively small and well isolated (Harrington, 2009; Cummins and Weiss, 2014).

We discuss how risks in the insurance sector could affect its stability and be transmitted to the rest of the economy through the corporate bond market, households, firms, and banks. Our discussion is qualitative because the available data and our current state of knowledge do not allow us to make accurate quantitative assessments. Quantifying the different channels is an important direction for future research.

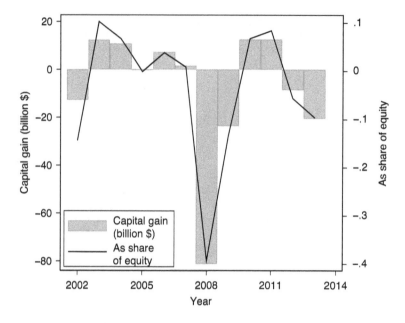

FIGURE 2.6. Capital Gain for Insurers with Securities Lending Agreements. Copyright Oxford University Press; reprint of Koijen and Yogo (2017, figure 4) with permission. This figure shows the total capital gain from investment activity in total dollars and as a share of equity in the previous year. The sample consists of A.M. Best financial groups with a positive amount of admitted assets subject to securities lending agreements in the previous year.

2.6.1   Corporate Bond Market

Figure 1.4 shows that insurers are among the largest institutional investors in the corporate bond market. Therefore, any shock to their balance sheets could interact with risk-based capital regulation to cause a significant shift in demand and price impact. Falling bond prices and rising volatility could cause value-at-risk constraints to bind for other institutional investors, leading to fire-sale dynamics (Brunnermeier and Pedersen, 2009). Lower bond prices ultimately matter for the real economy through higher borrowing costs for firms. In an illustrative exercise, Ellul et al. (2022) build a portfolio-choice model with a risk-based capital constraint and simulate fire-sale scenarios that arise from shocks to asset prices and variable annuity liabilities.

There is substantial evidence in the literature that shifts in bond demand, when insurers become financially constrained, have a price impact. Ellul, Jotikasthira, and Lundblad (2011) find that life insurers sell downgraded corporate bonds to improve their risk-based capital, temporarily depressing prices. Merrill et al. (2021) find similar evidence for downgraded residential MBSs during the global financial crisis. Ellul et al. (2015) find that life insurers sold corporate bonds with the highest unrealized gains, carried at historical cost according to the statutory accounting principles, to improve their risk-based capital during the global financial crisis. These examples show that poorly designed accounting standards and risk-based capital regulation could have unintended consequences. Insurers may have an incentive to sell bonds in depressed markets, even though they would be the natural long-term investors given their liability structure. Such incentives could exacerbate the transmission of shocks through fire-sale dynamics.

2.6.2   Households

A shock to insurers could transmit to households through the insurance product market. For example, demand for insurance products could collapse if households become concerned about the solvency of insurers because of variable annuities or shadow insurance. Instead of purchasing insurance, households may self-insure idiosyncratic risk through precautionary saving. This could have a potentially important impact on aggregate savings and household welfare (Koijen, Van Nieuwerburgh, and Yogo, 2016).

2.6.3   Firms

A shock to property and casualty insurers could transmit to firms and the real economy because liability insurance is necessary for some types of business activity. The HIH Insurance Group, which was the second largest insurer in Australia, collapsed in 2001 as a consequence of poor underwriting and risk management (Damiani, Bourne, and Foo, 2015). Its collapse caused several months of disruptions throughout the Australian economy. Legal and accounting professionals could not operate without liability insurance. Without accident and liability insurance, community and sporting events had to be canceled, and construction had to be halted.

2.6.4   Banks

Insurers are interconnected to banks through at least three channels. First, banks are counterparties in derivatives and securities lending transactions. The experience of AIG suggests that counterparty risk could be significant in bad times (Peirce, 2014; McDonald and Paulson, 2015). Second, insurers provide an important source of funding for banks through the corporate bond market. Any reduction in funding could lead to liquidity problems for banks, at least in the short run. Finally, banks fund a significant share of captive reinsurance through letters of credit. Therefore, a systematic shock to insurance liabilities (e.g., variable annuities) could trigger drawdowns of letters of credit, which expose banks to liquidity and credit risk.

3

Insurance Pricing

IN SECTION 3.1, we start with evidence on the extraordinary pricing of fixed annuities and life insurance during the global financial crisis. Insurers reduced the prices of term annuities, life annuities, and guaranteed universal life insurance from November 2008 to February 2009, when falling interest rates implied that they should have instead raised prices. The average markup, relative to the actuarial value, was −16% for 30-year term annuities and −19% for life annuities at age 60. Similarly, the average markup was −57% for guaranteed universal life insurance at age 30. In the cross section of policies, pricing was lower for policies with looser statutory reserve requirements. In the cross section of insurers, pricing was lower for insurers that suffered larger balance sheet shocks.

This extraordinary pricing behavior is a consequence of two unusual circumstances. First, as we discuss in Chapter 2, the global financial crisis had an adverse impact on insurers' balance sheets, especially insurers with variable annuity liabilities. Second, as we discuss in Section 3.2, statutory reserve regulation allowed insurers to record far less than a dollar of reserve per dollar of economic liability around December 2008. Thus, insurers could generate accounting profits by selling policies at a price far below actuarial value as long as that price was above the reserve value.

In Section 3.3, we extend the insurance pricing model in Section 1.5 to multiple types of policies with different statutory reserve requirements. The model explains the extraordinary pricing behavior during the global financial crisis. In the cross section of policies, the model predicts lower pricing for policies with looser statutory reserve requirements. In the cross section of insurers, the model predicts lower pricing for insurers that are more constrained.

In Section 3.4, we use the insurance pricing model to estimate the marginal cost of capital for the cross section of insurers. Relative to other industries, life insurance presents a unique opportunity to identify the marginal cost of capital for two reasons. First, we can accurately estimate the frictionless marginal cost of fixed annuities and life insurance as the actuarial value. Second, statutory reserve regulation specifies a constant discount rate for reserve valuation, regardless of the maturity of the policy. This mechanical rule generates exogenous variation in required reserves across policies of different maturities, which acts as relative shifts in the supply curve that are plausibly exogenous.

In Section 3.5, we find that the holding companies that are parents of the insurers in our sample appear constrained during the global financial crisis. These holding companies applied for government assistance, issued public equity, or suspended dividends. Thus, capital injections from these holding companies to their subsidiaries could have been limited by frictions in external capital markets.

3.1   Annuity and Life Insurance Prices

3.1.1   Summary Statistics

As we discuss in Section 1.3.2, the data on term and life annuity prices are from the WebAnnuities Insurance Agency, and the data on life insurance premiums are from Compulife Software. These data sources draw from the larger insurers in the industry with an A.M. Best rating of A− or higher and agency- or broker-based marketing (instead of direct sales). In 2011, our sample covers 47 of 275 insurers with an A.M. Best rating of A− or higher and agency- or broker-based marketing. These insurers represented 61% of the immediate annuity market and 42% of the life insurance market (Koijen and Yogo, 2015, table 1).

Table 3.1 summarizes the data on annuity and life insurance prices. We have 870 semiannual observations on 10-year term annuities from January 1989 to July 2011. The markup, defined as the percent deviation of the quoted price from the actuarial value, has a mean of 7.0% and a median of 7.2%. We can rule out adverse selection as a source of this markup because term annuities are essentially straight bonds. Instead, the markup must arise from market power, financial frictions, or marketing and administrative costs. The price of 10-year term annuities varies significantly across insurers, summarized by a standard deviation of 4.2%.

TABLE 3.1. Summary of Annuity and Life Insurance Prices

Type of policy	Sample begins	Frequency	Observations	Markup (%)		
				Mean	Median	Standard deviation
Term annuities:						
5 years	December 1992	Semiannual	646	6.5	6.7	3.7
10 years	January 1989	Semiannual	870	7.0	7.2	4.2
15 years	May 1998	Semiannual	394	4.4	4.5	4.7
20 years	May 1998	Semiannual	390	4.1	4.0	5.7
25 years	May 1998	Semiannual	318	3.7	3.7	6.7
30 years	May 1998	Semiannual	309	3.1	3.2	7.9
Life annuities:						
Life only	January 1989	Monthly	13,675	7.9	8.4	7.6
10-year guarantee	May 1998	Monthly	10,221	4.2	4.9	6.7
20-year guarantee	May 1998	Semiannual	6,248	4.5	4.9	6.5
Universal life insurance	January 2005	Monthly	31,226	−5.8	−6.5	16.0

Copyright American Economic Association; reprint of Koijen and Yogo (2015, table 2) with permission. The markup is defined as the percent deviation of the quoted price from the actuarial value. The actuarial value is based on the appropriate basic mortality table from the American Society of Actuaries and the zero-coupon Treasury yield curve. The sample covers insurers with an A.M. Best rating of A− or higher from January 1989 to July 2011.

We have 13,675 monthly observations on life annuities from January 1989 to July 2011. The average markup is 7.9% with a standard deviation of 7.6%. Although the average markup is high, the large price dispersion means that the cheapest annuities are better than actuarially fair. Therefore, the high average markup does not necessarily justify a low participation rate for life annuities (Friedman and Warshawsky, 1990). The puzzle is rather that many policy-holders do not buy cheaper annuities, similar to the puzzle that demand across S&P 500 index funds is only weakly correlated with the fee (Hortaçsu and Syverson, 2004).

The pricing data on life annuities with guarantees are available from May 1998. For 10-year guaranteed annuities, the average markup is 4.2% with a standard deviation of 6.7%. For 20-year guaranteed annuities, the average markup is 4.5% with a standard deviation of 6.5%.

We have 31,226 monthly observations on guaranteed universal life insurance from January 2005 to July 2011. The average markup is −5.8% with a standard deviation of 16.0%. The negative average markup does not mean that insurers lose money on these policies. With a constant premium and a rising mortality rate, policyholders are essentially prepaying for coverage later in life. When a life insurance policy is lapsed after the acquisition costs have been recovered, the insurer earns a windfall profit because the present value of the remaining premiums is typically less than the present value of the future death benefit. Since there is currently no agreed-upon standard for lapsation pricing, our calculation of the actuarial value does not account for lapsation. We are not especially concerned that the average markup might be slightly mismeasured because our analysis focuses on the variation in markups over time and across policies of different maturities.

3.1.2   Pricing during the Global Financial Crisis

Figure 3.1 shows the average markup on term annuities at various maturities, averaged across insurers and reported with a 95% confidence interval. The average markup usually varies between 0% and 10%, except around November 2008. The time variation in the average markup implies that insurers do not change annuity prices to perfectly offset interest rate movements (Charupat, Kamstra, and Milevsky, 2012).

For 30-year term annuities, the average markup fell to an extraordinary −15.7% in November 2008. Much of this large negative markup arises from price reductions for term annuities from May 2007 to November 2008, as

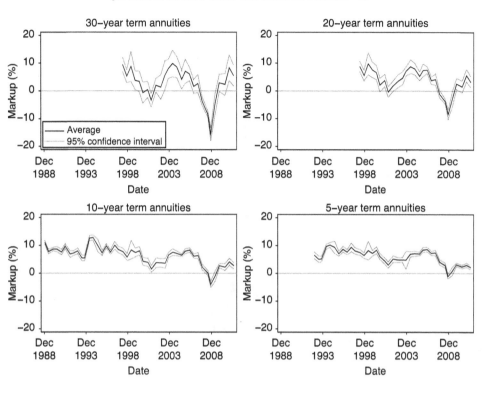

FIGURE 3.1. Average Markup on Term Annuities. Copyright American Economic Association; reprint of Koijen and Yogo (2015, figure 1) with permission. The markup is defined as the percent deviation of the quoted price from the actuarial value. The actuarial value is based on the zero-coupon Treasury yield curve. The sample covers insurers with an A.M. Best rating of A− or higher from January 1989 to July 2011.

we discuss below. In November 2008, the magnitude of the average markup is monotonically related to the maturity of the term annuity. The average markup was −8.5% for 20-year, −4.0% for 10-year, and −1.1% for 5-year term annuities. Excluding the extraordinary period around November 2008, the average markup was negative for 30-year term annuities only twice before in our semiannual sample (in October 2000 and October 2001).

Figure 3.2 shows the average markup on life annuities for males at various ages. Our findings are similar to those for term annuities. For life annuities at age 60, the average markup fell to an extraordinary −19.0% in December 2008. The magnitude of the average markup is monotonically related to age, which is negatively related to the effective maturity. The average markup on life annuities was −14.7% at age 65, −10.3% at age 70, and −5.7% at age 75.

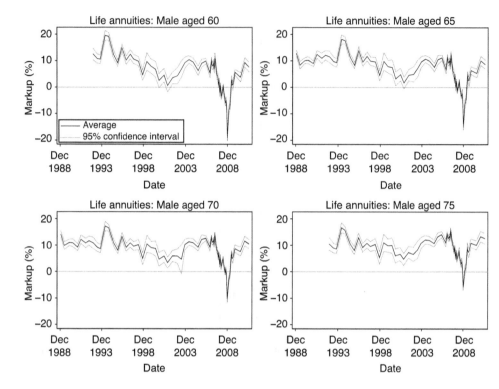

FIGURE 3.2. Average Markup on Life Annuities. Copyright American Economic Association; reprint of Koijen and Yogo (2015, figure 2) with permission. The markup is defined as the percent deviation of the quoted price from the actuarial value. The actuarial value is based on the appropriate basic mortality table from the American Society of Actuaries and the zero-coupon Treasury yield curve. The sample covers insurers with an A.M. Best rating of A— or higher from January 1989 to July 2011.

Figure 3.3 shows the average markup on guaranteed universal life insurance for males at various ages. Our findings are similar to those for term and life annuities. For guaranteed universal life insurance at age 30, the average markup fell to an extraordinary −57.0% in December 2008. The magnitude of the average markup is monotonically related to age. The average markup on guaranteed universal life insurance was −50.2% at age 40, −42.1% at age 50, and −27.5% at age 60.

Figure 3.4 shows the cross-sectional relation between changes in annuity prices from May 2007 to November 2008 and four measures of balance sheet shocks at fiscal year-end 2008. The figure reveals two important facts. First, most insurers reduced prices during this period, which is remarkable given that falling interest rates implied rising actuarial values. Second, the price

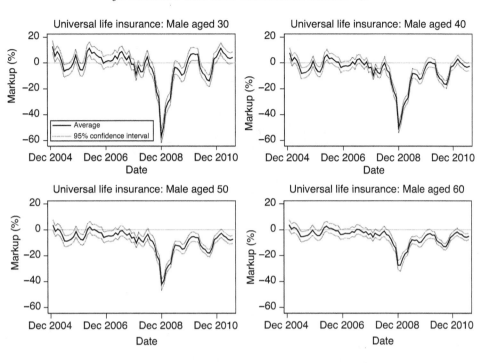

FIGURE 3.3. Average Markup on Life Insurance. Copyright American Economic Association; reprint of Koijen and Yogo (2015, figure 3) with permission. The markup is defined as the percent deviation of the quoted price from the actuarial value. The actuarial value is based on the appropriate basic mortality table from the American Society of Actuaries and the zero-coupon Treasury yield curve. The monthly sample covers insurers with an A.M. Best rating of A− or higher from January 2005 to July 2011.

reductions were larger for insurers with lower asset growth, a higher leverage ratio, lower risk-based capital relative to guideline, and a higher ratio of deferred annuity liabilities to equity. Deferred annuities include fixed and variable annuities, whose minimum return guarantees were unprofitable during the global financial crisis. The fact that the price reductions were larger for insurers that suffered larger balance sheet shocks suggests financial frictions as a potential explanation.

3.1.3   Evidence against Default Risk

Pricing below the actuarial value could reflect the possibility that policyholders may not receive the full face value of policies in the event of future default. However, the only scenario in which a policyholder would not be fully repaid is if all insurers associated with the state guaranty association were to default

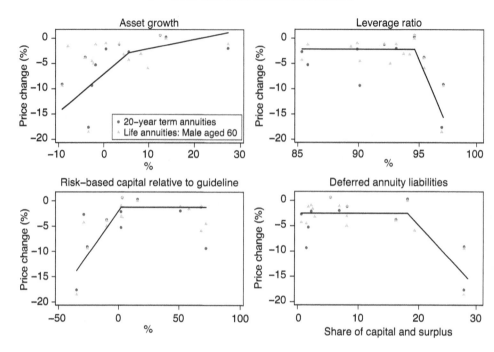

FIGURE 3.4. Relation between Price Changes and Balance Sheet Shocks. Copyright
American Economic Association; reprint of Koijen and Yogo (2015, figure 4) with
permission. The percent change in annuity prices is from May 2007 to November 2008.
Asset growth is from fiscal year-end 2007 to 2008. The leverage ratio, risk-based capital
relative to guideline, and the ratio of deferred annuity liabilities to equity are at fiscal
year-end 2008. The best-fitting monotone linear spline with one knot weights the
observations by total admitted assets at fiscal year-end 2007.

and the federal government were to provide no additional support. During
the global financial crisis, the pricing of annuities and life insurance remained
linear around the guaranteed amount, and pricing was uniform across states
with different guaranty provisions. The absence of kinks in pricing around
the guaranteed amount rules out idiosyncratic default risk that affects only
some insurers, but it does not rule out systematic default risk in which the
state guaranty fund fails.

Suppose that we were to entertain an extreme scenario in which the state
guaranty fund fails. Since insurers are subject to risk-based capital regulation, risky assets (e.g., non-investment-grade bonds, common and preferred
stocks, nonperforming mortgages, and real estate) account for only 16% of
their assets (Ellul, Jotikasthira, and Lundblad, 2011). The remainder of their

assets are in safe asset classes such as cash, Treasury bonds, and investment-grade bonds. Under an extreme assumption that the risky assets lose their value entirely, a reasonable upper bound on the loss ratio is 16%. To further justify this loss ratio, the asset deficiency in past cases of insolvency typically ranges from 5% to 10% and very rarely exceeds 15% (Gallanis, 2009).

Let $\pi_t(l)$ be the risk-neutral default probability between year $l-1$ and l at time t, and let θ be the loss ratio conditional on default. Then the market value of an M-year term annuity per dollar of income is

$$V_t(M) = \sum_{m=1}^{M} \frac{1 - \theta + \theta \prod_{l=1}^{m}(1 - \pi_t(l))}{(1 + y_t(m))^m}. \qquad (3.1)$$

Panel B of Table 3.2 reports the term structure of default probabilities implied by the markups on term annuities in Panel A. For MetLife Investors USA Insurance Company, an annual default probability of 24.4% at the 1- to 5-year horizon and 17.9% at the 6- to 10-year horizon justifies the markups on 5- and 10-year term annuities. There are no default probabilities that can justify the markups on term annuities with a maturity greater than 15 years. This is because equation (3.1) implies that the markup cannot be less than the loss ratio of 16%, which is clearly violated for term annuities with a maturity greater than 25 years.

Panel C of Table 3.2 presents further evidence against default risk based on the term structure of risk-neutral default probabilities implied by credit default swaps on the holding company of the respective subsidiary in Panel B. First, the 6- to 10-year default probability implied by term annuities is higher than that implied by credit default swaps for all companies, except American General Life Insurance Company. This finding is inconsistent with default risk given that the policyholders of a subsidiary are senior to the creditors of its holding company. Second, term annuities imply an upward-sloping term structure of default probabilities, which does not match the downward-sloping term structure implied by credit default swaps. Finally, the relative ranking of default probabilities across the subsidiaries in Panel B does not align with the relative ranking across the respective holding companies in Panel C.

3.2 Statutory Reserve Regulation

When an insurer sells an annuity or life insurance policy, its assets increase by the purchase price of the policy. At the same time, the insurer must record

TABLE 3.2. Default Probabilities Implied by Term Annuities versus Credit Default Swaps

Company	Maturity (years)					
	5	10	15	20	25	30
Panel A. Markup (%)						
Allianz Life Insurance of North America	0.4	−2.9	−7.7	−12.8	−18.2	−21.7
Lincoln Benefit Life	−1.4	−4.6	−6.3	−7.8	−9.9	−12.6
MetLife Investors USA Insurance		−9.2	−12.1	−14.5	−17.3	−20.9
Genworth Life Insurance	0.0	−2.6	−4.0	−5.9	−8.7	−12.4
Aviva Life and Annuity	0.1	−1.5	−2.1	−4.3	−7.9	−11.9
American General Life Insurance	−2.4	−3.3	−4.6	−7.8	−10.6	−14.2
Panel B. Default probabilities implied by term annuities (%)						
Allianz Life Insurance of North America	0.0	72.6	100.0	100.0	100.0	100.0
Lincoln Benefit Life	3.2	19.6	16.5	100.0	100.0	100.0
MetLife Investors USA Insurance	24.4	17.9	100.0	100.0	100.0	100.0
Genworth Life Insurance	0.1	15.4	14.5	100.0	100.0	100.0
Aviva Life and Annuity	0.0	8.4	10.1	100.0	100.0	100.0
American General Life Insurance	5.4	1.6	78.6	100.0	100.0	100.0
Panel C. Default probabilities implied by credit default swaps (%)						
Allianz Group	1.9	1.8				
Allstate	4.6	3.7				
MetLife	10.0	6.0				
Genworth Financial	32.8	4.8				
Aviva	2.8	2.7				
American International Group	20.3	5.8				

Copyright American Economic Association; reprint of Koijen and Yogo (2015, table 7) with permission. Panel B reports the term structure of annual risk-neutral default probabilities that justify the markups on term annuities in Panel A. An implied default probability of 100% means that the markups are too low to be justified by default risk, given a loss ratio of 16%. Panel C reports the term structure of annual risk-neutral default probabilities implied by 5- and 10-year credit default swaps on the holding company of the respective subsidiary in Panel B.

reserves on the liability side of its balance sheet to cover future claims. The amount of required reserves for each type of policy is governed by state law, but all states essentially follow recommended guidelines known as the Standard Valuation Law (National Association of Insurance Commissioners, 2011a, appendix A-820). The Standard Valuation Law establishes mortality tables and discount rates that are to be used for reserve valuation.

We describe the statutory reserve regulation for annuities and life insurance. Because these policies essentially have no market risk exposure, finance theory implies that the market value of these policies is determined by the term structure of riskless interest rates. However, the Standard Valuation Law requires that the reserve value of these policies be calculated using a mechanical discount rate that is a function of the Moody's composite yield on seasoned corporate bonds. Insurers care about the reserve value of policies insofar as it is used by rating agencies and state regulators to determine capital adequacy (A.M. Best Company, 2011, p. 31). Following the discussion in Section 1.4.2, low statutory capital could lead to a rating downgrade or regulatory action.

3.2.1 Term Annuities

Let $\bar{y}_t$ be the 12-month moving average of the Moody's composite yield on seasoned corporate bonds, over the period ending on June 30 prior to issuance of the policy. For an annuity issued at date t, the Standard Valuation Law specifies the following discount rate for reserve valuation:

$$\widehat{y}_t = 0.03 + 0.8(\bar{y}_t - 0.03), \tag{3.2}$$

which is rounded to the nearest 25 basis point. This is a constant discount rate that applies to all expected claims, regardless of maturity. The exogenous variation in required reserves that this mechanical rule generates, both over time and across policies of different maturities, allows us to identify financial frictions.

Figure 3.5 shows the discount rate for annuities together with the 10-year zero-coupon Treasury yield. The discount rate for annuities has generally fallen over the sample period as nominal interest rates have fallen. However, the discount rate for annuities has fallen more slowly than the 10-year Treasury yield. This means that statutory reserve requirements for annuities have become looser over time because a high discount rate implies low reserve valuation.

The reserve value of an M-year term annuity per dollar of income is

$$\widehat{V}_t(M) = \sum_{m=1}^{M} \frac{1}{(1+\widehat{y}_t)^m}. \tag{3.3}$$

Figure 3.6 shows the ratio of reserve to actuarial value for term annuities (i.e., $\widehat{V}_t(M)/V_t(M)$) at maturities of 5 to 30 years. Whenever this ratio is equal to one, the insurance liabilities are marked to market. That is, the insurer records a dollar of reserve per dollar of future claims in present value. Whenever this ratio is above one, the reserve valuation is more conservative than

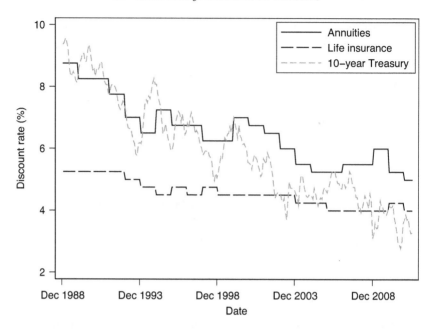

FIGURE 3.5. Discount Rates for Annuities and Life Insurance. Copyright American Economic Association; reprint of Koijen and Yogo (2015, figure 5) with permission. This figure shows the discount rates used for statutory reserve valuation of annuities and life insurance, together with the 10-year zero-coupon Treasury yield. The monthly sample covers January 1989 to July 2011.

mark-to-market. Conversely, whenever this ratio is below one, the reserve valuation is more aggressive than mark-to-market.

For 30-year term annuities, the ratio of reserve to actuarial value reaches a peak of 1.20 in November 1994 and a trough of 0.73 in January 2009. If an insurer were to sell a 30-year term annuity at the actuarial value in November 1994, its reserves would increase by $1.20 per dollar of policies sold. This implies a loss of $0.20 in accounting equity per dollar of policies sold. In contrast, if an insurer were to sell a 30-year term annuity at the actuarial value in January 2009, its reserves would only increase by $0.73 per dollar of policies sold. This implies a gain of $0.27 in accounting equity per dollar of policies sold.

3.2.2   Life Annuities

The reserve valuation of life annuities requires mortality tables. The American Society of Actuaries produces two versions of mortality tables, which are

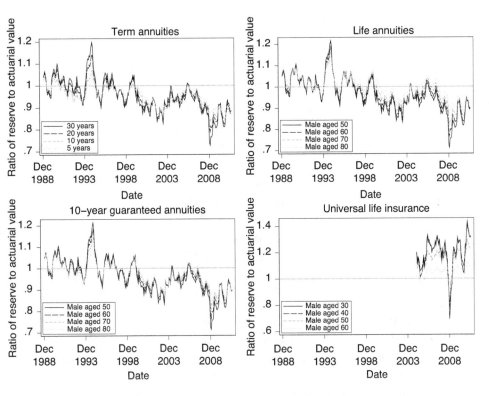

FIGURE 3.6. Reserve to Actuarial Value for Annuities and Life Insurance. Copyright
American Economic Association; reprint of Koijen and Yogo (2015, figure 6) with
permission. The reserve value is based on the appropriate loaded mortality table from the
American Society of Actuaries and the discount rate from the Standard Valuation Law. The
actuarial value is based on the appropriate basic mortality table from the American Society of
Actuaries and the zero-coupon Treasury yield curve. The monthly sample covers January
1989 to July 2011 for annuities and January 2005 to July 2011 for life insurance.

called basic and loaded. The loaded tables, which are used for reserve valuation, are conservative versions of the basic tables that underestimate the
mortality rates. The loaded tables ensure that insurers have adequate reserves,
even if the actual mortality rates turn out to be lower than those projected by
the basic tables. For calculating the reserve value, we use the 1983 Annuity
Mortality Table before January 1999 and the 2000 Annuity Mortality Table
since January 1999.

Let $\widehat{\pi}_n$ be the one-year survival probability at age n, and let N be the maximum attainable age according to the appropriate loaded mortality table. The
reserve value of a life annuity with an M-year guarantee at age n per dollar of

income (Lombardi, 2006, p. 204) is

$$\widehat{V}_t(n, M) = \sum_{m=1}^{M} \frac{1}{(1+\widehat{y}_t)^m} + \sum_{m=M+1}^{N-n} \frac{\prod_{l=0}^{m-1} \widehat{\pi}_{n+l}}{(1+\widehat{y}_t)^m}, \tag{3.4}$$

where the discount rate is given by equation (3.2).

Figure 3.6 shows the ratio of reserve to actuarial value for life annuities and 10-year guaranteed annuities for males aged 50 to 80 (every 10 years in between). The time variation in reserve to actuarial value for life annuities is quite similar to that for term annuities. In particular, the ratio reaches a peak in November 1994 and a trough in January 2009. Since the reserve valuation of term annuities depends only on the discount rates, the similarity to term annuities implies that discount rates, rather than mortality tables, have a predominant effect on the reserve valuation of life annuities.

3.2.3   Life Insurance

Let $\bar{y}_t$ be the minimum of the 12-month and the 36-month moving average of the Moody's composite yield on seasoned corporate bonds, over the period ending on June 30 prior to issuance of the policy. For life insurance with a guaranteed term greater than 20 years issued at date t, the Standard Valuation Law specifies the following discount rate for reserve valuation:

$$\widehat{y}_t = 0.03 + 0.35(\min\{\bar{y}_t, 0.09\} - 0.03) + 0.175(\max\{\bar{y}_t, 0.09\} - 0.09), \tag{3.5}$$

which is rounded to the nearest 25 basis point.

As with life annuities, the American Society of Actuaries produces basic and loaded mortality tables for life insurance. The loaded tables, which are used for reserve valuation, are conservative versions of the basic tables that overestimate the mortality rates. For calculating the reserve value, we use the 2001 Commissioners Standard Ordinary Mortality Table. The reserve value of life insurance at age n per dollar of death benefit (Lombardi, 2006, pp. 67–68) is

$$\widehat{V}_t(n) = \left(1 + \sum_{m=1}^{N-n-1} \frac{\prod_{l=0}^{m-1} \widehat{\pi}_{n+l}}{(1+\widehat{y}_t)^m}\right)^{-1}$$

$$\times \left(\sum_{m=1}^{N-n} \frac{\prod_{l=0}^{m-2} \widehat{\pi}_{n+l}(1 - \widehat{\pi}_{n+m-1})}{(1+\widehat{y}_t)^m}\right) - \frac{1 - \widehat{\pi}_n}{(1+\widehat{y}_t)}. \tag{3.6}$$

Figure 3.6 shows the ratio of reserve to actuarial value for guaranteed universal life insurance for males aged 30 to 60 (every 10 years in between). Our earlier caveat regarding lapsation applies to this figure as well, so that we focus on the variation in reserve to actuarial value over time and across policies of different maturities. The reserve value falls significantly relative to the actuarial value around December 2008. Figure 3.5 shows that this is because the discount rate for life insurance stays constant during this period, while the 10-year Treasury yield falls significantly. If an insurer were to sell guaranteed universal life insurance to a 30-year-old male in December 2008, its reserves would only increase by $0.69 per dollar of policies sold. This implies a gain of $0.31 in accounting equity per dollar of policies sold.

3.3 Insurance Pricing Model

We extend the insurance pricing model in Section 1.5 in three ways to explain the evidence in Section 3.1. First, the insurer chooses the prices for multiple types of policies with different statutory reserve requirements. Second, we model financial frictions as a leverage constraint on statutory capital, which better captures the sharp nature of the pricing behavior during the global financial crisis. Third, we change the objective function to the present value of profits to allow for pricing to depend on the possibility of future binding constraints.

The model predicts that the insurer reduces prices, even below the actuarial value, when the leverage constraint binds. In the cross section of policies, the model predicts lower pricing for policies with looser statutory reserve requirements. In the cross section of insurers, the model predicts lower pricing for insurers that are more constrained.

3.3.1 Insurance Market

An insurer sells various types of policies indexed by $i = 1, \ldots, I$. The different types of policies include annuities and life insurance, which are differentiated not only by maturity but also by sex and age of the insured. The insurer faces a separate demand function for each type of policy that depends on its own price and the prices of its competitors. The demand function is continuously differentiable and strictly decreasing in its own price.

In period t, the insurer chooses the price $P_{i,t}$ for each type of policy and sells $Q_{i,t}$ policies. As we discuss in Section 1.2, the actuarial value per policy is $V_{i,t}$. As we discuss in Section 3.2, the reserve value per policy is $\widehat{V}_{i,t}$.

3.3.2 Balance Sheet Dynamics

We describe how the sale of policies affects the balance sheet. Let A_{t-1} be the assets at the beginning of period t, and let $R_{A,t}$ be an exogenous gross asset return in period t. The assets at the end of period t, after the sale of policies, are

$$A_t = R_{A,t}A_{t-1} + \sum_{i=1}^{I} P_{i,t}Q_{i,t}. \tag{3.7}$$

The insurer must also record reserves on the liability side of its balance sheet. Let L_{t-1} be the reserves at the beginning of period t, and let $R_{L,t}$ be an exogenous gross return on reserves in period t. The reserves at the end of period t, after the sale of policies, are

$$L_t = R_{L,t}L_{t-1} + \sum_{i=1}^{I} \widehat{V}_{i,t}Q_{i,t}. \tag{3.8}$$

We define statutory capital as equity minus required capital, which is proportional to reserves:

$$K_t = \underbrace{A_t - L_t}_{\text{equity}} - \underbrace{\phi_t L_t}_{\text{required capital}}, \tag{3.9}$$

where $\phi_t > 0$ is a risk charge on liabilities under risk-based capital regulation. Substituting equations (3.7) and (3.8) into equation (3.9), the law of motion for statutory capital is

$$K_t = R_{K,t}K_{t-1} + \sum_{i=1}^{I} \left(P_{i,t} - (1+\phi_t)\widehat{V}_{i,t} \right) Q_{i,t}, \tag{3.10}$$

where

$$R_{K,t} = \frac{A_{t-1}}{K_{t-1}}R_{A,t} - \frac{(1+\phi_t)L_{t-1}}{K_{t-1}}R_{L,t} \tag{3.11}$$

is the return on statutory capital.

3.3.3 Financial Frictions

Following the discussion in Section 1.4.2, low statutory capital could lead to a rating downgrade or regulatory action, which has adverse consequences in both retail and capital markets. Moreover, financial frictions make equity issuance costly. We model financial frictions as a leverage constraint on statutory capital:

$$K_t \geq 0 \Leftrightarrow \frac{L_t}{A_t} \leq \frac{1}{1+\phi_t} \Leftrightarrow \frac{A_t - L_t}{\phi_t L_t} \geq 1. \tag{3.12}$$

The leverage constraint has three equivalent formulations. The first equation states that statutory capital must be positive. The second equation states that the leverage ratio must be less than $1/(1+\phi_t)$. The third equation states that the risk-based capital ratio must be greater than one. Under the third interpretation, ϕ_t is the risk charge on liabilities.

3.3.4   Optimal Pricing

The insurer's profit from selling policies is

$$D_t = \sum_{i=1}^{I} (P_{i,t} - V_{i,t}) Q_{i,t}. \tag{3.13}$$

Firm value is the present value of profits:

$$J_t = D_t + \mathbb{E}_t[M_{t+1} J_{t+1}], \tag{3.14}$$

where M_{t+1} is the stochastic discount factor. The insurer chooses the price $P_{i,t}$ for each type of policy to maximize firm value subject to the law of motion for statutory capital (3.10) and the leverage constraint (3.12). Let $c_t \geq 0$ be the Lagrange multiplier on the leverage constraint. The Lagrangian for the insurer's maximization problem is

$$\mathcal{L}_t = J_t + c_t K_t. \tag{3.15}$$

To simplify the exposition, we present the optimality conditions for a single insurer with the understanding that all insurers have the same optimality conditions in a Nash equilibrium. To simplify the notation, we define the demand elasticity as $\epsilon_{i,t} = -\partial \log(Q_{i,t})/\partial \log(P_{i,t})$. We also define the marginal cost of capital as

$$\bar{c}_t = -\left(\frac{\partial K_t}{\partial P_{i,t}}\right)^{-1} \frac{\partial D_t}{\partial P_{i,t}} = c_t + \mathbb{E}_t\left[M_{t+1}\frac{\partial J_{t+1}}{\partial K_t}\right]. \tag{3.16}$$

It measures the marginal reduction in profits that the insurer is willing to accept to raise its statutory capital by a dollar. Alternatively, it measures the importance of statutory capital for relaxing the leverage constraint today through c_t or at some future state through $\mathbb{E}_t[M_{t+1}\partial J_{t+1}/\partial K_t]$.

The first-order condition for the price of policy i is

$$\frac{\partial \mathcal{L}_t}{\partial P_{i,t}} = \frac{\partial J_t}{\partial P_{i,t}} + c_t \frac{\partial K_t}{\partial P_{i,t}} = \frac{\partial D_t}{\partial P_{i,t}} + \bar{c}_t \frac{\partial K_t}{\partial P_{i,t}}$$

$$= Q_{i,t} + \frac{\partial Q_{i,t}}{\partial P_{i,t}}(P_{i,t} - V_{i,t}) + \bar{c}_t \left(Q_{i,t} + \frac{\partial Q_{i,t}}{\partial P_{i,t}} \left(P_{i,t} - (1+\phi_t)\widehat{V}_{i,t} \right) \right)$$

$$= (1+\bar{c}_t)Q_{i,t} + \frac{\partial Q_{i,t}}{\partial P_{i,t}} \left((1+\bar{c}_t)P_{i,t} - V_{i,t} - \bar{c}_t(1+\phi_t)\widehat{V}_{i,t} \right) = 0.$$

$$(3.17)$$

We rearrange equation (3.17) to solve for the optimal price of policy i:

$$P_{i,t} = \left(1 - \frac{1}{\epsilon_{i,t}}\right)^{-1} \frac{1 + \bar{c}_t(1+\phi_t)\frac{\widehat{V}_{i,t}}{V_{i,t}}}{1+\bar{c}_t} V_{i,t}. \qquad (3.18)$$

The optimal price is the product of three terms. The first term is the markup that is inversely related to the demand elasticity. The second term arises from financial frictions. The third term is the actuarial value or the frictionless marginal cost.

3.3.5   Empirical Implications

Equation (3.18) explains the evidence in Section 3.1. In the cross section of policies, the model predicts lower pricing for policies with looser statutory reserve requirements (i.e., lower $\widehat{V}_{i,t}/V_{i,t}$). Consistent with this prediction, the differences in pricing across policies of different maturities during the global financial crisis (see Figures 3.1 to 3.3) align with the differences in statutory reserve requirements (see Figure 3.6). The model also explains why the extraordinary pricing behavior was so short-lived. Figure 3.6 shows that the reserve value was significantly lower than the actuarial value from November 2008 to February 2009, which was a relatively short window of opportunity for insurers to raise statutory capital by selling policies.

In the cross section of insurers, the model predicts lower pricing for insurers with a higher marginal cost of capital (3.16). The insurer may reduce prices, sacrificing current economic profits, to relax current or future leverage constraints. Figure 3.4 supports this prediction if the insurers that suffered larger balance sheet shocks were more constrained and had a higher marginal cost of capital.

Equation (3.18) predicts that a constrained insurer chooses low prices on policies for which $\widehat{V}_{i,t}/V_{i,t} < 1/(1+\phi_t)$. It also predicts that the same insurer chooses high prices on policies for which $\widehat{V}_{i,t}/V_{i,t} > 1/(1+\phi_t)$. In Section 4.1, we show that the same insurers that reduced fixed annuity prices simultaneously raised variables annuity fees during the global financial crisis, for which $\widehat{V}_{i,t}/V_{i,t}$ are high.

Ge (2022) studies how the life subsidiary responds when an insurance group becomes constrained due to operating losses on its property and casualty subsidiary. She uses severe weather events at the state level as an instrument for the property and casualty subsidiary's operating losses. The life subsidiary raises the price of 10-year term life insurance and reduces the price of guaranteed universal life insurance. This finding is consistent with equation (3.18) because $\widehat{V}_{i,t}/V_{i,t}$ is higher for term life insurance than guaranteed universal life insurance. It is also consistent with liquidity constraints because term life insurance has higher acquisition costs as a share of premiums and hence a lower initial cash flow than guaranteed universal life insurance. In addition, she finds that the life subsidiary transfers capital to the property and casualty subsidiary, which suggests that financial and liquidity constraints operate through internal capital markets.

3.4 Estimating the Insurance Pricing Model

3.4.1 Empirical Specification

Let i index the type of policy, n index the insurer, and t index time. Equation (3.18) implies a nonlinear regression model for the markup:

$$\log\left(\frac{P_{i,n,t}}{V_{i,t}}\right) = -\log\left(1 - \frac{1}{\epsilon_{i,n,t}}\right) + \log\left(\frac{1 + \bar{c}_{n,t}\frac{A_{n,t}}{L_{n,t}}\frac{\widehat{V}_{i,t}}{V_{i,t}}}{1 + \bar{c}_{n,t}}\right) + v_{i,n,t}, \quad (3.19)$$

where $v_{i,n,t}$ is an error term with zero conditional mean. This equation substitutes $1 + \phi_{n,t} = A_{n,t}/L_{n,t}$ when the leverage constraint binds.

We do not have quantity data by type of policy that are necessary to estimate a differentiated product demand system. Therefore, we model the demand elasticity in reduced form as

$$\epsilon_{i,n,t} = 1 + \exp(-\boldsymbol{\beta}'\mathbf{y}_{i,n,t}), \quad (3.20)$$

where $y_{i,n,t}$ is a vector of policy and insurer characteristics. The policy characteristics in our specification are sex and age. The insurer characteristics are the A.M. Best rating, log assets, asset growth, leverage ratio, risk-based capital relative to guideline, current liquidity, and operating return on equity (see Appendix A.2). We interact each of these variables with a dummy variable that allows their impact on the demand elasticity to differ between annuities and life insurance. We also include year-quarter and domiciliary-state fixed effects to capture additional variation in the demand elasticity.

We model the marginal cost of capital as

$$\bar{c}_{n,t} = \exp(\gamma' z_{n,t}), \tag{3.21}$$

where $z_{n,t}$ is a vector of insurer characteristics. Motivated by the reduced-form evidence in Figure 3.4, the insurer characteristics are log assets, asset growth, leverage ratio, risk-based capital relative to guideline, and net equity inflow (see Appendix A.2). We capture time variation in the marginal cost of capital through the yield spread between Moody's Aaa corporate bonds and 20-year constant-maturity Treasury bonds. The corporate yield spread is an important measure of borrowing costs that is closely related to time-varying risk premia in financial markets. Our specification also includes year-quarter fixed effects that allow the marginal cost of capital to be zero, by essentially turning off both insurer characteristics and the corporate yield spread.

3.4.2   Identifying Assumptions

If the demand elasticity is correctly specified, equation (3.19) implies that the markup has a positive conditional mean whenever the marginal cost of capital is zero. Therefore, a positive marginal cost of capital is identified by the combination of a negative conditional mean for the markup and a ratio of reserve to actuarial value that is less than the leverage ratio (i.e., $\widehat{V}_{i,t}/V_{i,t} < L_{n,t}/A_{n,t}$).

Even if the demand elasticity is misspecified, the Standard Valuation Law generates relative shifts in supply across different types of policies that an insurer sells, which are sufficient to identify the marginal cost of capital. To illustrate this point, we approximate equation (3.19) through a first-order Taylor approximation as

$$\log\left(\frac{P_{i,n,t}}{V_{i,t}}\right) \approx \alpha_{n,t} + \bar{c}_{n,t}\frac{A_{n,t}}{L_{n,t}}\frac{\widehat{V}_{i,t}}{V_{i,t}} + \omega_{i,n,t}, \tag{3.22}$$

where

$$\omega_{i,n,t} = -\alpha_{n,t} - \bar{c}_{n,t} - \log\left(1 - \frac{1}{\epsilon_{i,n,t}}\right) + \nu_{i,n,t} \qquad (3.23)$$

is an error term with zero conditional mean. For a given insurer n at a given time t, the regression coefficient $\bar{c}_{n,t}$ is identified by exogenous variation in the ratio of reserve to actuarial value across different types of policies. Intuitively, the markups are more sensitive to the ratio of reserve to actuarial value when the marginal cost of capital is high.

3.4.3 Marginal Cost of Capital

Panel A of Table 3.3 reports the estimated coefficients in the model for the demand elasticity (i.e., β in equation (3.20)). The positive coefficient on the dummy for the A.M. Best rating implies that insurers rated A or A− face a lower demand elasticity and have higher average markups than those rated A++ or A+. Similarly, the positive coefficients on log assets and the leverage ratio imply that larger and more leveraged insurers face a lower demand elasticity and have higher average markups.

Panel B of Table 3.3 reports the estimated coefficients in the model for the marginal cost of capital (i.e., γ in equation (3.21)). In the time series, the marginal cost of capital is positively related to the corporate yield spread. A standard deviation increase in the corporate yield spread is associated with a 66% increase in the marginal cost of capital. In the cross section of insurers, the marginal cost of capital is positively related to the leverage ratio, risk-based capital relative to guideline, and net equity inflow. It is negatively related to log assets and asset growth. The most important of these characteristics is the leverage ratio by an order of magnitude. A standard deviation increase in the leverage ratio is associated with a 155% increase in the marginal cost of capital.

Figure 3.7 shows the marginal cost of capital for the average company (i.e., at the mean of the insurer characteristics). The marginal cost of capital is positive around the 2001 recession and during the global financial crisis. Our point estimate of the marginal cost of capital is $0.96 per dollar of statutory capital in November 2008. That is, the average company was willing to accept a marginal reduction of $0.96 in profits to raise its statutory capital by a dollar. The 95% confidence interval for the marginal cost of capital ranges from $0.66 to $1.39 per dollar of statutory capital.

TABLE 3.3. Estimated Insurance Pricing Model

Explanatory variable	Coefficient	
Panel A. Demand Elasticity		
A.M. Best rating of A or A−	0.102	(0.021)
Log assets	0.197	(0.014)
Asset growth	0.011	(0.006)
Leverage ratio	0.168	(0.019)
Risk-based capital relative to guideline	−0.022	(0.010)
Current liquidity	0.067	(0.014)
Operating return on equity	0.082	(0.011)
Female	0.003	(0.003)
Age 50	0.060	(0.050)
Age 55	0.116	(0.046)
Age 60	0.170	(0.040)
Age 65	0.247	(0.039)
Age 70	0.353	(0.039)
Age 75	0.435	(0.040)
Age 80	0.438	(0.046)
Age 85	0.559	(0.054)
Interaction effects for life insurance		
A.M. Best rating of A or A−	−2.896	(0.482)
Log assets	−3.600	(0.472)
Asset growth	−1.172	(0.192)
Leverage ratio	−0.216	(0.053)
Risk-based capital relative to guideline	−0.118	(0.040)
Current liquidity	−0.232	(0.102)
Operating return on equity	−0.862	(0.141)
Female	−0.074	(0.045)
Age 30	−6.522	(1.257)
Age 40	−6.997	(1.274)
Age 50	−6.930	(1.259)
Age 60	−6.801	(1.258)
Age 70	−6.439	(1.248)
Age 80	−6.419	(1.247)
Panel B. Marginal cost of capital		
Corporate yield spread	0.660	(0.052)
Log assets	−0.240	(0.034)
Asset growth	−0.255	(0.030)
Leverage ratio	1.545	(0.130)
Risk-based capital relative to guideline	0.393	(0.047)
Net equity inflow	0.085	(0.024)
R^2	0.232	
Observations	45,430	

This table reports the coefficients in the models for the demand elasticity (3.20) and the marginal cost of capital (3.21). The omitted categories for the dummy variables are term annuities, A.M. Best ratings of A++ or A+, and male. The model for the demand elasticity also includes year-quarter and domiciliary-state fixed effects, which are not reported for brevity. The model for the marginal cost of capital also includes year-quarter fixed effects, which are not reported for brevity. Robust standard errors clustered by insurer, type of policy, sex, and age are reported in parentheses. The sample covers insurers with an A.M. Best rating of A− or higher from May 1998 to July 2011.

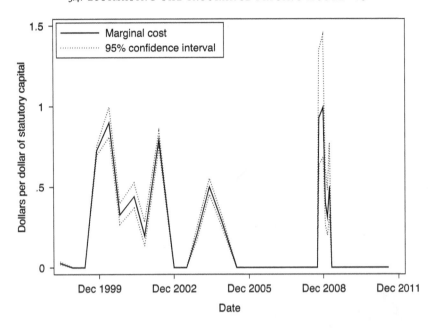

FIGURE 3.7. Marginal Cost of Capital. Copyright American Economic Association; reprint of Koijen and Yogo (2015, figure 7) with permission. This figure shows the marginal cost of capital for the average company, implied by the estimated insurance pricing model. The 95% confidence interval is based on robust standard errors clustered by insurer, type of policy, sex, and age. The sample covers insurers with an A.M. Best rating of A− or higher from May 1998 to July 2011.

Table 3.4 reports the marginal cost of capital for the cross section of insurers in our sample in November 2008. The marginal cost of capital varies significantly across insurers. At the top of the list is MetLife Investors USA Insurance Company, whose marginal cost of capital was $5.53 per dollar of statutory capital with a standard error of $1.52. Its assets shrank by 9% in 2008, and its leverage ratio was 97% at fiscal year-end 2008. The relative weakness of MetLife's balance sheet is remarkable, given that it raised new capital in 2008 that was 163% of its equity at fiscal year-end 2007. The last column of the table shows that MetLife was not the only company that raised an extraordinary amount of capital through capital injections from the holding company and a reduction of stockholder dividends (Berry-Stölzle, Nini, and Wende, 2014; Niehaus, 2016).

Near the bottom of Table 3.4 is American General Life Insurance Company with a marginal cost of capital of $0.13 per dollar of statutory capital. Its assets

TABLE 3-4. Marginal Cost of Capital in November 2008

Insurer	Holding company	Marginal cost (dollars)		Asset growth (%)	Leverage ratio (%)	Net equity inflow (%)
MetLife Investors USA Insurance	MetLife	5.53	(1.52)	−9	97	163
Pruco Life Insurance	Prudential Financial	5.38	(1.39)	−19	97	43
National Integrity Life Insurance		5.37	(1.20)	10	95	59
John Hancock Life Insurance of New York	Manulife Financial	5.02	(1.39)	−15	96	134
Pruco Life Insurance of New Jersey	Prudential Financial	4.97	(1.26)	−13	97	0
AXA Equitable Life Insurance	AXA	4.52	(1.12)	−22	97	0
John Hancock Life Insurance (USA)	Manulife Financial	3.87	(1.09)	−18	98	25
Lincoln National Life Insurance	Lincoln National	3.50	(0.82)	−17	96	−7
Sun Life Assurance of Canada (US)	Sun Life Financial	3.31	(0.88)	−11	97	95
Phoenix Life Insurance	Phoenix Companies	3.06	(0.64)	−8	94	−7
OM Financial Life Insurance	Old Mutual	2.88	(0.66)	−4	95	44
Aviva Life and Annuity of New York	Aviva	2.75	(0.61)	4	94	25
Allianz Life Insurance of North America	Allianz Group	2.75	(0.70)	−3	97	22
Texas Life Insurance		2.44	(0.51)	5	93	0
United States Life Insurance in City of New York	AIG	2.19	(0.51)	0	94	90
EquiTrust Life Insurance	FBL Financial Group	2.18	(0.47)	14	95	20
Integrity Life Insurance		2.07	(0.40)	3	92	25
OM Financial Life Insurance of New York	Old Mutual	1.96	(0.42)	−2	93	0
Companion Life Insurance		1.92	(0.39)	4	91	0
Sun Life Insurance and Annuity of New York	Sun Life Financial	1.85	(0.37)	−2	92	69
Genworth Life Insurance of New York	Genworth Financial	1.80	(0.38)	8	94	40
Aviva Life and Annuity	Aviva	1.65	(0.36)	12	95	7
Protective Life and Annuity Insurance	Protective Life	1.50	(0.35)	21	94	0

TABLE 3.4. (*Continued*)

North American for Life and Health Insurance		1.49	(0.30)	27	93	30
Cincinnati Life Insurance	Cincinnati Financial	1.36	(0.30)	−3	88	0
Genworth Life and Annuity Insurance	Genworth Financial	1.28	(0.25)	−11	92	39
Security Life of Denver Insurance	ING Group	1.26	(0.28)	0	94	14
ReliaStar Life Insurance of New York	ING Group	1.21	(0.26)	−1	92	29
C.M. Life Insurance		1.13	(0.21)	−13	90	0
Metropolitan Life Insurance	MetLife	1.08	(0.25)	−3	94	−8
Kansas City Life Insurance	Kansas City Life Insurance	1.07	(0.21)	−8	89	−2
United of Omaha Life Insurance		1.06	(0.20)	−3	90	−8
William Penn Life Insurance of New York	Legal and General Group	1.03	(0.20)	−1	90	0
Lincoln Life and Annuity of New York	Lincoln National	0.94	(0.18)	−6	90	0
Ohio National Life Assurance Corporation		0.93	(0.18)	2	90	0
Protective Life Insurance	Protective Life	0.87	(0.18)	0	92	5
Penn Mutual Life Insurance		0.68	(0.17)	−8	86	0
Lincoln Benefit Life	Allstate	0.59	(0.13)	−37	87	0
Illinois Mutual Life Insurance		0.58	(0.12)	1	89	0
West Coast Life Insurance	Protective Life	0.57	(0.12)	9	90	47
Genworth Life Insurance	Genworth Financial	0.50	(0.10)	0	90	9
Banner Life Insurance	Legal and General Group	0.19	(0.05)	3	84	42
American National Insurance	American National Insurance	0.18	(0.04)	−2	86	−3
American General Life Insurance	AIG	0.13	(0.03)	6	85	142
AAA Life Insurance		0.10	(0.03)	25	81	14

grew by 6% in 2008, and its leverage ratio was 85% at fiscal year-end 2008. The relative strength of American General's balance sheet is due to new capital that it received from its holding company in 2008 as part of the government bailout of AIG.

3.5   Evidence for Financial Frictions

An insurer that is part of a holding company can be constrained only if its parent is also constrained due to frictions in external capital markets, or its parent does not inject enough capital due to frictions in internal capital markets. We discuss these two possibilities to further support financial frictions as an explanation.

3.5.1   Frictions in External Capital Markets

Table 3.5 lists all publicly held holding companies that are parents of the subsidiaries in Table 3.4. For each holding company, the table describes recapitalization activity from September 2008 to July 2009. We define recapitalization activity as an application for government assistance, issuance of public equity, or reduction or suspension of dividends.

At the top of Table 3.5 are seven companies that applied for TARP and the ING Group, which received similar assistance from the Dutch government. Only the most constrained companies would ordinarily apply for government assistance because it comes with tighter capital regulation (e.g., forced suspension of dividends), restrictions on executive compensation, and potential loss of reputation in both product and capital markets. The six companies that applied for TARP could be subdivided into two categories. Allstate, AIG, and Prudential Financial were already bank holding companies that were eligible for TARP. Genworth Financial, Lincoln National, the Phoenix Companies, and Protective Life were originally insurance holding companies that had to acquire a bank to become eligible. Becoming a bank holding company means that they would be subject to Federal Reserve supervision, so these four companies were presumably constrained to take such a drastic step.

The second group in Table 3.5 consists of Manulife Financial and MetLife, which did not apply for government assistance but issued public equity during the global financial crisis. For these companies as well as Protective Life and Prudential Financial, which ultimately issued public equity after withdrawing their application for TARP, we estimate the announcement effect of equity issuance on the stock price (e.g., Gron and Lucas, 1998). The announcement effect has two potential interpretations. The first is that the announcement effect reflects the cost of external capital that arises from debt overhang. Equity issuance could signal that existing equity within the holding company and new capital that is raised will be used to repay the existing debtholders, including the policyholders of the subsidiaries. The second interpretation is that the announcement effect merely reflects private information about profitability, which would eventually be revealed to capital markets (Myers and Majluf, 1984). With this caveat in mind, the final column of Table 3.5 reports the announcement effect as an imperfect measure of the cost of external capital.

To illustrate our calculation with an example, MetLife announced an equity issuance at the close of trading on October 7, 2008. Its market capitalization was $26,170 million, and its abnormal return on the following day was −24.34%, according to the capital asset pricing model. Therefore, the announcement was associated with a $6,370 = 0.2434 × $26,170 million reduction in market capitalization. MetLife raised $2,286 million in new capital, which implies an average cost of $2.79 = $6,370/$2,286 per dollar of capital. This *average* cost of external capital for the holding company is the same order of magnitude as the *marginal* cost of internal capital for its subsidiaries in Table 3.4. Any difference between the two may be justified by convexity in the cost of equity issuance and frictions in internal capital markets, as we discuss below.

The third group in Table 3.5 consists of five companies that did not issue public equity but reduced or suspended dividends during the global financial crisis. These companies could have been constrained, but it is difficult to tell based on changes in the dividend policy alone. The final group in the table consists of five companies for whom there was no recapitalization activity. These companies were presumably unconstrained.

3.5.2 *Frictions in Internal Capital Markets*

The Insurance Holding Company System Regulatory Act (National Association of Insurance Commissioners, 2011a, appendix A-440) restricts the movement of capital within a holding company as well as the payment of stockholder dividends to the parent. Through these laws, state regulators protect the interests of policyholders by preventing holding companies from extracting too much capital from their subsidiaries. However, these laws could also lead to frictions in internal capital markets.

TABLE 3.5. Recapitalization Activity by the Holding Companies

Holding company	Date	Significant activity	Announcement effect (dollars)
Panel A. Applied for government assistance			
Allstate	11/14/2008	Applies for TARP.	
	2/25/2009	Reduces quarterly dividend from $0.41 to $0.20 per share.	
	5/15/2009	Receives approval for TARP.	
	5/19/2009	Withdraws application for TARP.	
AIG	9/22/2008	Suspends dividends under an $85 billion credit agreement with the New York Fed.	
	11/25/2008	Issues $40 billion of preferred equity to the US Treasury under TARP.	
Genworth Financial	11/1/2008	Suspends dividends.	
	11/16/2008	Applies for TARP with plans to acquire InterBank, FSB.	
	4/9/2009	Is rejected for TARP and cancels the acquisition of InterBank, FSB.	
ING Group	10/19/2008	Issues 10 billion euros of preferred equity to the Dutch government.	
	10/19/2008	Suspends dividends.	
Lincoln National	10/10/2008	Reduces quarterly dividend from $0.415 to $0.21 per share.	
	11/13/2008	Applies for TARP with plans to acquire Newton County Loan and Savings, FSB.	
	2/24/2009	Reduces quarterly dividend from $0.21 to $0.01 per share.	
	6/22/2009	Issues $690 million of common equity.	
	7/10/2009	Issues $950 million of preferred equity to the US Treasury under TARP.	
Phoenix Companies	1/15/2009	Applies for TARP with plans to acquire American Sterling Bank.	
	2/7/2009	Suspends dividends.	
	4/20/2009	Withdraws application for TARP after failing to acquire American Sterling Bank.	
Protective Life	11/3/2008	Reduces quarterly dividend from $0.235 to $0.12 per share.	
	1/15/2009	Applies for TARP with plans to acquire Bonifay Holding Company.	
	4/1/2009	Withdraws application for TARP after failing to acquire Bonifay Holding Company.	
	5/20/2009	Issues $133 million of common equity.	0.76

TABLE 3-5 (*Continued*)

Prudential Financial	10/1/2008	Applies for TARP.	
	11/11/2008	Reduces annual dividend from $1.15 to $0.58 per share.	
	5/14/2009	Receives approval for TARP.	
	6/1/2009	Withdraws application for TARP.	
	6/9/2009	Issues $1,438 million of common equity.	1.18
Panel B. Issued public equity			
Manulife Financial	12/11/2008	Issues $2,275 million of common equity.	0.72
	3/4/2009	Issues $450 million of preferred equity.	
	6/3/2009	Issues $350 million of preferred equity.	
	8/6/2009	Reduces quarterly dividend from $0.26 to $0.13 per share.	
MetLife	10/15/2008	Issues $2,286 million of common equity.	2.79
Panel C. Reduced or suspended dividends			
Allianz Group	2/26/2009	Reduces annual dividend from 5.50 to 3.50 euros per share.	
AXA	4/30/2009	Reduces annual dividend from 1.20 to 0.40 euros per share.	
FBL Financial Group	5/21/2009	Reduces quarterly dividend from $0.125 to $0.0625 per share.	
Legal and General Group	3/25/2009	Reduces final dividend from 4.10 to 2.05 pence per share.	
Old Mutual	3/4/2009	Suspends dividends.	
Panel D. No significant activity			
American National Insurance			
Aviva			
Cincinnati Financial			
Kansas City Life Insurance			
Sun Life Financial			

Copyright American Economic Association; reprint of Koijen and Yogo (2015, table 6) with permission. This table reports recapitalization activity by the holding companies from September 2008 to July 2009. The holding companies are grouped into those that applied for government assistance through the Troubled Asset Relief Program (TARP) or similar foreign programs, those that issued public equity, those that reduced or suspended dividends, and those with no significant activity.

The A.M. Best Company (2011, p. 21) raises regulatory uncertainty over the ability to extract capital as an important source of risk for holding companies. Any capital that a holding company injects into its subsidiary may not be paid back as dividends, at least in the foreseeable future. Moreover, this risk is greater in bad times when insurers are subject to more regulatory scrutiny. Importantly, regulatory uncertainty could alter the ex ante incentives of a holding company to inject capital into its subsidiary. While difficult to prove or quantify, we raise frictions in internal capital markets as another possibility for why the capital injections may have been limited during the global financial crisis.

4

Modeling Supply and Demand

THIS CHAPTER presents a complete model of insurance markets in which financial frictions and market power are important determinants of pricing, contract characteristics, and the degree of market completeness. The model explains how insurers choose prices and contract characteristics and why they may not offer insurance, addressing the same questions as Rothschild and Stiglitz (1976). However, we focus on financial frictions and market power instead of informational frictions as the important determinants of market equilibrium. The model could apply to other insurance markets in which insurers bear significant aggregate risk such as long-term care insurance (Cutler, 1996) and catastrophe insurance of climate or cyber risk.

In Section 4.1, we start with aggregate facts about the variable annuity market. Quarterly sales of variable annuities grew robustly from $22 billion in 2005:1 to $41 billion in 2007:4 and then decreased to $27 billion in 2009:2. At the same time, the average annual fee on contracts with minimum return guarantees increased from 2.04% of account value in 2007:4 to 2.38% in 2009:2, suggesting an important role for a supply shock. After the global financial crisis, insurers made the minimum return guarantees less generous or stopped offering guarantees to reduce risk exposure. The share of contracts with minimum return guarantees decreased from 36% in 2007:4 to 20% in 2011:4.

In Section 4.2, we extend the insurance pricing model in Section 1.5 to contract design. The insurer competes in an oligopolistic market by choosing the fee and the rollup rate subject to a risk-based capital or an economic risk constraint. The model explains the aggregate facts in Section 4.1. An adverse shock to the valuation of existing liabilities increases the marginal cost of capital and drives up the marginal cost of issuing contracts. The insurer reduces risk exposure not only by raising the fee but also by reducing the rollup rate. When the shadow cost of capital is sufficiently high, the insurer stops offering minimum return guarantees to avoid additional risk exposure.

Variation in fees and rollup rates across insurers and over time could come from a combination of supply- and demand-side effects. A model of variable annuity demand is necessary to disentangle these effects and quantify the importance of financial frictions in explaining variable annuity supply. In Section 4.3, we model variable annuity demand through a differentiated product demand system, which implies estimates of demand elasticities to the fee and the rollup rate. The average demand elasticity to the fee decreased after the global financial crisis, while the average demand elasticity to the rollup rate remained nearly constant. However, the lower demand elasticity to the fee cannot fully explain the higher fees after the global financial crisis.

In Section 4.4, we decompose the time variation in fees and rollup rates through the insurer's optimality conditions. The 34-basis-point increase in the average annual fee from 2007:4 to 2009:2 reflects an increase of 1 basis point in the markup, 16 basis points in the option value, and 17 basis points in the shadow cost of capital. Thus, financial frictions are just as important as the option pricing channel for explaining the increase in fees during the global financial crisis. The increase in the shadow cost of capital partly explains the decrease in rollup rates. More importantly, contracts with generous guarantees became too capital intensive because the option value was more sensitive to the rollup rate, which explains why insurers stopped offering minimum return guarantees.

4.1 Aggregate Facts about the Variable Annuity Market

We use the data on the variable annuity market from Section 1.3.2. Figure 4.1 shows quarterly sales of variable annuities across all contracts from 1999:1 to 2015:4. Sales grew robustly from $22 billion in 2005:1 to a peak of $41 billion in 2007:4. Sales then decreased during the global financial crisis to $27 billion in 2009:2, partly rebounded to $34 billion in 2011:2, and decreased again to $20 billion in 2015:4. For comparison, the figure also shows the aggregate sales of US open-end stock and bond mutual funds (excluding money market funds and funds of funds), which is a larger market and hence shown on a different scale. Interestingly, sales of variable annuities and mutual funds moved closely together through 2008, but the two time series diverge thereafter as mutual fund sales grew.

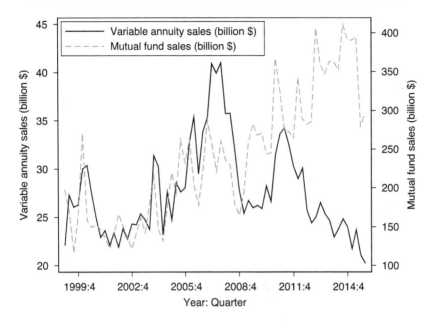

FIGURE 4.1. Variable Annuity Sales. Copyright American Finance Association; reprint of
Koijen and Yogo (2022a, figure 3) with permission. The left axis shows quarterly sales
of variable annuities across all contracts from 1999:1 to 2015:4. The right axis shows the
aggregate sales of US open-end stock and bond mutual funds (excluding money
market funds and funds of funds).

The decrease in variable annuity sales after 2008 is partly explained by
insurers that stopped offering minimum return guarantees. Figure 4.2 shows
the number of insurers and contracts offering minimum return guarantees
from 1999:1 to 2015:4. Eleven insurers stopped offering minimum return
guarantees from 2008 to 2015, during which six insurers stopped selling variable annuities altogether (see Table 2.1). Thus, some insurers chose to remain
in the variable annuity market but stopped offering minimum return guarantees. Without minimum return guarantees, variable annuities are essentially
mutual funds with longevity insurance and a potential tax advantage.

Panel A of Figure 4.3 shows the average annual fee on open (for sale)
minimum return guarantees from 1999:1 to 2015:4. The increase in fees during the global financial crisis coincides with the decrease in sales, suggesting
an important role for a supply shock. The average annual fee on minimum
return guarantees increased from 0.59% of account value in 2007:4 to 0.97%
in 2009:2. Including the base contract expense, the total annual fee increased

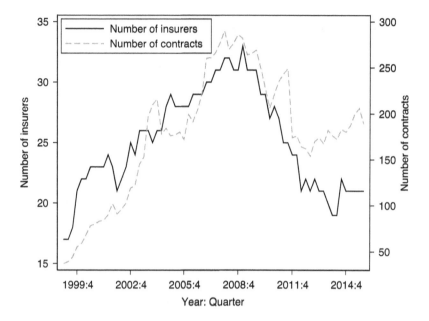

FIGURE 4.2. Number of Insurers and Contracts with Minimum Return Guarantees.
Copyright American Finance Association; reprint of Koijen and Yogo (2022a, figure 4)
with permission. The sample includes all contracts with minimum return guarantees
from 1999:1 to 2015:4.

from 2.04% in 2007:4 to 2.38% in 2009:2. Since then, fees have remained stable. The average annual fee on minimum return guarantees was 1.08% (2.33%
including the base contract expense) in 2015:4.

Panel B of Figure 4.3 summarizes the rollup rates on open contracts from
1999:1 to 2015:4. Conditional on offering a minimum return guarantee, the
average rollup rate increased from 2.4% in 2005:1 to 4.0% in 2007:4, coincid-
ing with the period of robust sales growth. The average rollup rate remained
high through the global financial crisis and decreased only after 2011. However, the share of contracts with minimum return guarantees decreased after
the global financial crisis from 36% in 2007:4 to 20% in 2011:4, consistent
with Figure 4.2. Thus, many insurers responded to the global financial crisis through the extensive margin by not offering minimum return guarantees
rather than through the intensive margin by reducing rollup rates.

To summarize Figures 4.1 to 4.3, variable annuity sales decreased, fees
increased, and many insurers stopped offering minimum return guarantees
in response to the global financial crisis. This evidence is consistent with a

Panel A. Fee

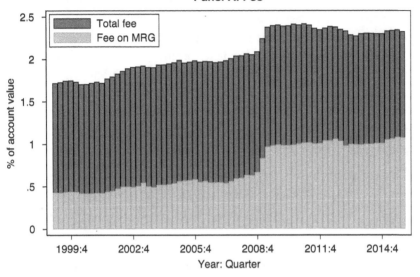

Panel B. Rollup rate

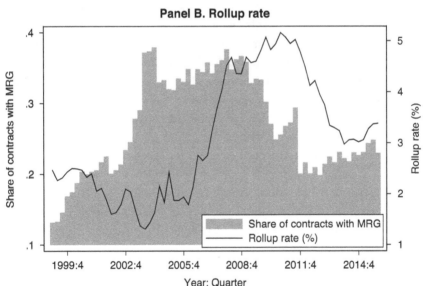

FIGURE 4.3. Fees and Rollup Rates on Minimum Return Guarantees. Copyright American Finance Association; reprint of Koijen and Yogo (2022a, figure 5) with permission. Panel A shows the annual fee on open minimum return guarantees, averaged across contracts with sales weighting. The total annual fee includes the base contract expense. Panel B shows the rollup rate on open minimum return guarantees, averaged across contracts with sales weighting, and the share of contracts with minimum return guarantees. The sample includes all contracts with minimum return guarantees from 1999:1 to 2015:4.

supply shock as a consequence of tightening risk-based capital and economic risk constraints. Two factors could explain why variable annuity supply did not fully recover long after the global financial crisis. First, as we discuss in Section 2.3.1, insurers may have been more cautious because of the difficulty of managing interest rate risk in the low interest rate environment. Second, as we discuss in Section 1.4.3, Actuarial Guideline 43 increased the capital requirements for variable annuities. Despite the enormous attention that Actuarial Guideline 43 received in the industry, its impact on variable annuity supply is difficult to identify because of its gradual implementation from 2009 to 2012.

4.2   A Model of Variable Annuity Supply

Risk-based capital and economic risk constraints are important determinants of variable annuity supply and explain the evidence in Section 4.1. Insurers suffered an adverse shock to risk-based capital from the increased valuation of existing liabilities during the global financial crisis. Moreover, insurers could have made risk management more conservative in response to higher model uncertainty. As the shadow cost of capital increased, insurers raised fees to pass through a higher marginal cost. Insurers also reduced rollup rates or stopped offering minimum return guarantees to reduce risk exposure. Higher fees and lower rollup rates make variable annuities less attractive to policyholders, which explains the decrease in sales.

To formalize this narrative, we extend the insurance pricing model in Section 1.5 to contract design. The insurer competes in an oligopolistic market by choosing the fee and the rollup rate subject to a risk-based capital or an economic risk constraint. The insurer could reduce the rollup rate or stop offering minimum return guarantees to reduce risk exposure. From the policyholder's perspective, the insurance market becomes incomplete when insurers stop offering minimum return guarantees. Thus, we develop a more complete theory of the supply side of insurance markets that explains pricing, contract characteristics, and the degree of market completeness.

4.2.1   Variable Annuity Market

There is a mutual fund, whose price evolves exogenously over time. To simplify the notation, we assume no portfolio expense on the mutual fund. Let S_t be the mutual fund price per share in period t. By the absence of arbitrage, there exists a strictly positive stochastic discount factor $M_{t,t+s}$ that discounts a payoff in period $t+s$ to its price in period t. Therefore, the mutual fund price satisfies $S_t = \mathbb{E}_t[M_{t,t+s}S_{t+s}]$.

In period t, an insurer sells a variable annuity, which is a combination of the mutual fund and a minimum return guarantee. The variable annuity fee is P_t per dollar of account value, which we assume is paid upfront as a lump sum for simplicity. The minimum return guarantee is over two periods, and the rollup rate r_t is the guaranteed return per period. Thus, the payoff of the minimum return guarantee in period $t+2$ is

$$X_{t,t+2} = \max\left\{(1+r_t)^2 - \frac{S_{t+2}}{S_t}, 0\right\}. \tag{4.1}$$

The minimum return guarantee is a long-maturity put option, whose strike price is the cumulative rollup rate. When $r_t = -1$, the variable annuity is a mutual fund because the put option is always worthless. We assume that the policyholder cannot insure downside market risk over long horizons outside of the variable annuity market, so the insurance market is incomplete when $r_t = -1$.

The option value of the minimum return guarantee in period t is

$$V_{t,t} = \mathbb{E}_t[M_{t,t+2}X_{t,t+2}] \tag{4.2}$$

per dollar of account value. More generally, $V_{t-s,t}$ denotes the option value in period t of a minimum return guarantee that was issued in period $t-s$. Although this notation is slightly cumbersome, it is important to distinguish the option value of existing liabilities $V_{t-1,t}$ from the option value of new contracts $V_{t,t}$. For the purposes of our theory, we do not need parametric assumptions about the option pricing model (e.g., Black and Scholes, 1973). We assume that the partial derivatives of the option value have the conventional signs. The option value decreases in the mutual fund price, decreases in the riskless interest rate, and increases in volatility. Furthermore, we assume that the first two partial derivatives of the option value with respect to the rollup rate are positive (i.e., $\partial V_{t,t}/\partial r_t > 0$ and $\partial^2 V_{t,t}/\partial r_t^2 > 0$).

We also do not need parametric assumptions about variable annuity demand. We assume that demand is continuous, continuously differentiable, strictly decreasing in the fee, and strictly increasing in the rollup rate. In an oligopolistic market, the demand for a contract depends on the fees and the rollup rates of all competing contracts. To simplify the notation, we denote the demand for a contract as Q_t with the understanding that it depends on the fees and the rollup rates of all competing contracts.

An institutional feature of the variable annuity market is that the rollup rate is positive (i.e., $r_t \geq 0$) or $r_t = -1$ in the case of mutual funds without minimum return guarantees. Insurers do not offer a variable annuity with a negative rollup rate presumably because policyholders have a psychological aversion to "negative interest rates." To model this institutional feature, we assume that the rollup rate is constrained to be in the set $\mathcal{R} = \{-1\} \bigcup (-0.01, \infty)$. A lower bound slightly less than zero ensures that $r_t = 0$ is an interior solution and that $r_t = -1$ is the only corner solution.[1]

4.2.2   Balance Sheet Dynamics

Let B_t be the total account value of mutual funds, or separate accounts in actuarial terms, at the end of period t. Let A_t be the general account assets at the end of period t. Let L_t be the general account liabilities, which represents the option value of existing minimum return guarantees, at the end of period t. The following T account summarizes the balance sheet.

Assets	Liabilities	
B_t	B_t	separate account
A_t	L_t	general account
	$A_t - L_t$	equity

There is no risk mismatch for mutual funds in the separate account. The insurer's equity fluctuates because of risk mismatch between assets and minimum return guarantees in the general account.

We describe how variable annuity sales affect the balance sheet. Let Q_t be the account value of new contracts, excluding the option value of minimum return guarantees, that the insurer sells in period t. The account value evolves according to

$$B_t = \frac{S_t}{S_{t-1}} B_{t-1} + Q_t. \tag{4.3}$$

The current account value is the previous account value revalued at the current mutual fund price plus the account value of new contracts.

---

1. By making the rollup rate a continuous choice, the model is not designed to match the discreteness of the empirical distribution of rollup rates. Among contracts with a GLWB, the frequency of a 0% rollup rate is similar to that of a 5% rollup rate. This fact motivates our assumption that a 0% rollup rate is an interior solution.

The general account assets evolve according to

$$A_t = R_{A,t}A_{t-1} + P_tQ_t, \qquad (4.4)$$

where $R_{A,t}$ is an exogenous gross asset return in period t. Current assets are the gross return on previous assets plus the fees on new contracts. As we discuss in Section 2.2, insurers do not fully hedge variable annuity risk for various economic and institutional reasons. Following that discussion, we assume that $R_{A,t}$ could be imperfectly correlated with the option value of existing liabilities, leading to risk mismatch.

The general account liabilities evolve according to

$$L_t = \frac{V_{t-1,t}}{V_{t-1,t-1}}L_{t-1} + V_{t,t}Q_t. \qquad (4.5)$$

Current liabilities are previous liabilities revalued at the current option value plus the cost of new contracts. The principle of reserving requires that the cost $V_{t,t}$ be recorded on the liability side to back the fees P_t on the asset side.

We define statutory capital as equity minus required capital, which is proportional to liabilities:

$$K_t = \underbrace{A_t - L_t}_{\text{equity}} - \underbrace{\phi_t L_t}_{\text{required capital}}. \qquad (4.6)$$

For simplicity, we assume that $\phi_t > 0$ is an exogenous parameter that does not depend on the fee or the rollup rate. Following the discussion in Section 1.4.3, $1 + \phi_t$ represents the ratio of reserve to market value under Actuarial Guideline 43. Alternatively, ϕ_t represents the risk weight on minimum return guarantees under the C-3 Phase II regulatory standard. Through equation (4.5), required capital increases in the option value of existing liabilities $V_{t-1,t}$. Therefore, required capital increases when the stock market falls, interest rates fall, or volatility rises. Required capital also increases in the option value of new contracts $V_{t,t}$. Therefore, required capital for new contracts increases in the rollup rate, decreases in interest rates, and increases in volatility.

Substituting equations (4.4) and (4.5) into equation (4.6), the law of motion for statutory capital is

$$K_t = R_{K,t}K_{t-1} + (P_t - (1 + \phi_t)V_{t,t})Q_t, \qquad (4.7)$$

where

$$R_{K,t} = \frac{A_{t-1}}{K_{t-1}} R_{A,t} - \frac{(1+\phi_t)L_{t-1}}{K_{t-1}} \frac{V_{t-1,t}}{V_{t-1,t-1}} \tag{4.8}$$

is the return on statutory capital.

4.2.3   Financial Frictions

Following the discussion in Section 1.5.3, we model the cost of financial frictions through a cost function:

$$C_t = C(K_t). \tag{4.9}$$

This cost function is continuous, twice continuously differentiable, strictly decreasing, and strictly convex. The cost function is decreasing because higher statutory capital reduces the likelihood of a rating downgrade or regulatory action. The cost function is convex because these benefits of higher statutory capital have diminishing returns.

An alternative interpretation of the cost function is that the insurer has an economic risk constraint, such as the value-at-risk constraint in Section 1.4.2. As a consequence of the global financial crisis, the insurer learned that model uncertainty is higher than previously recognized and made risk management more conservative. An increase in ϕ_t could capture a tighter economic risk constraint. A permanent increase in ϕ_t could lead to persistent effects on variable annuity supply that are consistent with the evidence in Section 4.1.

4.2.4   Optimal Fee and Rollup Rate

The insurer's profit from variable annuity sales is

$$D_t = (P_t - V_{t,t})Q_t. \tag{4.10}$$

The insurer chooses the fee P_t and the rollup rate $r_t \in \mathcal{R}$ to maximize firm value, which is the profit minus the cost of financial frictions:

$$J_t = D_t - C_t. \tag{4.11}$$

We could have specified firm value as the present value of profits as in equation (3.14), but we opt for the simpler presentation because the key insights do not depend on dynamics.

To simplify the exposition, we present the optimality conditions for a single insurer with the understanding that all insurers have the same optimality conditions in a Nash equilibrium. To simplify the notation, we define the semi-elasticity of demand to the fee as $\epsilon_t^P = -\partial \log(Q_t)/\partial P_t$ and to the rollup rate as $\epsilon_t^r = \partial \log(Q_t)/\partial r_t$. We also define the marginal cost of capital as

$$c_t = -\frac{\partial C_t}{\partial K_t} > 0. \tag{4.12}$$

The marginal cost of capital represents the importance of financial frictions, which decreases in statutory capital by the convexity of the cost function.

OPTIMAL FEE

The first-order condition for the fee is

$$\frac{\partial J_t}{\partial P_t} = \frac{\partial D_t}{\partial P_t} + c_t \frac{\partial K_t}{\partial P_t}$$

$$= Q_t + \frac{\partial Q_t}{\partial P_t}(P_t - V_{t,t}) + c_t \left(Q_t + \frac{\partial Q_t}{\partial P_t}(P_t - (1 + \phi_t)V_{t,t}) \right)$$

$$= (1 + c_t)Q_t + \frac{\partial Q_t}{\partial P_t}((1 + c_t)(P_t - V_{t,t}) - c_t\phi_t V_{t,t}) = 0. \tag{4.13}$$

We rearrange this equation to solve for the optimal fee:

$$P_t = \frac{1}{\epsilon_t^P} + \underbrace{\lambda_t V_{t,t}}_{\text{marginal cost}}, \tag{4.14}$$

where the shadow cost of capital is

$$\lambda_t = \frac{1 + c_t(1 + \phi_t)}{1 + c_t} > 1. \tag{4.15}$$

The optimal fee (4.14) is the sum of two terms. The first term is the markup, which is inversely related to the demand elasticity to the fee. The second term is the marginal cost of issuing contracts, which is the product of the shadow cost of capital and the option value. The marginal cost is greater than the option value because of financial frictions. The shadow cost of capital decreases in statutory capital through c_t and increases in the risk weight ϕ_t.

Equation (4.14) is identical to equation (1.17), but they may appear different for two reasons. First, ϵ_t^P is the semi-elasticity of demand in equation (4.14), while ϵ_t is the full elasticity of demand in equation (1.17). Semi-elasticity is the natural formulation here because the fee is expressed as a percentage of the account value. Second, we have folded the ratio of reserve to actuarial value into $1 + \phi_t$, so that $\widehat{V}_t/V_t$ does not appear in equation (4.14).

OPTIMAL ROLLUP RATE

The first-order condition for the rollup rate is

$$\frac{\partial J_t}{\partial r_t} = \frac{\partial D_t}{\partial r_t} + c_t \frac{\partial K_t}{\partial r_t}$$

$$= -\frac{\partial V_{t,t}}{\partial r_t} Q_t + \frac{\partial Q_t}{\partial r_t} (P_t - V_{t,t})$$

$$+ c_t \left(-(1 + \phi_t) \frac{\partial V_{t,t}}{\partial r_t} Q_t + \frac{\partial Q_t}{\partial r_t} (P_t - (1 + \phi_t) V_{t,t}) \right)$$

$$= -(1 + c_t(1 + \phi_t)) \frac{\partial V_{t,t}}{\partial r_t} Q_t + \frac{\partial Q_t}{\partial r_t} ((1 + c_t)(P_t - V_{t,t}) - c_t \phi_t V_{t,t})$$

$$= -(1 + c_t(1 + \phi_t)) \frac{\partial V_{t,t}}{\partial r_t} Q_t - (1 + c_t) \frac{\partial Q_t}{\partial r_t} \left(\frac{\partial Q_t}{\partial P_t} \right)^{-1} Q_t = 0,$$

$$\tag{4.16}$$

where the last line follows from substituting equation (4.13). At an interior solution, the rollup rate satisfies

$$\frac{\epsilon_t^r}{\epsilon_t^P} = \lambda_t \frac{\partial V_{t,t}}{\partial r_t}. \tag{4.17}$$

Otherwise, $r_t = -1$ is optimal.

The optimal rollup rate depends on three terms in equation (4.17). On the left side is the demand channel through which the insurer optimally chooses the rollup rate to exploit market power. The first term on the right side is the shadow cost of capital. The second term on the right side is the slope of the option value with respect to the rollup rate, which increases in the rollup rate because $\partial^2 V_{t,t}/\partial r_t^2 > 0$.

Equation (4.16) clarifies why the demand elasticity to the fee ϵ_t^P appears in equation (4.17). The intuition is that the insurer earns a higher markup when the demand elasticity to the fee is lower, so variable annuities are less capital intensive per unit sold. This slackness in statutory capital allows the insurer to offer a higher rollup rate to increase demand and profits.

The intuition for the right side of equation (4.17) is simple for the logit model of demand, in which case the left side is constant. In this case, the optimal rollup rate decreases in the shadow cost of capital. An insurer that faces a higher shadow cost of capital must reduce risk exposure by reducing the rollup rate on new contracts. When the shadow cost of capital is sufficiently high, the insurer offers mutual funds without minimum return guarantees (i.e., $r_t = -1$). That is, the insurer stops offering minimum return guarantees to avoid additional risk exposure. The general insight is that financial frictions affect contract characteristics and could even lead to market incompleteness in the extreme case.

The model provides a narrative for the aggregate facts in Figures 4.1 to 4.3. Insurers suffered an adverse shock to risk-based capital during the global financial crisis and could have made risk management more conservative in response to higher model uncertainty. As the shadow cost of capital increased, insurers raised their fees to pass through a higher marginal cost. Insurers also reduced their rollup rates or stopped offering minimum return guarantees to reduce risk exposure. Higher fees and lower rollup rates make variable annuities less attractive to policyholders, which explains the decrease in sales.

4.2.5   Evidence from the Cross Section of Insurers

We provide reduced-form evidence from the cross section of insurers that supports the model's predictions. A measurement challenge is that the shadow cost of capital is not directly observed. However, the reserve valuation is a relevant empirical proxy that we describe in Section 1.3.1. The reserve valuation most closely corresponds to $(1 + \phi_t)V_{t-1,t}$ in the model, which is positively related to the shadow cost of capital:

$$\frac{\partial \lambda_t}{\partial (1 + \phi_t)V_{t-1,t}} = -\frac{\phi_t L_{t-1}}{(1 + c_t)^2 K_{t-1}V_{t-1,t-1}} \frac{\partial c_t}{\partial K_t}$$

$$= \frac{\phi_t L_{t-1}}{(1 + c_t)^2 K_{t-1}V_{t-1,t-1}} \frac{\partial^2 C_t}{\partial K_t^2} > 0. \qquad (4.18)$$

We look for broad patterns at the insurer level that could be summarized by a scatter plot and leave a more formal analysis at the contract level to Section 4.4.

Depending on the contract characteristics of existing liabilities, different insurers experienced different shocks to the reserve valuation during the global financial crisis. Insurers that sold more generous guarantees before the global financial crisis suffered larger increases in the reserve valuation than those that sold less generous guarantees. Moreover, insurers that sold more generous guarantees could have made risk management more conservative after the global financial crisis as they learned that model uncertainty is higher than previously recognized. Thus, changes in the reserve valuation should be negatively related to sales growth in the cross section of insurers.

Panel A of Figure 4.4 is a scatter plot of sales growth versus the change in the reserve valuation from 2007 to 2010. The linear regression line shows that sales growth is negatively related to the change in the reserve valuation. On the bottom right are insurers like AXA and Genworth that essentially closed their variable annuity business as they suffered large increases in the reserve valuation. On the left side are six insurers (Fidelity Investments, MassMutual, New York Life, Northwestern, Ohio National, and Thrivent Financial) that did not offer a GLWB in 2007, which tends to be the most generous guarantee among guaranteed living benefits. The reserve valuation did not change much for these insurers because they sold less generous guarantees.

As we discuss in Section 1.4.3, variable annuity reserves under the statutory accounting principles increase relative to those under GAAP after a period of high volatility. If insurers that suffered large increases in the reserve valuation were constrained, they had an incentive to move variable annuity reserves off the balance sheet through reinsurance. Panel B of Figure 4.4 is a scatter plot of the change in the reinsurance share of variable annuities versus the change in the reserve valuation from 2007 to 2010. The linear regression line shows that the change in the reinsurance share of variable annuities is positively related to the change in the reserve valuation. On the top right are insurers like AXA and Genworth that reinsured more variable annuity liabilities as they suffered large increases in the reserve valuation. This evidence suggests an important role for a risk-based capital constraint rather than an economic risk constraint.

4.3 Estimating Variable Annuity Demand

Variation in fees and rollup rates across insurers and over time could come from supply- or demand-side effects. A model of variable annuity demand is necessary to disentangle these effects and quantify the importance of financial frictions in explaining variable annuity supply. Therefore, we estimate a differentiated product demand system for the variable annuity market at the contract level, which provides an internally consistent framework to model market equilibrium and decompose the fee into the markup and marginal cost.

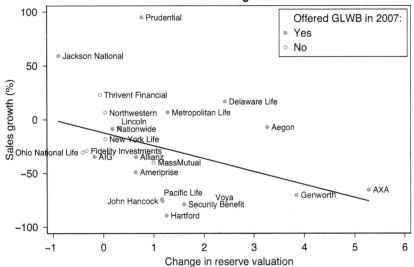

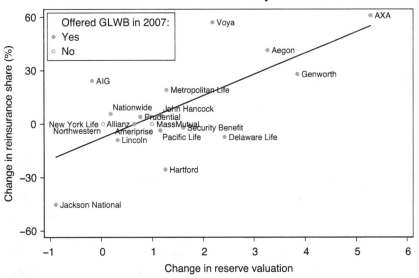

FIGURE 4.4. Cross Section of Insurers during the Global Financial Crisis. Copyright American Finance Association; reprint of Koijen and Yogo (2022a, figure 6) with permission. Panel A is a scatter plot of sales growth versus the change in the reserve valuation from 2007 to 2010. Panel B is a scatter plot of the change in the reinsurance share of variable annuities versus the change in the reserve valuation from 2007 to 2010. Both panels report a linear regression line through the scatter points. The sample includes all insurers with at least $1 billion of variable annuity sales in 2007.

4.3.1   A Model of Variable Annuity Demand

A life-cycle model of consumption and portfolio choice is a fully structural approach to modeling variable annuity demand (Horneff et al., 2009, 2010; Koijen, Nijman, and Werker, 2011). These models can explain the demand for variable annuities relative to other savings products, but they are not designed to explain heterogeneous demand across insurers and contracts. Moreover, we do not have data on the demographics of policyholders who purchase variable annuities at the contract level. For these reasons, we take a different approach and model variable annuity demand through the random coefficients logit model (Berry, Levinsohn, and Pakes, 1995), which is a tractable and microfounded model of product differentiation and market power.

Let $P_{i,t}$ be the annual fee and $r_{i,t}$ be the rollup rate on contract i in period t. Let $\mathbf{x}_{i,t}$ be a vector of other observed characteristics of contract i in period t, which are determinants of demand. Let $\xi_{i,t}$ be an unobserved (to the econometrician) characteristic of contract i in period t. For a consumer with a realized coefficient α_P on the fee, the indirect utility from buying contract i in period t is

$$U_{i,t} = \alpha_P P_{i,t} + \alpha_r r_{i,t} + \boldsymbol{\beta}' \mathbf{x}_{i,t} + \xi_{i,t} + \varepsilon_{i,t}, \qquad (4.19)$$

where $\varepsilon_{i,t}$ is a logit error drawn from a type 1 extreme value distribution. The probability that the consumer buys contract i in period t is

$$q_{i,t}(\alpha_P) = \frac{\exp(-\alpha_P P_{i,t} + \alpha_r r_{i,t} + \boldsymbol{\beta}' \mathbf{x}_{i,t} + \xi_{i,t})}{1 + \sum_{j=1}^{I} \exp(-\alpha_P P_{j,t} + \alpha_r r_{j,t} + \boldsymbol{\beta}' \mathbf{x}_{j,t} + \xi_{j,t})}, \qquad (4.20)$$

where I is the total number of contracts across all insurers. The denominator of equation (4.20) captures how demand for a contract depends on the fees and characteristics of all competing contracts. If the consumer does not buy a variable annuity, she buys an outside asset instead, which occurs with probability $1 - \sum_{i=1}^{I} q_{i,t}(\alpha_P)$.

Let $F(\alpha_P)$ be the cumulative distribution function for the coefficient on the fee, which is independently and identically distributed over time. The coefficient on the fee α_P is lognormally distributed, ensuring a positive demand elasticity. Integrating equation (4.20) over the distribution of consumers, the market share for contract i in period t is

$$Q_{i,t} = \int q_{i,t}(\alpha_P) \, dF(\alpha_P). \qquad (4.21)$$

The semi-elasticity of demand to the fee for contract i in period t is

$$\epsilon_{i,t}^{P} = \frac{1}{Q_{i,t}} \int \alpha_P q_{i,t}(\alpha_P)(1 - q_{i,t}(\alpha_P)) \, dF(\alpha_P). \qquad (4.22)$$

Through equation (4.14), the markup is inversely related to the demand elasticity to the fee.

The demand elasticity to the fee varies over time through changing contract characteristics, interacting with the distribution of random coefficients on the fee. When the fee increases or the rollup rate decreases, the more price elastic consumers substitute into competing contracts with lower fees or the outside asset. Thus, the demand elasticity to the fee decreases because the remaining consumers are less price elastic on average. In Panel A of Figure 4.3, fees could have increased after the global financial crisis not only because of an increasing shadow cost of capital but also because of a decreasing demand elasticity.

The estimation sample comprises all variable annuity contracts from 2005:1 to 2015:4. Because sales are at the contract level, we measure the total annual fee as the sum of the annual base contract expense and the annual fee on the minimum return guarantee. We assign a type of minimum return guarantee to each contract following the procedure in Section 1.3.2. The rollup rate is 0% for contracts with minimum return guarantees but no step ups and −100% for contracts without minimum return guarantees. This treatment of the rollup rate is consistent with the model of variable annuity supply in Section 4.2, in which we assume that demand is continuously differentiable in the rollup rate. We specify the outside asset as the sales of open-end stock and bond mutual funds (excluding money market funds and funds of funds).

The other contract characteristics in our specification are the number of investment options, a dummy for whether the contract offers a GLWB, and share class fixed effects. The number of investment options captures the menu or the complexity of options within contracts (Célérier and Vallée, 2017). A GLWB is the most common type and tends to be the most generous guarantee among guaranteed living benefits. The share class (i.e., A, B, C, I, L, O, or X) determines whether there is an initial sales charge or a surrender charge for early withdrawal. For example, B is the most common share class, and it has a surrender charge but no sales charge. The share class also determines the commission schedule for the investment advisor who sells the variable annuity. For example, investment advisors do not earn a commission on the I share class.

We also include the A.M. Best rating and insurer fixed effects to capture reputation in the retail market, which could vary across insurers and over time.

Consumers could substitute across insurers based on ratings, or they could substitute from variable annuities to the outside asset (i.e., mutual funds) if they are concerned about the stability of the insurance sector. The unobserved characteristic $\xi_{i,t}$ in equation (4.20) captures other demand factors that are difficult to measure, such as a relative tax advantage. Finally, the intercept captures the attractiveness (such as a tax advantage) of variable annuities relative to the outside asset.

4.3.2   Identifying Assumptions

According to the model of variable annuity supply in Section 4.2, the insurer optimally chooses the fee and the rollup rate, so they are jointly endogenous with demand. We start with the usual identifying assumption that observed characteristics other than the fee and the rollup rate are exogenous. Furthermore, we assume that the reserve valuation and the reinsurance share of variable annuities are valid instruments that affect the marginal cost, but they do not enter demand directly. To ensure exogeneity, we construct both instruments in year t based only on contracts that the insurer sold in prior years but are still on the balance sheet in year t. Thus, the instruments do not depend directly on sales or contract characteristics in year t. Because our specification includes insurer fixed effects, the demand elasticities are identified from the time variation in the instruments within each insurer.

We motivate the reserve valuation as a relevant and valid instrument, based on the model of variable annuity supply in Section 4.2. According to equation (4.18), the reserve valuation $(1 + \phi_t)V_{t-1,t}$ is a relevant instrument that is positively related to the shadow cost of capital. The reserve valuation depends on the option value of existing liabilities $V_{t-1,t}$, which is different from the option value of new contracts $V_{t,t}$. Even if the option value of existing liabilities were collinear with the option value of new contracts because the contract characteristics happen to be identical, $1 + \phi_t$ is another source of variation in the reserve valuation that could break the collinearity. Recall that $1 + \phi_t$ represents the ratio of reserve to market value under Actuarial Guideline 43. Therefore, the reserve valuation is an accounting value that does not coincide with the market value or the policyholders' valuation that enters demand. As we discuss in Section 1.4.3, insurers compute reserves and required capital as a conditional tail expectation using the insurance regulators' scenarios, which ultimately depend on contract characteristics. However, policyholders value these characteristics differently from insurers because their marginal utility depends on the usefulness of variable annuities for aggregate risk sharing, insuring longevity risk, and tax management. Therefore, contract characteristics enter demand differently from how they enter the insurer's conditional tail expectation. Thus, we have plausibly exogenous variation in the reserve valuation that affects demand only through the marginal cost, conditional on the contract characteristics in our specification.

We have a similar motivation for the reinsurance share of variable annuities as an instrument. As we discuss in Section 2.4, most reinsurance is shadow insurance that relaxes regulatory constraints and reduces tax liabilities. Thus, insurers reinsure a higher share of variable annuity reserves when the marginal cost is high, leading to a positive relation between the reinsurance share of variable annuities and the marginal cost for a given insurer. We assume that the reinsurance share of variable annuities does not affect demand directly conditional on the contract and insurer characteristics in our specification. This assumption is plausible insofar as policyholders have little motive or knowledge to condition demand on reinsurance activity beyond what is already reflected in ratings.

4.3.3   Estimation Methodology

We estimate the random coefficients logit model of variable annuity demand by the two-step generalized method of moments. Let $\mathbf{z}_{i,t}$ be a vector of instruments that includes the reserve valuation, the reinsurance share of variable annuities, and the square of these instruments to help identify the variance of the random coefficients on the fee. The moment condition is

$$\mathbb{E}[\xi_{i,t}|\mathbf{z}_{i,t}, \mathbf{x}_{i,t}] = 0. \tag{4.23}$$

Because $\xi_{i,t}$ is not analytical, we compute it numerically as follows.

We rewrite the market share (4.21) as

$$Q_{i,t}(\mu_P, \sigma_P^2, \delta_t) = \int \frac{\exp(-e^v P_{i,t} + \delta_{i,t})}{1 + \sum_{j=1}^{I} \exp(-e^v P_{j,t} + \delta_{j,t})} \, dF(v), \tag{4.24}$$

where

$$\delta_{i,t} = \alpha_r r_{i,t} + \boldsymbol{\beta}' \mathbf{x}_{i,t} + \xi_{i,t}, \tag{4.25}$$

$$v \sim \mathbb{N}\left(\mu_P - \frac{\sigma_P^2}{2}, \sigma_P^2\right), \tag{4.26}$$

and $\delta_t = (\delta_{1,t}, \ldots, \delta_{I,t})'$. Starting with an initial guess of the parameters $(\mu_P, \sigma_P^2, \alpha_r, \boldsymbol{\beta})$ and the vector of mean utility $\delta_t(1)$, the estimation proceeds as follows.

1. Iterate on the following equation until convergence, computing the market share (4.24) numerically through a simulation with 500 draws:

$$\delta_t(n+1) = \delta_t(n) + \log(\mathbf{Q}_t) - \log(\mathbf{Q}_t(\mu_P, \sigma_P^2, \delta_t(n))). \quad (4.27)$$

Let $\delta_t(N)$ be the converged vector of mean utility.

2. Compute $\xi_{i,t} = \delta_{i,t}(N) - \alpha_r r_{i,t} - \boldsymbol{\beta}' \mathbf{x}_{i,t}$ and evaluate the objective function corresponding to moment condition (4.23).

3. Stop if the objective function is minimized. Otherwise, update the parameters $(\mu_P, \sigma_P^2, \alpha_r, \boldsymbol{\beta})$ by Newton's method and go back to step 1.

4.3.4   Estimated Model of Variable Annuity Demand

Table 4.1 reports the estimated parameters for the random coefficients logit model of variable annuity demand. The estimate of the mean parameter is $\mu_P = 3.37$ with a standard error of 0.13. The estimate of the standard deviation parameter is $\sigma_P = 0.30$ with a standard error of 0.05. The coefficient on the rollup rate is 0.18 with a standard error of 0.01. The signs of the coefficients confirm that demand decreases in the fee and increases in the rollup rate.

Demand also increases in the number of investment options, the GLWB dummy, and the A.M. Best rating. The coefficient on the number of investment options is 0.18 with a standard error of 0.01. The coefficient on the GLWB dummy is 17.02 with a standard error of 2.64. The coefficient on the I share class is -13.82 with a standard error of 2.34, which means that the I share class has lower demand than the B share class. The coefficient on the A.M. Best rating, which is standardized, is 0.73 with a standard error of 0.10. This means that demand increases by 73% per one standard deviation increase in the rating.

We compute the semi-elasticity of demand for each contract through equation (4.22). For contracts with minimum return guarantees, the semi-elasticity of demand to the fee has a mean of 16.4 and a standard deviation of 0.8 across contracts in 2007:4. A semi-elasticity of 16.4 means that demand decreases by 16.4% per 1 basis point increase in the fee. The dynamics of sales

TABLE 4.1. Estimated Model of Variable Annuity Demand

Variable	Mean	Standard deviation
Fee	3.37	0.30
	(0.13)	(0.05)
Rollup rate	0.18	
	(0.01)	
Investment options	0.11	
	(0.01)	
GLWB	17.02	
	(2.64)	
Share class		
A	−9.01	
	(1.60)	
C	2.01	
	(0.62)	
I	−13.82	
	(2.34)	
L	4.99	
	(1.05)	
O	−5.60	
	(1.03)	
X	3.86	
	(0.82)	
A.M. Best rating	0.73	
	(0.10)	
Observations	32,419	

Copyright American Finance Association; reprint of Koijen and Yogo (2022a, table 4) with permission. The random coefficients logit model of variable annuity demand is estimated by the two-step generalized method of moments. The random coefficient on the fee is parameterized as $\log(\alpha_P) \sim \mathbb{N}(\mu_P - \sigma_P^2/2, \sigma_P^2)$, where the table reports estimates of μ_P and σ_P. For reporting purposes, the rollup rate is orthogonalized with respect to the number of investment options, the GLWB dummy, and share class fixed effects. B is the omitted category for the share class fixed effects. The specification includes insurer fixed effects, whose coefficients are not reported for brevity. The instruments are log reserve valuation, the reinsurance share of variable annuities, and the squares of these variables. Heteroscedasticity-robust standard errors are reported in parentheses. The sample includes all contracts from 2005:1 to 2015:4.

and fees during the global financial crisis are especially important for identifying the demand elasticity. Sales decreased and fees increased sharply during the global financial crisis, especially for contracts with minimum return guarantees. The average semi-elasticity of demand to the fee falls to 15.4 in 2009:2 and ultimately to 14.8 in 2015:4. As we discuss above, the demand elasticity to the fee varies over time through changing contract characteristics, interacting with the distribution of random coefficients on the fee.

The semi-elasticity of demand to the fee is 6 for S&P 500 index funds in 2000 (Hortaçsu and Syverson, 2004).[2] The demand for variable annuities may be more elastic than that for index funds for several reasons. First, variable annuity policyholders are wealthier and less risk averse than the average household (Brown and Poterba, 2006). Second, variable annuity policyholders may be more inclined to shop around because a variable annuity is a large investment that is costly to reverse. Third, financial frictions could interact with broker incentives to increase the demand elasticity. After the global financial crisis, insurers made the minimum return guarantees less generous or stopped offering guarantees to reduce risk exposure, which changed the composition of new contracts toward those for which brokers earn lower commissions. Thus, brokers may have had weaker incentives to sell variable annuities after the global financial crisis. The role of brokers in determining demand elasticities is an important area for future research, which recent work explores using new data on broker commissions (Bhattacharya, Illanes, and Padi, 2020; Egan, Ge, and Tang, 2022; Barbu, 2021).

For contracts with minimum return guarantees, the semi-elasticity of demand to the rollup rate has a mean of 0.18 across contracts in 2007:4. A semi-elasticity of 0.18 means that demand increases by 18% per one percentage point increase in the rollup rate. The demand elasticity to the rollup rate is nearly constant across contracts and over time. The coefficient on the rollup rate is constant in our specification, which implies that the demand elasticity to the rollup rate is not sensitive to changing contract characteristics.

Our baseline specification limits the random coefficients to the fee. For robustness, we estimate a richer model in which the coefficients on the rollup rate or the A.M. Best rating are also random. However, the standard deviation of the random coefficients converges to zero or has large standard errors indicating that the richer model is poorly identified. Thus, we find evidence for heterogeneity across policyholders in the demand elasticity to the fee but not to the rollup rate. The identification problem arises from the fact that the variation in market shares can only identify a limited covariance structure for the random coefficients.

---

2. This semi-elasticity is implied by an asset-weighted average fee of 32.2 basis points in 2000 (Hortaçsu and Syverson, 2004, table 2) and a marginal cost of 16 basis points (Hortaçsu and Syverson, 2004, column D of table 3).

4.3.5 Consumer Surplus

The large size of the variable annuity market reflects its importance for house-hold welfare. In theory, minimum return guarantees could facilitate efficient risk sharing across heterogeneous agents (Dumas, 1989; Chan and Kogan, 2002) or overlapping generations (Allen and Gale, 1997; Ball and Mankiw, 2007). Policyholders cannot easily replicate minimum return guarantees because traded options have shorter maturity and model uncertainty exposes them to basis risk in a dynamic hedging program. Therefore, insurers complete a missing market for long-maturity options by offering minimum return guarantees over long horizons. In addition, variable annuities are potentially useful for insuring longevity risk and tax management.

Following Small and Rosen (1981), we quantify these benefits of variable annuities through the consumer surplus:

$$\int \frac{\log(1 + \sum_{i=1}^{I} \exp(-\alpha_P P_{i,t} + \alpha_r r_{i,t} + \boldsymbol{\beta}' \mathbf{x}_{i,t} + \xi_{i,t}))}{\alpha_P} \, dF(\alpha_P). \quad (4.28)$$

Figure 4.5 shows the average consumer surplus for each dollar of investment, which naturally tracks variable annuity sales. The consumer surplus peaks at just above 4 cents per dollar of investment in 2007:3. After the global financial crisis, the consumer surplus steadily declines to just above 1 cent per dollar of investment in 2015:4. The decrease in sales, especially for contracts with minimum return guarantees, has significantly reduced the consumer surplus.

4.4 Estimating Variable Annuity Supply

4.4.1 Empirical Specification

For contract i sold by insurer n in period t, equation (4.14) for the optimal fee in logarithms is

$$\log\left(P_{i,n,t} - \frac{1}{\epsilon_{i,n,t}^P}\right) = \log(V_{i,n,t}) + \log(\lambda_{n,t}). \quad (4.29)$$

This equation decomposes marginal cost into the option value and the shadow cost of capital. The option value explains within-insurer variation in the marginal cost along contract characteristics, while the shadow cost of capital explains between-insurer variation in the marginal cost along insurer characteristics.

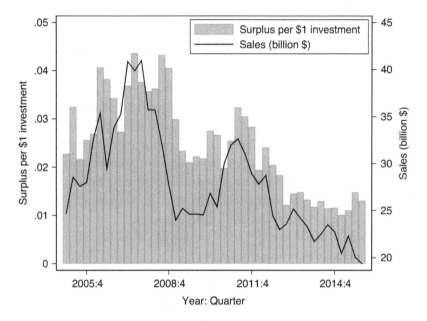

FIGURE 4.5. Consumer Surplus from Variable Annuities. The left axis shows the average
consumer surplus for each dollar of investment from 2005:1 to 2015:4. The right
axis shows the quarterly sales of variable annuities across all contracts.

For contract i sold by insurer n in period t, equation (4.17) for the optimal
rollup rate in logarithms is

$$\log\left(\frac{\epsilon^r_{i,n,t}}{\epsilon^P_{i,n,t}}\right) - \log(\lambda_{n,t}) - \log\left(\frac{\partial V_{i,n,t}}{\partial r_{i,n,t}}\right) = \omega_{i,n,t} \geq 0. \qquad (4.30)$$

At an interior solution (i.e., $\omega_{i,n,t} = 0$), the marginal benefit of a higher rollup
rate through demand is equal to the marginal cost of a higher rollup rate
through financial frictions. The black line in Figure 4.6, which represents
the left side of equation (4.30) as a function of the rollup rate, illustrates an
interior solution. The line is downward sloping because of the third term
on the left side of equation (4.30). The negative of the slope of the option
value with respect to the rollup rate decreases in the rollup rate because
$\partial^2 V_{i,n,t}/\partial r^2_{i,n,t} > 0$.

At a corner solution, the marginal benefit of a higher rollup rate through
demand is greater than the marginal cost of a higher rollup rate through financial frictions. The gray line in Figure 4.6 illustrates a corner solution when
the relative demand elasticities minus the shadow cost of capital is low. The

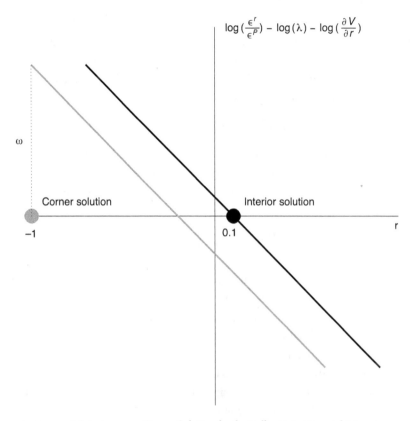

FIGURE 4.6. Interior versus Corner Solution for the Rollup Rate. Copyright American Finance Association; reprint of Koijen and Yogo (2022a, figure 7) with permission. When the relative demand elasticities minus the shadow cost of capital is high, the optimal rollup rate is at an interior solution (i.e., $r = 0.1$), as illustrated by the black line. When the relative demand elasticities minus the shadow cost of capital is low, the optimal rollup rate is at a corner solution (i.e., $r = -1$), as illustrated by the gray line.

insurer would like to reduce its risk exposure by reducing the rollup rate, but the constraint prevents the insurer from choosing a negative rollup rate that would be the unconstrained optimum. Therefore, the insurer offers mutual funds without minimum return guarantees, so that equation (4.30) holds at $r_{i,n,t} = -1$ with $\omega_{i,n,t} > 0$.

Because the same shadow cost of capital enters both equations (4.29) and (4.30), both fees and rollup rates contribute toward the identification of the shadow cost of capital. Intuitively, a high shadow cost of capital must simultaneously lead to high fees and low rollup rates across all contracts that an insurer offers.

We take three steps to transform equations (4.29) and (4.30) into estimation equations. First, we parameterize the option value to depend on the rollup rate and a vector $\mathbf{y}_{i,n,t}$ of other contract characteristics, which are the number of investment options, the GLWB dummy, and share class fixed effects. The option value of contract i in period t is

$$V_{i,n,t} = \exp(\boldsymbol{\delta}' \mathbf{y}_{i,n,t} + \exp(\boldsymbol{\Delta}' \mathbf{y}_{i,n,t}) r_{i,n,t} + v_{i,n,t}). \qquad (4.31)$$

The vector $\boldsymbol{\delta}$ contains coefficients that determine the level of option value. The residual $v_{i,n,t}$ represents unobserved (to the econometrician) contract characteristics that affect the level of option value. The slope of the option value with respect to the rollup rate is

$$\frac{\partial V_{i,n,t}}{\partial r_{i,n,t}} = \exp(\boldsymbol{\Delta}' \mathbf{y}_{i,n,t}) V_{i,n,t}. \qquad (4.32)$$

The vector $\boldsymbol{\Delta}$ contains the coefficients that determine the slope of the option value with respect to the rollup rate.

An alternative to our econometric approach in equation (4.31) is an option pricing model (Milevsky and Salisbury, 2006; Bauer, Kling, and Russ, 2008). However, long-horizon volatility is a key input in option pricing, which we cannot estimate from traded options that have much shorter maturity than the minimum return guarantees. An insight that we offer for this literature is that the fee actually includes a markup and the shadow cost of capital, according to equation (4.14). Therefore, one should not estimate an option pricing model directly on the fee without first taking out the markup and the shadow cost of capital. An interesting area for future research is to estimate long-horizon implied volatility using our estimates of option value for a large cross section of contracts.

Second, we parameterize the shadow cost of capital to depend on a vector $\mathbf{z}_{n,t}$ of insurer characteristics, which are the A.M. Best rating, log reserve valuation, and the reinsurance share of variable annuities. The shadow cost of capital for insurer n in period t is

$$\lambda_{n,t} = \exp(\boldsymbol{\Gamma}' \mathbf{z}_{n,t} + \boldsymbol{\gamma}' \mathbf{1}_n). \qquad (4.33)$$

The vector $\boldsymbol{\Gamma}$ contains the coefficients on insurer characteristics. The vector $\boldsymbol{\gamma}$ contains the coefficients on the insurer fixed effects, which capture permanent differences in the shadow cost of capital across insurers. For example, stock companies have a more complex financial structure than mutual companies that allows for shadow insurance. We do not have time fixed effects, so the only time variation in the shadow cost of capital comes from insurer characteristics. This assumption is conservative in that we do not overattribute time variation in marginal cost to the shadow cost of capital rather than the option value.

Third, we derive equations (4.14) and (4.17) under the assumption that the insurer offers only one contract. In reality, the insurer offers multiple contracts and presumably chooses the fees and the rollup rates accounting for demand elasticities across contracts. In Appendix B, we derive a more general version of equations (4.14) and (4.17) for a multiproduct insurer and describe how to compute the semi-elasticities of demand from the estimated model of variable annuity demand.

Taking these three steps, equations (4.29) and (4.30) become

$$v_{i,n,t} = \log\left(P_{i,n,t} - \frac{1}{\epsilon_{i,n,t}^P}\right) - \delta' y_{i,n,t} - \exp(\Delta' y_{i,n,t}) r_{i,n,t} - \Gamma' z_{n,t} - \gamma' 1_n,$$

$$(4.34)$$

$$\omega_{i,n,t} = \log\left(\frac{\epsilon_{i,n,t}^r}{\epsilon_{i,n,t}^P}\right) - \log\left(P_{i,n,t} - \frac{1}{\epsilon_{i,n,t}^P}\right) - \Delta' y_{i,n,t}.$$

$$(4.35)$$

After subtracting marginal cost, equation (4.35) for the optimal rollup rate identifies only the slope of the option value with respect to the rollup rate. This clean separability comes from the fact that the optimal rollup rate depends on the shadow cost of capital only through marginal cost, given our parametric assumptions.

4.4.2 Estimation Methodology

The moment conditions for the optimal fee are

$$\mathbb{E}\left[v_{i,n,t}\begin{pmatrix} y_{i,n,t} \\ y_{i,n,t} r_{i,n,t} \\ z_{n,t} \\ 1_n \end{pmatrix}\right] = 0.$$

$$(4.36)$$

Since the vector of contract characteristics satisfies $y_{i,n,t} \geq 0$ in our specification, the moment inequalities for the optimal rollup rate are

$$\mathbb{E}[\omega_{i,n,t} y_{i,n,t}] \geq 0.$$

$$(4.37)$$

We transform this equation into moment equalities as

$$\mathbb{E}[\operatorname{diag}(\omega_{i,n,t}\mathbf{1} - \mathbf{\Omega})\mathbf{y}_{i,n,t}] = \mathbf{0}, \qquad (4.38)$$

where $\mathbf{\Omega} \geq \mathbf{0}$ is a vector of auxiliary parameters that captures the slackness of the inequality.

We plug in the point estimates of demand elasticities in equations (4.34) and (4.35). We then estimate equations (4.36) and (4.38) by the two-step generalized method of moments. Moon and Schorfheide (2009) discuss identification issues related to our model that has both moment equalities and inequalities. If $\mathbf{\Omega} = \mathbf{0}$, the model is overidentified, and the moment condition for the optimal rollup rate is informative about the slope of the option value with respect to the rollup rate. If $\mathbf{\Omega} > \mathbf{0}$, the model is exactly identified, and the moment condition for the optimal rollup rate is uninformative about the slope of the option value with respect to the rollup rate. Between these extreme cases, only a subset of the moments in equation (4.38) may be informative about the slope of the option value with respect to the rollup rate.

The intercept in equation (4.34) is the unconditional mean of marginal cost, from which we cannot separately identify the unconditional mean of the option value versus the shadow cost of capital. This issue is inconsequential for our main findings, which concern the time variation in the option value and the shadow cost of capital. For the purposes of presentation, we normalize the unconditional mean of the shadow cost of capital so that $\log(\lambda_{n,t}) = 0$ for the lowest realized value in our sample. This procedure leads to an upper bound on the option value and a lower bound on the shadow cost of capital for each contract.

4.4.3   Estimated Model of Variable Annuity Supply

Table 4.2 reports the estimated model of variable annuity supply. The signs of the coefficients on the insurer characteristics are consistent with the hypothesis that they capture the shadow cost of capital. That is, the shadow cost of capital decreases in the A.M. Best rating and increases in log reserve valuation and the reinsurance share of variable annuities. These estimates also validate the "first stage" of the demand estimation in Table 4.1, which relies on log reserve valuation and the reinsurance share of variable annuities as relevant instruments for fees and rollup rates.

The average value of the shadow cost of capital is $\lambda_t = 1.52$ for the cross section of insurers in 2008:4. We check the internal consistency of this

TABLE 4.2. Estimated Model of Variable Annuity Supply

Variable	Coefficient	Standard error
Panel A. Level of option value		
Investment options	0.44	(0.02)
GLWB	46.05	(0.25)
Share class		
A	−44.01	(0.93)
C	11.53	(0.36)
I	−78.83	(1.39)
L	18.78	(0.26)
O	−19.08	(1.13)
X	16.06	(0.33)
Panel B. Slope of option value		
Investment options	2.90	(0.13)
GLWB	−21.67	(0.91)
Share class		
A	29.41	(5.15)
C	5.09	(1.31)
I	89.48	(1.85)
L	−28.94	(2.51)
O	13.92	(10.15)
X	−16.88	(3.45)
Panel C. Shadow cost of capital		
A.M. Best rating	−2.08	(0.25)
Reserve valuation	0.48	(0.25)
Variable annuities reinsured	0.97	(0.20)
Panel D. Constraint on the rollup rate		
Investment options	0.00	
GLWB	0.00	
Share class		
A	26.73	(4.63)
C	0.00	
I	0.00	
L	25.44	(1.89)
O	15.50	(9.17)
X	12.81	(2.73)
Constant	14.14	(0.60)
Observations	32,419	

A model of variable annuity supply is estimated by the two-step generalized method of moments. For reporting purposes, the rollup rate is orthogonalized with respect to the number of investment options, the GLWB dummy, and share class fixed effects. B is the omitted category for the share class fixed effects. In Panel C, the shadow cost of capital depends on the A.M. Best rating, log reserve valuation, the reinsurance share of variable annuities, and insurer fixed effects, whose coefficients are not reported for brevity. In Panel D, the auxiliary parameters for the moments corresponding to the number of investment options, the GLWB dummy, and share class fixed effects for C and I are set to zero because their inequality constraints are binding. Heteroscedasticity-robust standard errors are reported in parentheses. The sample includes all contracts from 2005:1 to 2015:4.

estimate with the estimated marginal cost of capital in Section 3.4.3 through a back-of-the-envelope calculation. In equation (4.15), the shadow cost of capital depends on the marginal cost of capital c_t and the risk weight ϕ_t, which is an unknown value that depends on the overall risk profile of minimum return guarantees. Based on a relevant case study that provides a sense of magnitudes, the required capital for a GLWB under the C-3 Phase II regulatory standard is 8.2% of account value, while the required capital under Actuarial Guideline 43 is 4.4% of account value (Junus and Motiwalla, 2009, table 9). Assuming that the reserve value under Actuarial Guideline 43 is conservative and greater than the market value, a lower bound on the risk weight is $\phi_t = 8.2/4.4 - 1 = 0.86$. This implies that the marginal cost of capital is

$$c_t = \frac{\lambda_t - 1}{\phi_t - \lambda_t + 1} = 1.53 \qquad (4.39)$$

when $\lambda_t = 1.52$ and $\phi_t = 0.86$. According to Figure 3.7, the average value of the marginal cost of capital is $c_t = 0.96$ for the cross section of insurers in 2008:4. Moreover, 1.53 is well within the range of estimates for the cross section of variable annuity insurers in Table 3.4.

Through the estimated model for the optimal fee, we decompose the total annual fee for contracts with minimum return guarantees, averaged across contracts with sales weighting. Figure 4.7 reproduces the total annual fee from Panel A of Figure 4.3 and shows its decomposition into the markup, the option value, and the shadow cost of capital. The total annual fee was 2.04% of account value in 2007:4, which is the sum of 0.06% for the markup, 1.29% for the option value, and 0.69% for the shadow cost of capital. Thus, the profit was 0.75% of account value, which was mostly from financial frictions (0.69%) rather than market power (0.06%). The total annual fee increased by 34 basis points from 2.04% of account value in 2007:4 to 2.38% in 2009:2. This increase reflects an increase of 1 basis point in the markup, 16 basis points in the option value, and 17 basis points in the shadow cost of capital. Thus, financial frictions are just as important as the option pricing channel for explaining the increase in fees during the global financial crisis.

Rearranging equation (4.30) for the optimal rollup rate and taking the expectation across contracts, we have

$$\mathbb{E}\left[\log\left(\frac{\epsilon_{i,n,t}^r}{\epsilon_{i,n,t}^P}\right) - \log(\lambda_{n,t})\right] = \mathbb{E}\left[\log\left(\frac{\partial V_{i,n,t}}{\partial r_{i,n,t}}\right) + \omega_{i,n,t}\right]. \qquad (4.40)$$

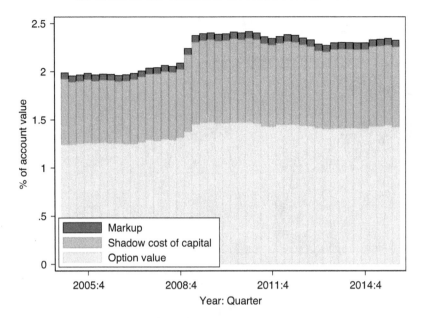

FIGURE 4.7. Decomposition of Fees. Copyright American Finance Association; reprint of Koijen and Yogo (2022a, figure 8) with permission. The total annual fee, averaged across contracts with sales weighting, is decomposed into the markup, the option value, and the shadow cost of capital. The sample includes all contracts with minimum return guarantees from 2005:1 to 2015:4.

We use this equation to decompose the time variation in the determination of the optimal rollup rates. Panel A of Figure 4.8 shows the two variables on the left side of equation (4.40), which is the relative demand elasticities minus the shadow cost of capital. Both variables are reported as deviations from their time-series mean. As we discuss in Section 4.3.4, the demand elasticity to the fee decreased, while the demand elasticity to the rollup rate remained nearly constant. Thus, the relative demand elasticities increased after the global financial crisis, which increases the optimal rollup rate. As we discuss in Section 4.2.4, the intuition is that insurers earn higher markups when the demand elasticity to the fee is lower, so variable annuities are less capital intensive per unit sold. The shadow cost of capital also increased during the global financial crisis, which reduces the optimal rollup rate. Between the two effects, the relative demand elasticities have larger time variation and play a more important role in the determination of rollup rates.

Panel B of Figure 4.8 shows the two variables on the right side of equation (4.40), which is the slope of the option value with respect to the rollup rate

Panel A. Left side of the equation

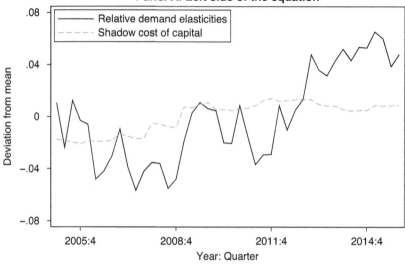

Panel B. Right side of the equation

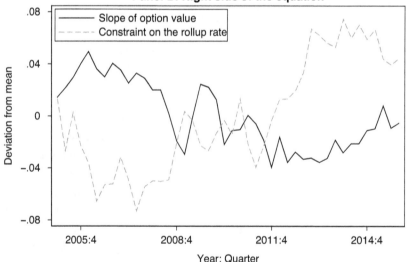

FIGURE 4.8. Decomposition of Rollup Rates. Copyright American Finance Association; reprint of Koijen and Yogo (2022a, figure 9) with permission. Panel A shows the two variables on the left side of equation (4.40), which is the relative demand elasticities minus the shadow cost of capital. Panel B shows the two variables on the right side of equation (4.40), which is the slope of the option value with respect to the rollup rate plus the constraint on the rollup rate. All variables are reported as deviations from their time-series mean. The sample includes all contracts from 2005:1 to 2015:4.

plus the constraint on the rollup rate. Both variables are reported as deviations from their time-series mean. The slope of the option value with respect to the rollup rate has a downward trend after the global financial crisis. The contracts with generous guarantees are too capital intensive after the global financial crisis because the option value is more sensitive to the rollup rate. At an interior optimum, insurers optimally reduce rollup rates to the point where the slope of the option value is sufficiently low to satisfy equation (4.17). The optimal rollup rate could be so low that the constraint on the rollup rate is binding, which explains why insurers stopped offering minimum return guarantees. The relative demand elasticities in Panel A closely track the constraint on the rollup rate in Panel B. Thus, insurers stopped offering minimum return guarantees despite the fact that the relative demand elasticities increased.

As we discuss in Section 4.1, two factors could explain why variable annuity supply did not fully recover long after the global financial crisis. First, insurers may have been more cautious because of the difficulty of managing interest rate risk in the low interest rate environment. Second, Actuarial Guideline 43 increased the capital requirements for variable annuities. These two factors ultimately drive up the shadow cost of capital, which is consistent with the evidence in Figures 4.7 and 4.8.

5

Reinsurance

IN SECTION 2.4, we document the rapid growth of shadow insurance after 2002, as a consequence of changes in life insurance regulation and captive laws that we summarize in Section 1.4.3. On the one hand, shadow insurance could increase leverage and risk for the insurance group because shadow reinsurers could hold less equity than the operating companies that sell policies. The limited data that we have for Iowa captives in Table 2.7 suggests that shadow reinsurers hold significantly less equity than the operating companies. On the other hand, shadow insurance could reduce the cost of regulatory frictions and thereby improve retail market efficiency. This chapter develops a framework to study this trade-off.

In Section 5.1, we show that ratings are unrelated to shadow insurance in the cross section of insurers, which raises the hypothesis that ratings do not adequately reflect the risk of shadow insurance. Therefore, we quantify the potential risk of shadow insurance by adjusting risk measures based on publicly available data and plausible assumptions. Our adjustment reduces risk-based capital by 53 percentage points (or three rating notches) and increases the 10-year cumulative default probability by a factor of 3.5 for the average company using shadow insurance.

In Section 5.2, we extend the insurance pricing model in Section 1.5 to study the trade-off posed by shadow insurance. A holding company consists of an operating company that sells policies and an affiliated reinsurer, whose only role is to assume reinsurance from the operating company. The key friction is that the operating company faces tighter capital regulation than the affiliated reinsurer. Affiliated reinsurance allows the holding company to reallocate liabilities between the two companies to reduce the overall cost of regulatory frictions. The model predicts that affiliated reinsurance reduces the operating company's marginal cost of issuing policies and increases the equilibrium supply in the retail market.

In Section 5.3, we quantify this effect by estimating a differentiated product demand system for the life insurance market. Our estimates imply that shadow insurance reduces life insurance premiums by 10% for the average company and increases annual life insurance issued by $6.8 billion for the industry, which is 7% of the market size in 2012.

5.1 Risk of Shadow Insurance

We show that ratings are unrelated to shadow insurance in the cross section of insurers. This finding is consistent with the hypothesis that rating agencies view shadow insurance as sufficiently safe to not require a meaningful adjustment to ratings. However, this finding is also consistent with an alternative hypothesis that ratings do not adequately reflect the risk of shadow insurance. Under the alternative hypothesis, we quantify the potential risk of shadow insurance by adjusting risk measures based on publicly available data and plausible assumptions.

5.1.1 Relation between Ratings and Shadow Insurance

According to the A.M. Best Company (2013), ratings and risk-based capital fully reflect the risk of shadow insurance. In Table 5.1, we empirically investigate the relation between ratings and shadow insurance, which reveals the perceived magnitude of risk. As we discuss in Appendix A.2, we convert the A.M. Best rating to a cardinal measure and standardize ratings and all regressors that are not dummy variables.

In column (1) of Table 5.1, we estimate the relation between ratings and a dummy for shadow insurance by ordinary least squares. Our simplest specification controls for only year and A.M. Best financial size category, whose coefficients are not reported for brevity. A coefficient of 0.03 on shadow insurance has the wrong sign if we expect shadow insurance to increase risk. However, the coefficient is economically small and statistically insignificant; ratings are only 0.03 standard deviations higher for insurers that use shadow insurance. In column (2), we show that the coefficient on shadow insurance is robust to controlling for the conventional determinants of ratings.

Because we do not know the proprietary model used by the A.M. Best Company, omitted variables could explain the absence of a negative relation

TABLE 5.1. Relation between Ratings and Shadow Insurance

	A.M. Best rating			Risk-based capital
	OLS		IV	
Variable	(1)	(2)	(3)	(4)
Shadow insurance	0.03	0.00	0.25	−0.02
	(0.06)	(0.06)	(0.34)	(0.05)
Log liabilities		0.17	0.13	0.15
		(0.04)	(0.06)	(0.05)
Risk-based capital		0.13	0.15	
		(0.02)	(0.02)	
Leverage		−0.01	0.01	−0.46
		(0.03)	(0.03)	(0.06)
Current liquidity		0.08	0.06	0.18
		(0.02)	(0.02)	(0.04)
Return on equity		0.03	0.03	0.01
		(0.02)	(0.02)	(0.02)
Stock company		0.05	0.02	0.12
		(0.06)	(0.07)	(0.06)
R^2	0.60	0.62	0.63	0.33
Observations	6,641	6,641	6,351	6,641

Copyright Econometric Society; reprint of Koijen and Yogo (2016, table E.1) with permission. Columns (1) and (2) estimate the relation between A.M. Best ratings and company characteristics by ordinary least squares (OLS). Column (3) estimates the same relation by instrumental variables (IV), where the instrument for shadow insurance is the market share for term life insurance in 1999, interacted with a dummy for a stock company in 1999. Column (4) estimates the relation between risk-based capital and company characteristics by OLS. All specifications include dummies for year and A.M. Best financial size category, whose coefficients are not reported for brevity. The coefficients are standardized, and robust standard errors clustered by insurance group are reported in parentheses. The sample consists of US life insurers from 2002 to 2012.

between ratings and shadow insurance. For example, the A.M. Best Company could have soft information that is positively related to both ratings and the use of shadow insurance, and shadow insurance is mostly used by less risky companies. We could address this concern through instrumental variables, but the challenge is that many known characteristics that correlate with shadow insurance are also direct determinants of ratings.

Our instrument is the market share of term life insurance in 1999, interacted with a dummy for a stock company in 1999. For each company, we calculate its market share as the face amount of term life insurance in force divided by the sum across all companies. The motivation for the instrument is that Regulation XXX had a stronger impact on insurers with a larger presence in the term life insurance market. The interaction accounts for the fact that among those companies affected by Regulation XXX, the stock companies have a stronger incentive to take advantage of the captive laws after 2002. The market share in 1999 is plausibly exogenous to ratings after 2002, conditional on the conventional determinants of ratings, because Regulation XXX applies only to new policies issued after 2000 and does not apply retroactively to existing liabilities.

In column (3) of Table 5.1, we estimate the relation between ratings and shadow insurance by instrumental variables.[1] The coefficient on shadow insurance again has the wrong sign. Ratings are 0.25 standard deviations higher for insurers that use shadow insurance, but this coefficient is statistically insignificant with a standard error of 0.34. Interestingly, the coefficients on the conventional determinants have the expected signs with higher ratings awarded to insurers that are larger and have higher risk-based capital, more liquid assets, and higher profitability. Overall, the evidence in Table 5.1 does not suggest an economically meaningful negative relation between ratings and shadow insurance.

In addition to ratings, the A.M. Best Company (2013) claims to adjust risk-based capital for shadow insurance. In column (4) of Table 5.1, we investigate the relation between risk-based capital and shadow insurance by ordinary least squares. Risk-based capital is negatively related to shadow insurance, but the coefficient is economically small and statistically insignificant. Risk-based capital is only 0.02 standard deviations lower for insurers that use shadow insurance.

5.1.2   Estimating Risk

The finding that ratings are unrelated to shadow insurance raises the possibility that ratings do not adequately reflect the risk of shadow insurance. We quantify the potential risk of shadow insurance by adjusting risk measures based on publicly available data and plausible assumptions. The fact that accurate risk assessments are difficult highlights the importance of more transparency.

---

1. In a first-stage regression that is not reported, the instrument is a highly relevant predictor of shadow insurance with an F-statistic of 21 (Stock and Yogo, 2005).

We start with accounting identities and a simple rating framework for an operating company that cedes reinsurance to a shadow reinsurer. Let A and L be the operating company's assets and liabilities, so its equity is $E = A - L$. We define leverage as L/A and risk-based capital as $\text{RBC} = E/(\phi L)$, where the risk charge $\phi > 0$ summarizes the risk profile of assets and liabilities. Let $\widehat{A}$ and $\widehat{L}$ be the shadow reinsurer's assets and liabilities, so its equity is $\widehat{E} = \widehat{A} - \widehat{L}$. Liabilities $\widehat{L}$ are observable based on the reinsurance ceded by the operating company to the shadow reinsurer. However, we do not observe $\widehat{E}$ (or equivalently $\widehat{A}$) or the risk profile of $\widehat{A}$ or $\widehat{L}$. Based on the evidence for Iowa captives in Table 2.7, we assume that shadow reinsurers do not have equity (i.e., $\widehat{E} = 0$). We also assume that the risk profile of reinsurance ceded is identical to assets and liabilities that remain on the balance sheet, so the risk charge on $\widehat{L}$ is ϕ.

We ask how the operating company's balance sheet would change if shadow insurance were moved back on the balance sheet. Our assumptions yield simple adjustments to risk-based capital and leverage based on publicly available data. The adjusted risk-based capital is

$$\frac{E + \widehat{E}}{\phi(L + \widehat{L})} = \frac{\text{RBC} \times L}{L + \widehat{L}}. \tag{5.1}$$

The adjusted leverage is

$$\frac{L + \widehat{L}}{A + \widehat{A}} = \frac{L + \widehat{L}}{A + \widehat{L}}. \tag{5.2}$$

Table 5.2 reports risk-based capital adjusted for shadow insurance, averaged across US life insurers using shadow insurance. Our adjustment reduces risk-based capital from 208% to 155%, or by 53 percentage points, for the average company using shadow insurance in 2012. According to equation (5.1), risk-based capital falls because equity does not change, but the capital required to support the additional liabilities (i.e., denominator of the ratio) rises. The difference between reported and adjusted risk-based capital has increased from 10 percentage points in 2002 to 53 percentage points in 2012 because shadow insurance $\widehat{L}$ has grown relative to liabilities L that remain on the balance sheet.

We ultimately do not know how ratings would be adjusted for shadow insurance because they are based on a proprietary model and soft information that are not publicly available. However, we could get a sense of the potential magnitude by assuming that ratings are a direct function of risk-based capital. Under this assumption, we first convert the A.M. Best rating to the equivalent

TABLE 5.2. Risk Measures Adjusted for Shadow Insurance

Year	Risk-based capital (%)			Rating		10-year default probability (%)		
	Reported	Adjusted	Difference	Reported	Adjusted	Reported	Adjusted	Ratio
2002	160	150	−10	A+	A	0.7	1.3	1.8
2003	170	156	−14	A+	A	0.7	1.3	2.0
2004	168	146	−22	A	A−	0.8	1.6	2.0
2005	197	166	−31	A	A−	0.9	1.8	2.0
2006	190	164	−25	A+	A−	0.7	1.5	2.3
2007	199	171	−28	A	B++	1.0	2.2	2.3
2008	199	174	−25	A	B++	0.8	2.1	2.6
2009	227	182	−45	A	B++	0.9	2.5	2.8
2010	250	197	−53	A	B+	0.9	2.8	3.1
2011	238	194	−44	A	B+	1.0	2.8	2.9
2012	208	155	−53	A	B+	0.9	3.0	3.5

The adjusted risk-based capital is based on equation (5.1). The adjusted rating converts the reported rating to the equivalent risk-based capital based on the guideline table (A.M. Best Company, 2011, p. 24) and then applies equation (5.1). The adjusted 10-year cumulative default probability is based on the adjusted rating. All risk measures are averaged across US life insurers using shadow insurance.

risk-based capital based on the guideline table (A.M. Best Company, 2011, p. 24). For example, a rating of A is equivalent to a risk-based capital of 145%. We then apply equation (5.1) to obtain the adjusted risk-based capital, which implies an adjusted rating by the same guideline table. In Table 5.2, the rating drops by three notches from A to B+ for the average company using shadow insurance in 2012.

In Koijen and Yogo (2016, appendix F), we estimate the term structure of default probabilities by A.M. Best rating. These estimates imply default probabilities for each company, corresponding to the reported rating and the adjusted rating. In Table 5.2, the adjusted rating implies a 10-year cumulative default probability of 3.0% for the average company using shadow insurance in 2012, which is 3.5 times higher than that implied by the reported rating.

5.1.3   Estimating Expected Loss

We can use the A.M. Best rating to estimate expected loss because it reflects an insurer's claims-paying ability without support from the state guaranty associations. Let $\Pr(m|\text{Rating})$ be the marginal default probability between years $m-1$ and m, conditional on the rating. Let θ be the loss ratio conditional on default, which we estimate to be 0.25 (Koijen and Yogo, 2016, appendix F). Let $y(m)$ be the zero-coupon Treasury yield at maturity m. For each company, we estimate the present value of expected loss as

$$\sum_{m=1}^{15} \frac{\Pr(m|\text{Rating})\theta L}{(1+y(m))^m}. \tag{5.3}$$

To estimate the expected loss adjusted for shadow insurance, we modify this formula by using the adjusted rating instead and replacing L with $L + \widehat{L}$.

Table 5.3 reports the expected loss adjusted for shadow insurance, aggregated across US life insurers. The expected loss based on reported ratings and liabilities is $4.9 billion for the industry in 2012. The expected loss increases to $14.4 billion when ratings and liabilities are adjusted for shadow insurance. The difference between adjusted and reported expected loss grew from $0.1 billion in 2002 to $9.5 billion in 2012. Since state guaranty associations ultimately pay off all liabilities by assessing the surviving companies, this expected loss represents an externality to the insurers not using shadow insurance. State taxpayers also bear a share of the cost because guaranty association assessments are tax deductible. The experience of TARP during the global financial

TABLE 5.3. Expected Loss Adjusted for Shadow Insurance

| Year | Expected loss (billion $) | | | Guaranty funds (billion $) |
	Reported	Adjusted	Difference	
2002	2.8	2.9	0.1	40.6
2003	2.6	2.9	0.3	38.0
2004	2.8	4.3	1.5	35.9
2005	2.8	4.2	1.4	33.4
2006	2.7	4.2	1.5	36.3
2007	3.1	6.6	3.5	38.7
2008	4.2	9.7	5.5	50.7
2009	3.7	11.5	7.7	47.6
2010	4.0	12.2	8.2	46.2
2011	4.7	13.5	8.8	49.2
2012	4.9	14.4	9.5	56.4

The expected loss is based on equation (5.3), aggregated across US life insurers. The adjusted expected loss is based on adjusted ratings and liabilities, the former of which is reported in Table 5.2. The total capacity of state guaranty funds is the maximum annual assessment aggregated across all states, projected to remain constant over the next 10 years (Gallanis, 2009).

crisis suggests that the federal government could also bear a share of the cost in a bailout.

To put these estimates of expected loss into perspective, we estimate the total capacity of state guaranty funds. All states cap annual guaranty association assessments, typically at 2% of recent life insurance and annuity premiums. Following Gallanis (2009), we estimate the total capacity of state guaranty funds as the maximum annual assessment aggregated across all states, projected to remain constant over the next 10 years. In Table 5.3, the expected loss for the industry grew from 7% in 2002 to 26% in 2012, as a share of the total capacity of state guaranty funds.

5.2   A Model of Insurance Pricing and Reinsurance

We extend the insurance pricing model in Section 1.5 to reinsurance to explain shadow insurance and its impact on the retail market. A holding company consists of an operating company that sells policies and an affiliated reinsurer, whose only role is to assume reinsurance from the operating company. Because the operating company faces tighter capital regulation than the affiliated reinsurer, the holding company can reduce the overall cost of regulatory frictions through reinsurance. Reinsurance reduces the operating company's marginal cost of capital and thereby reduces the marginal cost of issuing policies. However, reinsurance could also reduce the overall risk-based capital for the holding company.

For simplicity, we do not model unaffiliated reinsurance under the assumption that it is a more expensive way to raise statutory capital than affiliated reinsurance. We refer to Koijen and Yogo (2013) for a version of the model with unaffiliated reinsurance. We also do not model taxes because it is difficult to do so realistically, and the tax benefits of reinsurance are difficult to separately identify from the reduced cost of regulatory frictions. Estimating the tax benefits of reinsurance is a promising direction for future research.

5.2.1   Insurance Holding Company

The operating company sells just one type of insurance policy (e.g., life insurance). Insurers compete in an oligopolistic market and have market power because of product differentiation along policy characteristics other than the price, which we parameterize through a differentiated product demand system in Section 5.3.1. For now, we assume that the operating company faces a demand function that depends on its own price and the prices of its competitors. The demand function is continuously differentiable and strictly decreasing in its own price.

In period t, the operating company chooses the price P_t per policy and sells Q_t policies. The actuarial value per policy is V_t, which we assume is equal to the reserve value for simplicity. After the sale of policies, the operating company can cede reinsurance to the affiliated reinsurer. Let $B_t \geq 0$ be the quantity of reinsurance ceded by the operating company in period t. The holding company's profit is

$$D_t = (P_t - V_t)Q_t. \tag{5.4}$$

Reinsurance does not affect total profit under the maintained assumption of no tax effects.

5.2.2   Balance Sheet Dynamics

We describe how the sale of policies and reinsurance affect the balance sheet. Let A_{t-1} be the operating company's assets at the beginning of period t, and let $R_{A,t}$ be an exogenous gross asset return in period t. The operating company's assets at the end of period t, after the sale of policies and reinsurance, are

$$A_t = R_{A,t}A_{t-1} + V_t(Q_t - B_t) + D_t. \tag{5.5}$$

Let L_{t-1} be the operating company's liabilities at the beginning of period t, and let $R_{L,t}$ be an exogenous gross return on liabilities in period t. The operating company's liabilities at the end of period t are

$$L_t = R_{L,t}L_{t-1} + V_t(Q_t - B_t). \tag{5.6}$$

We define the operating company's statutory capital as equity minus required capital, which is proportional to reserves:

$$K_t = \underbrace{A_t - L_t}_{\text{equity}} - \underbrace{\phi L_t}_{\text{required capital}}, \tag{5.7}$$

where $\phi > 0$ is a risk charge on liabilities under risk-based capital regulation. As we discuss in Section 1.4.3, Regulation (A)XXX forced operating companies to hold more capital on newly issued life insurance policies. Thus, $1 + \phi$ also represents the ratio of reserve to actuarial value under Regulation (A)XXX.

For simplicity, we assume that the affiliated reinsurer faces the same returns on assets and liabilities as the operating company. The affiliated reinsurer's assets at the end of period t, after reinsurance, are

$$\widehat{A}_t = R_{A,t}\widehat{A}_{t-1} + V_t B_t. \tag{5.8}$$

The affiliated reinsurer's liabilities at the end of period t are

$$\widehat{L}_t = R_{L,t}\widehat{L}_{t-1} + V_t B_t. \tag{5.9}$$

As we discuss in Section 1.4.3, an affiliated reinsurer under the captive laws is not subject to Regulation (A)XXX or risk-based capital regulation. Thus, the affiliated reinsurer faces looser capital regulation than the operating company, which we model through a lower risk charge $\widehat{\phi} \in (0, \phi)$. The affiliated reinsurer's statutory capital is

$$\widehat{K}_t = \underbrace{\widehat{A}_t - \widehat{L}_t}_{\text{equity}} - \underbrace{\widehat{\phi}\,\widehat{L}_t}_{\text{required capital}}. \tag{5.10}$$

5.2.3   Financial Frictions

The Insurance Holding Company System Regulatory Act protects the interests of existing policyholders and the state guaranty associations by restricting the movement of capital within a holding company, including affiliated reinsurance (National Association of Insurance Commissioners, 2011a, appendix A-440). Furthermore, increased use of shadow insurance could draw regulatory scrutiny or intervention (Lawsky, 2013). We model these regulatory frictions through a cost function:

$$C_t = C\left(K_t, \widehat{K}_t\right). \qquad (5.11)$$

This cost function is continuous, twice continuously differentiable, strictly decreasing, and strictly convex. The cost function is decreasing because higher statutory capital reduces the likelihood of regulatory scrutiny or intervention. The cost function is convex because these benefits of higher statutory capital have diminishing returns.

We assume that financial frictions make equity issuance and unaffiliated reinsurance costly. For simplicity, we do not model equity issuance and unaffiliated reinsurance under the assumption that they are more expensive ways to raise statutory capital than affiliated reinsurance (Myers and Majluf, 1984).

5.2.4   Optimal Pricing and Reinsurance

The holding company chooses the insurance price P_t and reinsurance B_t to maximize firm value. Firm value is the present value of profits minus the cost of regulatory frictions:

$$J_t = D_t - C_t + \mathbb{E}_t[M_{t+1}J_{t+1}], \qquad (5.12)$$

where M_{t+1} is the stochastic discount factor.

To simplify the exposition, we present the optimality conditions for a single insurer with the understanding that all insurers have the same optimality conditions in a Nash equilibrium. To simplify the notation, we define the demand elasticity as $\epsilon_t = -\partial \log(Q_t)/\partial \log(P_t)$. We define the operating company's marginal cost of capital as

$$c_t = -\frac{\partial C_t}{\partial K_t} + \mathbb{E}_t\left[M_{t+1}\frac{\partial J_{t+1}}{\partial K_t}\right]. \qquad (5.13)$$

We also define the affiliated reinsurer's marginal cost of capital as

$$\widehat{c_t} = -\frac{\partial C_t}{\partial \widehat{K_t}} + \mathbb{E}_t\left[M_{t+1}\frac{\partial J_{t+1}}{\partial \widehat{K_t}}\right]. \tag{5.14}$$

The marginal cost of capital represents the importance of regulatory frictions, which decreases in statutory capital by the convexity of the cost function.

OPTIMAL PRICING

Following the same derivation as equation (1.17), the optimal insurance price is

$$P_t = \left(1 - \frac{1}{\epsilon_t}\right)^{-1} \underbrace{\lambda_t V_t,}_{\text{marginal cost}} \tag{5.15}$$

where the shadow cost of capital is

$$\lambda_t = \frac{1 + c_t(1 + \phi)}{1 + c_t} > 1. \tag{5.16}$$

The first term in equation (5.15) is the markup that is inversely related to the demand elasticity. The second term is the marginal cost of issuing policies, which is the product of the shadow cost of capital and the actuarial value. Marginal cost is greater than the actuarial value because of regulatory frictions. The shadow cost of capital decreases in the operating company's statutory capital through c_t and increases with tighter capital regulation (i.e., a higher ϕ).

OPTIMAL REINSURANCE

The first-order condition for reinsurance is

$$\frac{\partial J_t}{\partial B_t} = c_t\frac{\partial K_t}{\partial B_t} + \widehat{c_t}\frac{\partial \widehat{K_t}}{\partial B_t} \tag{5.17}$$

$$= (c_t\phi - \widehat{c_t}\widehat{\phi})V_t = 0.$$

At an interior optimum, reinsurance satisfies

$$c_t\phi = \widehat{c_t}\widehat{\phi}. \tag{5.18}$$

The holding company equates the marginal cost of capital across the two companies, appropriately weighted by the tightness of capital regulation. For example, suppose that the two companies have the same marginal cost of capital before reinsurance. Then the operating company cedes reinsurance to the affiliated reinsurer that faces looser capital regulation. The operating company's statutory capital rises relative to the affiliated reinsurer's, so that equation (5.18) holds with $c_t < \widehat{c}_t$ after reinsurance.

The partial derivative of marginal cost with respect to reinsurance is

$$
\frac{\partial (\lambda_t V_t)}{\partial B_t} = \left(\frac{\phi V_t}{1 + c_t} \right)^2 \frac{\partial c_t}{\partial K_t}
$$

$$
= \left(\frac{\phi V_t}{1 + c_t} \right)^2 \left(-\frac{\partial^2 C_t}{\partial K_t^2} + \mathbb{E}_t \left[M_{t+1} \frac{\partial J_{t+1}^2}{\partial K_t^2} \right] \right) < 0, \qquad (5.19)
$$

which follows by the convexity of the cost function and an additional assumption that demand does not depend on risk-based capital. Reinsurance reduces the operating company's marginal cost of capital and thereby reduces the marginal cost of issuing policies. A lower marginal cost implies a lower price through equation (5.15), provided that the demand elasticity does not decrease to more than offset the lower marginal cost. Thus, reinsurance could reduce the insurance price and increase the quantity of policies issued.

5.2.5 Holding Company's Risk-Based Capital

Although reinsurance could reduce the insurance price, it could reduce the overall risk-based capital for the holding company. We define the holding company's risk-based capital as

$$
E_t = A_t + \widehat{A}_t - (1 + \phi)(L_t + \widehat{L}_t)
$$

$$
= K_t + \widehat{K}_t - (\phi - \widehat{\phi})\widehat{L}_t. \qquad (5.20)
$$

Risk-based capital corresponds to the operating company's statutory capital if reinsurance were moved back on the balance sheet. This counterfactual is equivalent to our empirical exercise in Section 5.1.2.

The partial derivative of risk-based capital with respect to reinsurance is

$$
\frac{\partial E_t}{\partial B_t} = \frac{\partial K_t}{\partial B_t} + \frac{\partial \widehat{K}_t}{\partial B_t} - (\phi - \widehat{\phi}) \frac{\partial \widehat{L}_t}{\partial B_t}
$$

$$
= \frac{\partial P_t}{\partial B_t} \left(Q_t + (P_t - (1 + \phi)V_t) \frac{\partial Q_t}{\partial P_t} \right)
$$

$$
= \frac{\partial P_t}{\partial B_t} Q_t \epsilon_t \left(\frac{1}{\epsilon_t} - 1 + \frac{(1 + \phi)V_t}{P_t} \right). \qquad (5.21)
$$

Because the expression inside the parentheses is positive, $\partial E_t / \partial B_t < 0$ if $\partial P_t / \partial B_t < 0$. If reinsurance reduces the insurance price, it also reduces risk-based capital. The reason is that the marginal increase in equity from the additional business is less than the marginal increase in required capital to support the additional liabilities. If the holding company has limited liability, a reduction in risk-based capital increases the default probability.

5.3   Modeling the Life Insurance Market

We develop a model of the life insurance market to test the prediction that shadow insurance reduces the marginal cost of issuing policies and increases the equilibrium supply in the retail market. We focus on life insurance because Figure 2.5 shows that life insurance accounts for a larger share of shadow insurance than annuities. In addition, life insurance reserves under the statutory accounting principles are higher than those under GAAP under Regulation XXX. The estimation exercise in this section could be repeated for variable annuities if variable annuity reserves under the statutory accounting principles are higher than those under GAAP, as we discuss in Section 1.4.3.

5.3.1   A Model of Life Insurance Demand

As we discuss in Section 1.3.2, we use data on 10-year term life insurance premiums as representative of the life insurance market. Based on the financial statements, we estimate the sales of life insurance at the company level as the change in total gross life insurance reserves. We model life insurance demand through the random coefficients logit model. Since all companies sell the same type of policy, product differentiation is along company characteristics that capture differences in reputation and broker networks. Life insurance is a type of intermediated savings, so the natural alternative is all savings that are intermediated by financial institutions other than insurers. Therefore, we specify the outside asset as total annual saving by US households in savings deposits, money market funds, and mutual funds (Board of Governors of the Federal Reserve System, 2017, table F.100).

Let $P_{n,t}$ be the price of life insurance sold by company n in year t. Let $\mathbf{x}_{n,t}$ be a vector of observed characteristics of company n in year t, which are determinants of demand. The probability that a consumer with preference parameters $(\alpha, \boldsymbol{\beta})$ buys life insurance from company n in year t is

$$q_{n,t}(\alpha, \boldsymbol{\beta}) = \frac{\exp(-\alpha P_{n,t} + \boldsymbol{\beta}'\mathbf{x}_{n,t} + \xi_{n,t})}{1 + \sum_{m=1}^{N} \exp(-\alpha P_{m,t} + \boldsymbol{\beta}'\mathbf{x}_{m,t} + \xi_{m,t})}, \qquad (5.22)$$

where N is the total number of operating companies. The structural error $\xi_{n,t}$ captures company characteristics that are unobserved to the econometrician. If the consumer does not buy life insurance, he buys the outside asset instead, which occurs with probability $1 - \sum_{n=1}^{N} q_{n,t}(\alpha, \boldsymbol{\beta})$.

The company characteristics in our specification of $\mathbf{x}_{n,t}$ are the A.M. Best rating and the conventional determinants of ratings from Appendix A.2: log liabilities, risk-based capital, leverage, current liquidity, return on equity, and a dummy for a stock company. Thus, the marginal effect of the A.M. Best rating can be interpreted as soft information used in the rating process that is not captured by these other variables.

Let $F(\alpha, \boldsymbol{\beta})$ denote the distribution of preference parameters, which is multivariate normal with a diagonal covariance matrix. The market share for life insurance sold by company n in year t is

$$Q_{n,t} = \int q_{n,t}(\alpha, \boldsymbol{\beta}) \, dF(\alpha, \boldsymbol{\beta}). \tag{5.23}$$

The demand elasticity for life insurance sold by company n in year t is

$$\epsilon_{n,t} = -\frac{\partial \log(Q_{n,t})}{\partial \log(P_{n,t})} = \frac{P_{n,t}}{Q_{n,t}} \int \alpha q_{n,t}(\alpha, \boldsymbol{\beta})(1 - q_{n,t}(\alpha, \boldsymbol{\beta})) \, dF(\alpha, \boldsymbol{\beta}). \tag{5.24}$$

5.3.2 Empirical Specification for Marginal Cost

Equation (5.15) is the optimal pricing equation for each company in a Nash equilibrium. Marginal cost varies across operating companies because of differences in the shadow cost of capital. Let $\mathrm{SI}_{n,t}$ be a dummy that is one if company n uses shadow insurance in year t.[2] Let $\mathbf{1}_t$ be a vector of year fixed effects. We parameterize marginal cost for company n in year t as

$$\lambda_{n,t} V_t = \exp(\delta \mathrm{SI}_{n,t} + \boldsymbol{\Gamma}' \mathbf{x}_{n,t} + \boldsymbol{\gamma}' \mathbf{1}_t + \nu_{n,t}), \tag{5.25}$$

---

2. The dummy for shadow insurance is one if gross life and annuity reserves ceded to shadow reinsurers are positive. We have also considered the share of gross life and annuity reserves ceded to shadow reinsurers, which is a continuous measure between zero and one. Because there are relatively few companies that use shadow insurance, there is little cross-sectional variation in the intensive margin that is useful for identification. Therefore, we report the results based on the dummy for shadow insurance to make clear that our identification is coming from the extensive margin of whether the company uses shadow insurance.

where the structural error $v_{n,t}$ represents an unobserved cost shock. Shadow insurance reduces marginal cost so that $\delta \leq 0$. The company characteristics $\mathbf{x}_{n,t}$ in our specification of marginal cost are the same as those in the specification of demand. The vector $\boldsymbol{\gamma}$ contains the coefficients on the year fixed effects, which capture the time variation in marginal cost.

Because of year fixed effects, identification of marginal cost is based on the cross-sectional relation between marginal cost and shadow insurance across companies. This cross-sectional identification contrasts with the time-series identification in Section 4.3.2, where we use the reinsurance share of variable annuities as an instrument to estimate variable annuity demand. In that specification, we have insurer fixed effects, which means that identification is based on the time variation in the reinsurance share of variable annuities for a given insurer. We find that insurers increase the reinsurance share of variable annuities when marginal cost increases, leading to a positive relation between the two variables for a given insurer.

5.3.3 Identifying Assumptions

We need identifying assumptions because the insurance price and the structural error in demand are jointly endogenous. We estimate demand (5.23) and marginal cost (5.25) jointly under the moment conditions:

$$\mathbb{E}[\xi_{n,t}|SI_{n,t}, \mathbf{x}_{n,t}] = 0, \tag{5.26}$$

$$\mathbb{E}[v_{n,t}|SI_{n,t}, \mathbf{x}_{n,t}, \mathbf{1}_t] = 0. \tag{5.27}$$

Equation (5.26) states that shadow insurance is uncorrelated with demand, conditional on the observed characteristics. A motivation for this identifying assumption is that policyholders do not bother gathering information about shadow insurance beyond what is already reflected in the A.M. Best rating. This exclusion restriction is plausible because the negative attention from regulators and rating agencies came after 2012 (e.g., A.M. Best Company (2013), Lawsky (2013), Koijen and Yogo (2013), Robinson and Son (2013), and related media coverage). Equation (5.27) states that shadow insurance is uncorrelated with the cost shock, conditional on the observed characteristics and year fixed effects. The implicit assumption is that the observed characteristics capture all determinants of marginal cost that are also related to shadow insurance.

Given the mean and standard deviation of (α, β), we invert equation (5.23) to recover the structural errors $\xi_{n,t}$, approximating the integral through simulation. We then construct the moments for demand by interacting the structural error with a vector of instruments, which consists of shadow insurance, company characteristics, and squared characteristics. Given $(\delta, \boldsymbol{\gamma}, \boldsymbol{\Gamma})$, we invert equation (5.25) to recover the structural errors $v_{n,t}$. We then construct the moments for marginal cost by interacting the structural error with a vector of instruments, which consists of shadow insurance, company characteristics, and year fixed effects.

We stack the moments for demand and marginal cost and estimate the system by the two-step generalized method of moments. The weighting matrix in the first step is block diagonal in demand and marginal cost, where each block is the inverse of the quadratic matrix of the instruments. The optimal weighting matrix in the second step is robust to heteroscedasticity and correlation between the structural errors for demand and marginal cost.

5.3.4   Estimated Model of the Life Insurance Market

Columns (1) and (2) of Table 5.4 report the estimated mean and standard deviation of the random coefficients in demand (5.23). Our preferred specification limits the random coefficients to log liabilities, the A.M. Best rating, and leverage. The mean coefficient on price is -1.33 with a standard error of 0.50. This implies a demand elasticity of 2.18 for the average company in 2012. The mean coefficient on log liabilities is 2.71, and the mean coefficient on the A.M. Best rating is 0.13. That is, demand is positively related to both company size and the A.M. Best rating. The standard deviation of the random coefficient on log liabilities is 0.24 and statistically significant. Similarly, the standard deviation of the random coefficient on leverage is 0.33 and statistically significant.

Column (3) of Table 5.4 reports the estimated coefficients for marginal cost (5.25). Shadow insurance reduces marginal cost by 13% with a standard error of 3%. Other important determinants of marginal cost are the A.M. Best rating and leverage. Marginal cost decreases by 7% per one standard deviation increase in the A.M. Best rating. Similarly, marginal cost decreases by 4% per one standard deviation increase in leverage.

We have attempted to estimate a richer model in which price and risk-based capital also have random coefficients. However, the standard deviations of the random coefficients on price and risk-based capital converge to zero, and large standard errors reveal that the richer model is poorly identified. Similarly, we were not able to identify a richer model in which the covariance matrix for the

TABLE 5.4. Estimated Model of the Life Insurance Market

Variable	Demand		Marginal cost
	Mean	Standard deviation	
Price	−1.33		
	(0.50)		
Shadow insurance			−0.13
			(0.03)
Log liabilities	2.71	0.24	0.02
	(0.05)	(0.11)	(0.01)
A.M. Best rating	0.13	0.12	−0.07
	(0.08)	(0.58)	(0.03)
Risk-based capital	−0.07		0.01
	(0.07)		(0.02)
Leverage	0.11	0.33	−0.04
	(0.09)	(0.15)	(0.02)
Current liquidity	0.09		0.00
	(0.06)		(0.01)
Return on equity	−0.21		0.04
	(0.03)		(0.02)
Stock company	0.07		0.01
	(0.10)		(0.03)
Observations	1,711		

Copyright Econometric Society; reprint of Koijen and Yogo (2016, table D.1) with permission. The random coefficients logit model of demand (5.23) and marginal cost (5.25) are estimated jointly by generalized method of moments. The specification for marginal cost includes year fixed effects, whose coefficients are not reported for brevity. The instruments for demand are shadow insurance, company characteristics, and squared characteristics. The instruments for marginal cost are shadow insurance, company characteristics, and year fixed effects. The coefficients are standardized, and heteroscedasticity-robust standard errors are reported in parentheses. The sample consists of US life insurers from 2002 to 2012, which are matched to term life insurance premiums from Compulife Software.

random coefficients is not diagonal. The identification problem arises from the fact that the variation in aggregate market shares can only identify a limited covariance structure for the random coefficients.

5.3.5   Retail Market in the Absence of Shadow Insurance

The structural estimates in Table 5.4 allow us to estimate counterfactual insurance prices and market size in the absence of shadow insurance. We first set $SI_{n,t} = 0$ in equation (5.25) to estimate the counterfactual marginal cost for each company in the absence of shadow insurance. We do not alter ratings, risk-based capital, or leverage under the baseline assumption that these measures already reflect the risk of shadow insurance. We then solve for the new price vector that satisfies the equilibrium conditions for demand (5.23) and supply (5.25).

Marginal cost would increase by 13% for the average company using shadow insurance in 2012. In response to higher marginal cost, the average company would raise prices by 10%. The quantity of life insurance issued annually would fall by $7.2 billion for the operating companies using shadow insurance, while the other companies would gain $0.4 billion because of substitution effects. Higher prices mean that some consumers would stay out of the life insurance market. The industry as a whole would shrink by $6.8 billion, which is 7% of the market size of $91.5 billion in 2012.

We also consider an alternative assumption that ratings, risk-based capital, and leverage do not reflect the risk of shadow insurance. We update these measures based on the procedure in Section 5.1.2 and solve for the new price vector. Marginal cost would increase by 27% for the average company using shadow insurance in 2012. In response to higher marginal cost, the average company would raise prices by 21%. The quantity of life insurance issued annually would fall by $15.8 billion for the operating companies using shadow insurance, while the other companies would gain $0.9 billion because of substitution effects. The industry as a whole would shrink by $14.9 billion.

We have quantified the trade-off between the potential risk of shadow insurance and its impact on the retail market. However, we have not done a welfare analysis of this trade-off to derive the optimal regulation, which is a promising direction for future research. Regulators must balance the welfare of policyholders, insurance company shareholders, and state guaranty associations and taxpayers. Lower capital requirements benefit policyholders, who pay lower prices, and insurers that could expand through higher leverage. However, a more leveraged insurance sector increases the default probability, which is a cost to state guaranty associations and taxpayers.

6

Portfolio Choice and Asset Pricing

THE PREVIOUS chapters have focused on the liability side of the insurance sector. This chapter turns to the asset side with a focus on portfolio choice and the central role of the insurance sector in determining asset prices.

In Section 6.1, we start with aggregate facts about insurers' bond portfolios. An important fact is that both life insurers and property and casualty insurers allocate a larger share of their portfolio to corporate bonds than Treasury bonds, and this portfolio tilt has strengthened over time. Within the corporate bond portfolio, insurers tilt toward highly rated bonds relative to the market portfolio and thus have a preference for low-beta assets. The allocation to corporate bonds leads to credit risk mismatch because traditional liabilities are not sensitive to credit risk. Moreover, variable annuities are exposed to equity risk that is positively correlated with credit risk.

As we discuss in Section 6.2, the fact that insurers take on credit risk is puzzling from the perspective of the baseline model in Section 1.5. On the one hand, allocation to riskier assets requires additional capital and tightens the risk-based capital constraint. On the other hand, allocation to riskier assets has no benefit to shareholders if financial markets are efficient, so that risk-adjusted expected returns are equated across assets. Therefore, the theory predicts that insurers hold riskless bonds to minimize the impact on risk-based capital.

In Section 6.3, we develop an equilibrium asset pricing model that resolves the puzzle by predicting that insurers hold low-beta assets such as investment-grade corporate bonds. Households buy annuities to insure idiosyncratic longevity risk and save the remaining wealth in a portfolio of risky assets subject to a leverage constraint. Insurers invest the annuity premiums in a portfolio of risky assets and a riskless asset subject to a risk-based capital constraint. Other institutional investors also choose between risky assets and a riskless asset subject to a leverage constraint.

The presence of leverage constraints implies an important deviation from the Capital Asset Pricing Model (CAPM). The CAPM predicts that an asset's expected excess return is equal to the expected excess market return times its beta (i.e., covariance of an asset's returns with market returns divided by the variance of market returns). The empirical relation between average excess returns and betas is weaker than the theoretical prediction, meaning that the slope is actually less than the average excess market return. Thus, low-beta assets earn positive alpha (i.e., high risk-adjusted expected returns) and high-beta assets earn negative alpha relative to the CAPM. Leverage constraints are a potential explanation for this "low-beta anomaly" (Black, 1972; Frazzini and Pedersen, 2014).

In this environment, insurers maximize firm value by holding a leveraged portfolio of low-beta assets. Households and institutional investors cannot replicate the insurers' portfolio due to leverage constraints and instead hold the insurers' equity, which is equivalent to a highly leveraged portfolio of low-beta assets. This result holds even when capital regulation is not sensitive to risk. When capital regulation is sensitive to risk, the demand for low-beta assets strengthens. The model provides a unifying explanation of recent empirical findings on insurers' portfolio choice and its impact on asset prices (Ellul, Jotikasthira, and Lundblad, 2011; Ge and Weisbach, 2021; Becker, Opp, and Saidi, 2022). We conclude the chapter by discussing potential extensions.

This chapter is part of a growing literature on intermediary asset pricing. The theoretical literature studies the impact of institutional investors' agency frictions or leverage constraints for asset prices. The empirical literature focuses on frictions in a particular sector, such as risk factors that arise from broker-dealers' leverage constraints (Adrian, Etula, and Muir, 2014; He, Kelly, and Manela, 2017). We study the important role of insurers among other institutional investors who are subject to leverage constraints. A key implication of the model is that insurers hold low-beta assets in response to the leverage constraints of other institutional investors.

6.1   Insurers' Bond Portfolios

6.1.1   Portfolio Composition

Figure 6.1 shows the bond holdings of life insurers and property and casualty insurers from 1994 to 2019. We focus on insurers' bond holdings because

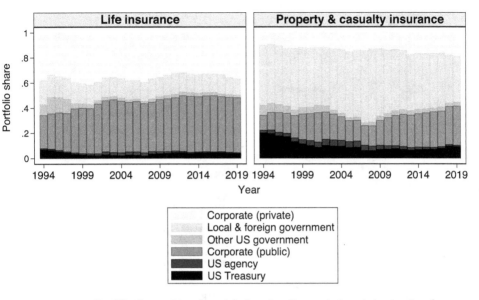

FIGURE 6.1. Portfolio Composition. Copyright American Economic Association; reprint of
Koijen and Yogo (2023, figure 2) with permission. The long-term bond holdings are from the
National Association of Insurance Commissioners (1994–2019, Schedule D Part 1). The
bottom three categories (US Treasury, US agency, and publicly traded corporate bonds)
represent publicly traded and non-asset-backed securities with coverage in Mergent (2021).
The top three categories include asset-backed securities, MBSs, and private placement bonds.

their equity holdings tend to be small, which can be partly explained by the
high capital requirements on equities. We break down the bond holdings
into US Treasury bonds, US agency bonds, publicly traded corporate bonds,
other US government bonds, local and foreign government bonds, and private corporate bonds. The first three categories represent publicly traded and
non-asset-backed securities with coverage in Mergent (2021).

Life insurers hold most of their portfolio in publicly traded and private corporate bonds instead of Treasury bonds. In the 1990s, property and casualty
insurers held a larger share of their portfolio in Treasury bonds than publicly
traded corporate bonds, but this relation has reversed in recent years. In 2019,
property and casualty insurers held 9% of their portfolio in Treasury bonds
and 31% in publicly traded corporate bonds. Because insurers' liabilities are
not directly exposed to credit risk, corporate bond holdings introduce credit
risk mismatch.

Figure 6.2 shows the corporate bond portfolios of life insurers and property
and casualty insurers by NAIC designation from 1994 to 2019. The NAIC

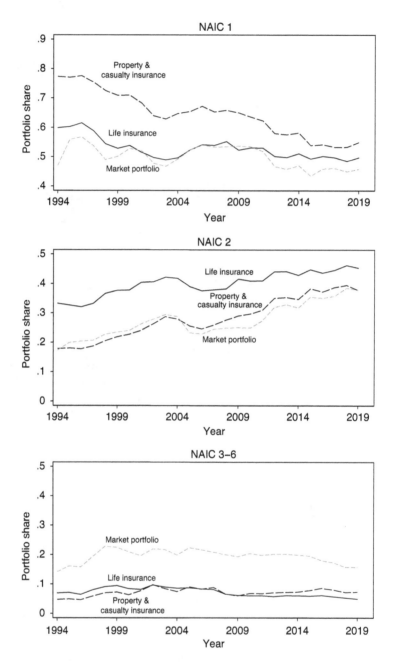

FIGURE 6.2. Corporate Bond Portfolio Composition. Copyright American Economic Association; reprint of Koijen and Yogo (2023, figure 3) with permission. This figure shows the corporate bond portfolio share by NAIC designation for life insurers and property and casualty insurers. It also shows the market portfolio weights for the universe of corporate bonds that are held by the insurance sector. The long-term bond holdings are from the National Association of Insurance Commissioners (1994–2019, Schedule D Part 1). The sample consists of corporate bonds in Mergent (2021) that are publicly traded and not asset-backed.

designates assets into six categories based on credit ratings, where NAIC 1 corresponds to the lowest risk and NAIC 6 corresponds to the highest risk. For
perspective, the figure also shows the market portfolio weights for the universe of corporate bonds that are held by the insurance sector. Life insurers
hold NAIC 1 bonds close to market weights but overweight NAIC 2 bonds.
Property and casualty insurers overweight NAIC 1 bonds but hold NAIC 2
bonds close to market weights. Both life insurers and property and casualty
insurers underweight corporate bonds that are NAIC 3 and below. Insurers
tilt toward highly rated corporate bonds relative to the market portfolio and
thus have a preference for low-beta assets.

Figure 6.2 shows that the distribution of corporate bonds has shifted from
NAIC 1 to NAIC 2 as credit risk has increased after the global financial crisis.
From 2007 to 2019, the market portfolio weight has decreased by 8% in NAIC
1, has increased by 13% in NAIC 2, and has decreased by 5% in NAIC 3 and
below. During the same period, life insurers have decreased their allocation
to NAIC 1 by 4%, have increased their allocation to NAIC 2 by 7%, and have
decreased their allocation to NAIC 3 and below by 3%. Property and casualty
insurers have decreased their allocation to NAIC 1 by 10%, have increased
their allocation to NAIC 2 by 12%, and have decreased their allocation to
NAIC 3 and below by 2%. The growth of the NAIC 2 share (particularly the
BBB-rated bonds) exposes insurers to the risk of a large-scale credit migration, in which these bonds are downgraded from investment to speculative
grade.

6.1.2 Duration

Figure 6.3 shows the weighted average duration of bond portfolios for life
insurers and property and casualty insurers from 1994 to 2019. This calculation is based on a sample of US Treasury, US agency, and corporate bonds
that are publicly traded and not asset-backed.

For life insurers, the weighted average duration increased from 6.3 years
in 1994 to 9.3 years in 2019. Part of the increase in duration is a mechanical
effect of falling interest rates during this period. To understand the magnitude
of this effect, we report an alternative calculation of weighted average duration
fixing bond yields by maturity and credit rating to their values in 2002. The
duration at 2002 bond yields increased from 6.2 years in 2002 to 7.4 years in
2019. Thus, the actual increase in duration that arises from portfolio choice is
more modest.

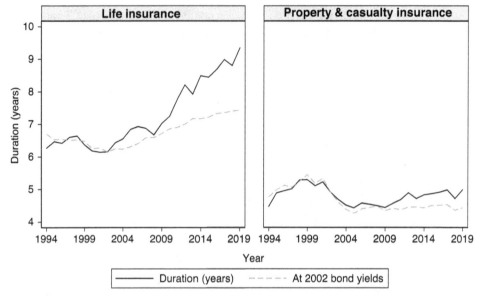

FIGURE 6.3. Average Duration of Bond Portfolios. This figure shows the weighted average duration of bond portfolios for life insurers and property and casualty insurers. The long-term bond holdings are from the National Association of Insurance Commissioners (1994–2019, Schedule D Part 1). The sample consists of US Treasury, US agency, and corporate bonds in Mergent (2021) that are publicly traded and not asset-backed. The duration for each bond is based on its coupon rate, coupon frequency, maturity, and the credit spread by rating category. An alternative calculation of the weighted average duration fixes bond yields by maturity and credit rating to their values in 2002.

Life insurers' assets have a short duration relative to their long-term liabilities, especially minimum return guarantees on variable annuities, leading to a negative duration gap. We do not have direct data on the maturity structure of the liabilities. However, the evidence on the interest risk exposure of variable annuity insurers' stock returns in Table 2.3 suggests a negative duration gap that is close to the duration of the 10-year Treasury bond. A possible reason for the negative duration gap is that corporate bonds have a shorter maturity distribution than Treasury bonds. By taking on credit risk, life insurers expose themselves to interest risk mismatch.

Property and casualty insurers' portfolios have a stable weighted average duration of four to five years, regardless of whether we use the actual yields or the 2002 yields. The shorter duration in their portfolio reflects the shorter maturity of their liabilities.

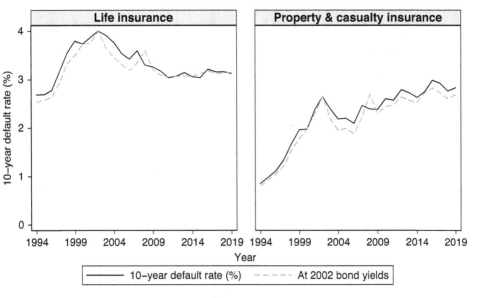

FIGURE 6.4. Credit Risk of Bond Portfolios. Copyright American Economic Association; reprint of Koijen and Yogo (2023, figure 4) with permission. This figure shows the weighted average 10-year cumulative default rate of bond portfolios for life insurers and property and casualty insurers. The long-term bond holdings are from the National Association of Insurance Commissioners (1994–2019, Schedule D Part 1). The sample consists of US Treasury, US agency, and corporate bonds in Mergent (2021) that are publicly traded and not asset-backed. The 10-year cumulative default rate is assigned to each bond based on the median of its S&P, Moody's, and Fitch ratings. An alternative calculation of the weighted average 10-year cumulative default rate fixes bond yields by maturity and credit rating to their values in 2002.

6.1.3 Credit Risk

Figure 6.4 shows the credit risk of bond portfolios for life insurers and property and casualty insurers from 1994 to 2019. We quantify credit risk by mapping credit ratings to 10-year cumulative default rates and computing the weighted average for the overall portfolio. This calculation is based on a sample of US Treasury, US agency, and corporate bonds that are publicly traded and not asset-backed. We assume that Treasury and agency bonds have no default risk for the purposes of this calculation. Thus, the overall credit risk depends on the allocation to corporate bonds and the portfolio choice across rating categories within corporate bonds.

For life insurers, the weighted average 10-year cumulative default rate is stable at 2% to 4%, which reflects the stable allocation to corporate bonds in

Figure 6.1. Figure 6.2 shows that the portfolio share increased for NAIC 2 and decreased for NAIC 3 and below from 2007 to 2019. The combination of these offsetting trends implies that the weighted average default rate has remained nearly constant after the global financial crisis.

For property and casualty insurers, the weighted average 10-year cumulative default rate increased from 0.9% in 1994 to 2.8% in 2019. This increase in credit risk is due to the shift from Treasury bonds to corporate bonds in Figure 6.1 and the shift from NAIC 1 to NAIC 2 in Figure 6.2. Property and casualty insurers have always taken less credit risk than life insurers, presumably because of the less predictable nature of their liabilities with tail risk. However, the difference in the level of credit risk between life insurers and property and casualty insurers is not a focus of this chapter.

In summary, there are two important facts about insurers' bond portfolios that the model in Section 6.3 explains. First and most importantly, both life insurers and property and casualty insurers allocate a large share of their portfolio to corporate bonds with credit risk. As we discuss in Section 6.2, this fact is puzzling from the perspective of a standard theory of insurance markets. Second, the credit risk of life insurers' bond portfolios has decreased relative to that of property and casualty insurers after the global financial crisis. In Section 6.4, we discuss a potential connection between this trend in relative credit risk, the low interest rate environment, and financial frictions in the life insurance sector.

6.2 A Portfolio Puzzle for Insurers

The baseline model in Section 1.5 assumes that insurers maximize firm value subject to a risk-based capital constraint. Let us introduce portfolio choice under the null hypothesis that financial markets are efficient and that insurers have no special ability to earn alpha. Then the insurer cannot affect firm value through portfolio choice because all portfolios have the same risk-adjusted expected value. In the absence of risk-based capital regulation, the optimal portfolio is indeterminate. In the presence of risk-based capital regulation, the optimal portfolio consists of only riskless bonds.

This prediction is inconsistent with the fact that insurers take credit risk and incur risk charges by allocating a larger share of their portfolio to corporate bonds than Treasury bonds. The literature proposes several resolutions to this puzzle. Chodorow-Reich, Ghent, and Haddad (2021) propose that the same asset has a higher value when held by insurers, which is an arbitrage opportunity from the insurers' perspective. Knox and Sørensen (2020) propose that insurers have a comparative advantage in earning a liquidity premium on corporate bonds and MBSs because of their long-term liability structure. In general, insurers may have market power or may be able to take advantage of mispricing in some markets because of their long-term liability structure. An interesting empirical question is whether insurers have a special ability to earn alpha beyond the standard anomalies such as the low-beta anomaly.

Another potential resolution is to modify the insurer's objective function, following the literature on intermediary asset pricing with value-at-risk constraints (Adrian and Shin, 2014; Coimbra and Rey, 2017). For example, Ellul et al. (2022) assume that insurers maximize expected value instead of risk-adjusted expected value. Although this model may explain portfolio choice, other decisions such as product pricing and capital structure may be more puzzling when insurers maximize expected value.

We propose a different resolution that does not rely on special ability or a different objective function. We introduce insurers to a standard asset pricing model with leverage constraints. An important insight is that insurers are highly leveraged institutions that have relatively cheap access to leverage through their underwriting activity. Therefore, insurers have a comparative advantage in holding a leveraged portfolio of low-beta assets and earn a positive alpha in equilibrium. Thus, insurers play an important role in financial markets by relaxing the leverage constraints of households and other institutional investors.

6.3   Asset Pricing with an Insurance Sector

We develop an asset pricing model with three types of investors: households, insurers, and other institutional investors (e.g., mutual funds, hedge funds, and pension funds). Households and institutional investors are subject to leverage constraints. Each investor chooses a portfolio of risky assets and a riskless asset in period 0, and the assets pay terminal dividends in period 1. We assume that each investor type is composed of a continuum of atomistic investors, so that investors do not account for price impact in choosing their portfolio.

Insurers have market power and earn profits by selling annuities to households at a markup. They also choose a portfolio of risky assets and a riskless asset subject to a risk-based capital constraint. In equilibrium, insurers derive their value from three sources. The first source is high expected returns on low-beta assets because households and institutional investors are leverage constrained. The second source is the cost of regulatory frictions due to the risk-based capital constraint. The third source is the underwriting profits that arise from market power.

6.3.1   Financial Assets

RISKLESS ASSET

All investors can hold a riskless asset with gross interest R_f from period 0 to 1.

ANNUITIES

Households do not have a bequest motive and survive in period 1 with probability π. Households can buy annuities from insurers in period 0 to insure longevity risk.[1] Annuities have a gross return of zero conditional on death and

$$R_L = \frac{1}{P_L} = \left(1 - \frac{1}{\epsilon}\right)\frac{R_f}{\pi} \qquad (6.1)$$

conditional on survival. P_L is the annuity price in period 0 per unit of death benefit. Insurers have market power and price annuities accounting for the demand elasticity $\epsilon > 1$. We assume that the demand elasticity is sufficiently high so that $R_L > R_f$. That is, annuities strictly dominate the riskless asset for households without bequest motives.

Insurers potentially face two sources of risk. The first source is idiosyncratic longevity risk from annuities. We assume that the insured pool is sufficiently large for the law of large numbers to apply. Alternatively, insurers can perfectly diversify longevity risk through a state guaranty association. The second source is systematic risk from portfolio choice. We assume that the insurers' dividends can be negative to ensure full payment of annuity claims. Thus, annuities are riskless from the households' perspective.

RISKY ASSETS

Insurers pay out dividends d_I in period 1, which is endogenously determined by their optimal portfolio choice in period 0. Other firms pay exogenous

---

1. We could modify the model so that some households have a bequest motive, which generates a demand for life insurance. Similarly, a tax advantage could generate additional demand for annuities.

dividends $\mathbf{d}$ in period 1, where each element of the N-dimensional vector corresponds to a firm's dividend. The dividends have a factor structure:

$$\mathbf{d} = \mathbb{E}[\mathbf{d}] + \boldsymbol{\beta} F + \boldsymbol{v}, \tag{6.2}$$

where $\boldsymbol{\beta} > \mathbf{0}$ is a vector of factor loadings. The common factor F has the moments $\mathbb{E}[F] = 0$ and $\text{Var}(F) = \sigma_F^2$. The vector of idiosyncratic shocks has the moments $\mathbb{E}[\boldsymbol{v}] = \mathbf{0}$ and $\text{Var}(\boldsymbol{v}) = \text{diag}(\sigma_v^2)$, where σ_v^2 is a vector of idiosyncratic variance. Thus, the covariance matrix of dividends is

$$\text{Var}(\mathbf{d}) = \sigma_F^2 \boldsymbol{\beta} \boldsymbol{\beta}' + \text{diag}(\sigma_v^2). \tag{6.3}$$

We stack the dividends of insurers and other firms in a vector as $\mathbf{D} = (\mathbf{d}', d_I)'$. We denote the moments of dividends as $\boldsymbol{\mu} = \mathbb{E}[\mathbf{D}]$ and $\boldsymbol{\Sigma} = \text{Var}(\mathbf{D})$. We denote the price of risky assets in period 0 as p_I for insurers, $\mathbf{p}$ for other firms, and $\mathbf{P} = (\mathbf{p}', p_I)'$. We normalize the supply of all risky assets to one unit.

6.3.2   Insurers

Insurers allocate their assets to $\mathbf{X}_I = (\mathbf{x}_I', 0)'$ units of risky assets, where the last element is zero under the assumption that insurers cannot invest in other insurers. Insurers are subject to risk-based capital regulation that limits risk-shifting motives that could arise from limited liability and the presence of state guaranty associations. We assume that the NAIC designation (i.e., 1 through 6) increases in beta, so that riskier assets require more capital.[2] Let $\exp(\phi \boldsymbol{\beta})$ be a diagonal matrix of risk weights with nth diagonal element $\exp(\phi \beta(n))$. We define required capital as

$$\sqrt{\mathbf{x}_I' \exp(\phi \boldsymbol{\beta}) \mathbf{x}_I} = \sqrt{\sum_{n=1}^{N} \exp(\phi \beta(n)) x_I(n)^2}. \tag{6.4}$$

We assume that the cost of regulatory frictions is a quadratic function of required capital:

$$C(\mathbf{x}_I) = \frac{\mathbf{x}_I' \exp(\phi \boldsymbol{\beta}) \mathbf{x}_I}{2}. \tag{6.5}$$

---

2. We abstract from the fact that the NAIC designation does not perfectly correspond to credit risk for corporate bonds (Becker and Ivashina, 2015) or MBSs (Hanley and Nikolova, 2021; Becker, Opp, and Saidi, 2022).

The assumption that the matrix of risk weights is diagonal ignores the impact of correlation between assets on required capital. The parameter $\phi \geq 0$ captures the interaction between the riskiness of assets and liabilities. Insurers with riskier liabilities (e.g., variable annuities) have higher values of ϕ. Thus, the marginal impact of holding riskier assets is greater for insurers with riskier liabilities.

Insurers have initial equity E and sell Q units of annuities to households at the price P_L. The insurers' assets in period 0 are

$$A_{I,0} = E - C(\mathbf{x}_I) + P_L Q. \tag{6.6}$$

Insurers pay out their equity in period 1 as dividends. The dividends are equal to the gross return on their assets minus the annuity claims:

$$
\begin{aligned}
d_I &= \mathbf{d}'\mathbf{x}_I + R_f(A_{I,0} - \mathbf{p}'\mathbf{x}_I) - \pi Q \\
&= \mathbf{d}'\mathbf{x}_I + R_f(E - C(\mathbf{x}_I) - \mathbf{p}'\mathbf{x}_I) + (R_f P_L - \pi)Q, \tag{6.7}
\end{aligned}
$$

where the second equality follows from substituting equation (6.6).

The last term of equation (6.7) represents the underwriting profits, which insurers maximize by choosing the annuity price P_L. The price and the quantity of annuities enter equation (6.7) only through the underwriting profits, which are known in period 0. We differentiate the underwriting profits with respect to P_L to derive the optimal annuity price. Equation (6.1) is the resulting expression for the optimal annuity price with $\epsilon = -\partial \log(Q)/\partial \log(P_L)$. Substituting equation (6.1) in equation (6.7), the dividends are

$$d_I = \mathbf{d}'\mathbf{x}_I + R_f(E - C(\mathbf{x}_I) - \mathbf{p}'\mathbf{x}_I) + \frac{\pi Q}{\epsilon - 1}. \tag{6.8}$$

If insurers were to hold only the riskless asset, their dividends would be the riskless return on their initial equity plus the underwriting profits (i.e., $d_I = R_f E + \pi Q/(\epsilon - 1)$).

6.3.3 Portfolio-Choice Problem

HOUSEHOLDS

Households allocate initial wealth $A_{H,0}$ to $\mathbf{X}_H$ units of risky assets and Q units of annuities subject to the budget constraint:

$$A_{H,0} = \mathbf{P}'\mathbf{X}_H + P_L Q. \tag{6.9}$$

Conditional on survival, their wealth in period 1 is

$$A_{H,1} = \mathbf{D}'\mathbf{X}_H + Q$$
$$= \mathbf{D}'\mathbf{X}_H + R_L(A_{H,0} - \mathbf{P}'\mathbf{X}_H), \qquad (6.10)$$

where the second equality follows from equation (6.9) and $P_L = 1/R_L$.

In the absence of bequest motives, households have mean-variance preferences over wealth conditional on survival:

$$\mathbb{E}[A_{H,1}] - \frac{\gamma_H}{2}\mathrm{Var}(A_{H,1}), \qquad (6.11)$$

where $\gamma_H > 0$ is risk aversion. Households choose $\mathbf{X}_H$ to maximize this objective function subject to the intertemporal budget constraint (6.10) and a leverage constraint:

$$\mathbf{P}'\mathbf{X}_H \leq A_{H,0}. \qquad (6.12)$$

This leverage constraint implies that households cannot short annuities.

INSTITUTIONAL INVESTORS

There are J types of institutional investors, indexed as $j = 1, \ldots, J$. For example, there are mutual funds, hedge funds, pension funds, and so on. Institutional investors allocate their initial wealth $A_{j,0}$ to $\mathbf{X}_j$ units of risky assets and the remainder in the riskless asset. Their wealth in period 1 is

$$A_{j,1} = \mathbf{D}'\mathbf{X}_j + R_f(A_{j,0} - \mathbf{P}'\mathbf{X}_j). \qquad (6.13)$$

Institutional investors have mean-variance preferences over wealth:

$$\mathbb{E}[A_{j,1}] - \frac{\gamma_j}{2}\mathrm{Var}(A_{j,1}), \qquad (6.14)$$

where $\gamma_j > 0$ is risk aversion. Institutional investors choose $\mathbf{X}_j$ to maximize this objective function subject to the intertemporal budget constraint (6.13) and a leverage constraint:

$$\mathbf{P}'\mathbf{X}_j \leq \frac{A_{j,0}}{\omega_j}. \qquad (6.15)$$

The leverage constraint limits risk-shifting motives that could arise from limited liability and moral hazard. In practice, margin requirements operate as a leverage constraint. The parameter $\omega_j > 0$ captures the tightness of the leverage constraint, which could be heterogeneous across investors.

6.3.4   *Optimal Portfolio Choice*

We solve the model in three steps. First, we solve the portfolio-choice problem for households and institutional investors. Second, we impose market clearing to solve for asset prices conditional on the insurers' portfolio. Finally, we solve the insurers' portfolio-choice problem that maximizes firm value.

HOUSEHOLDS

The Lagrangian for the households' portfolio-choice problem is

$$\mathcal{L}_H = \mathbb{E}[A_{H,1}] - \frac{\gamma_H}{2}\mathrm{Var}(A_{H,1}) + \lambda_H(A_{H,0} - \mathbf{P}'\mathbf{X}_H)$$

$$= \boldsymbol{\mu}'\mathbf{X}_H + (R_L + \lambda_H)(A_{H,0} - \mathbf{P}'\mathbf{X}_H) - \frac{\gamma_H}{2}\mathbf{X}_H'\boldsymbol{\Sigma}\mathbf{X}_H, \qquad (6.16)$$

where $\lambda_H \geq 0$ is the Lagrange multiplier on the leverage constraint. The first-order condition implies optimal portfolio choice:

$$\mathbf{X}_H = \frac{1}{\gamma_H}\boldsymbol{\Sigma}^{-1}(\boldsymbol{\mu} - (R_L + \lambda_H)\mathbf{P}). \qquad (6.17)$$

A binding leverage constraint $\lambda_H > 0$ is equivalent to a higher annuity return, which reduces the allocation to risky assets.

INSTITUTIONAL INVESTORS

The Lagrangian for institution j's portfolio-choice problem is

$$\mathcal{L}_j = \mathbb{E}[A_{j,1}] - \frac{\gamma_j}{2}\mathrm{Var}(A_{j,1}) + \lambda_j(A_{j,0} - \mathbf{P}'\mathbf{X}_j)$$

$$= \boldsymbol{\mu}'\mathbf{X}_j + (R_f + \lambda_j)\left(\frac{A_{j,0}}{\omega_j} - \mathbf{P}'\mathbf{X}_j\right) - \frac{\gamma_j}{2}\mathbf{X}_j'\boldsymbol{\Sigma}\mathbf{X}_j, \qquad (6.18)$$

where $\lambda_j \geq 0$ is the Lagrange multiplier on the leverage constraint. The first-order condition implies optimal portfolio choice:

$$\mathbf{X}_j = \frac{1}{\gamma_j}\boldsymbol{\Sigma}^{-1}(\boldsymbol{\mu} - (R_f + \lambda_j)\mathbf{P}). \qquad (6.19)$$

A binding leverage constraint $\lambda_j > 0$ is equivalent to a higher riskless rate, which reduces the allocation to risky assets.

6.3.5   Asset Prices

By market clearing, the sum of the demand across all investors equals supply:

$$\mathbf{X}_I + \mathbf{X}_H + \sum_{j=1}^{J} \mathbf{X}_j = 1. \tag{6.20}$$

Substituting the optimal demand of households (6.17) and institutional investors (6.19), we have

$$\mathbf{X}_I + \frac{1}{\gamma} \boldsymbol{\Sigma}^{-1} (\boldsymbol{\mu} - (R + \lambda)\mathbf{P}) = 1, \tag{6.21}$$

where

$$\frac{1}{\gamma} = \frac{1}{\gamma_H} + \sum_{j=1}^{J} \frac{1}{\gamma_j}, \tag{6.22}$$

$$R = \frac{\gamma}{\gamma_H} R_L + \sum_{j=1}^{J} \frac{\gamma}{\gamma_j} R_f, \tag{6.23}$$

$$\lambda = \frac{\gamma}{\gamma_H} \lambda_H + \sum_{j=1}^{J} \frac{\gamma}{\gamma_j} \lambda_j. \tag{6.24}$$

Thus, asset prices conditional on the insurers' portfolio are

$$\mathbf{P}(\mathbf{X}_I) = \frac{1}{R + \lambda} (\boldsymbol{\mu} - \gamma \boldsymbol{\Sigma}(1 - \mathbf{X}_I)). \tag{6.25}$$

OTHER FIRMS

We break up equation (6.25) into two blocks, representing the asset prices of other firms and insurers separately. The asset prices of other firms are

$$\mathbf{p} = \frac{1}{R + \lambda} (\mathbb{E}[\mathbf{d}] - \gamma (\mathrm{Var}(\mathbf{d})(1 - \mathbf{x}_I) + \mathrm{Cov}(\mathbf{d}, d_I)))$$

$$= \frac{1}{R + \lambda} (\mathbb{E}[\mathbf{d}] - \gamma \mathrm{Var}(\mathbf{d})\mathbf{1}), \tag{6.26}$$

where the second equality uses the definition of the insurers' dividends (6.8). The insurers' portfolio choice affects the asset prices of other firms only through the aggregate Lagrange multiplier λ. That is, insurers can affect asset prices by relaxing the other investors' leverage constraints.

The insurers' equity price is

$$p_I = \frac{1}{R+\lambda}\left(\mathbb{E}[d_I] - \gamma\left(\text{Cov}(\mathbf{d}, d_I)'(\mathbf{1} - \mathbf{x}_I) + \text{Var}(d_I)\right)\right)$$

$$= \frac{1}{R+\lambda}\left(\mathbb{E}[d_I] - \gamma\mathbf{1}'\text{Var}(\mathbf{d})\mathbf{x}_I\right). \tag{6.27}$$

Substituting the insurers' dividends (6.8) in this equation, we have

$$p_I = \frac{1}{R+\lambda}\left((\mathbb{E}[\mathbf{d}] - \gamma\text{Var}(\mathbf{d})\mathbf{1} - R_f\mathbf{p})'\mathbf{x}_I + R_f(E - C(\mathbf{x}_I)) + \frac{\pi Q}{\epsilon - 1}\right). \tag{6.28}$$

Substituting the asset prices of other firms (6.26) in this equation, we have

$$p_I = \frac{1}{R+\lambda}\left(\underbrace{\frac{R - R_f + \lambda}{R+\lambda}(\mathbb{E}[\mathbf{d}] - \gamma\text{Var}(\mathbf{d})\mathbf{1})'\mathbf{x}_I +}_{\text{portfolio choice}} \underbrace{R_f(E - C(\mathbf{x}_I))}_{\text{regulatory frictions}} \right.$$

$$\left. + \underbrace{\frac{\pi Q}{\epsilon - 1}}_{\text{underwriting profits}}\right). \tag{6.29}$$

Equation (6.29) shows that insurers derive their value from three sources. The first source is the portfolio choice $\mathbf{x}_I$. Suppose that insurance markets are competitive (i.e., $\epsilon \to \infty$) and that there is no longevity risk (i.e., $\pi = 1$). Then the first term in parentheses simplifies to

$$\frac{\lambda}{R_f + \lambda}(\mathbb{E}[\mathbf{d}] - \gamma\text{Var}(\mathbf{d})\mathbf{1})'\mathbf{x}_I, \tag{6.30}$$

which increases in the tightness of the leverage constraints as captured by λ. Holding the insurers' equity is equivalent to holding a highly leveraged portfolio of the assets that insurers hold. Insurers maximize firm value by holding low-beta assets, which relaxes the other investors' leverage constraints.

In the presence of longevity risk (i.e., $\pi < 1$), portfolio choice matters for the insurers' equity price, even if the leverage constraints do not bind (i.e., $\lambda = 0$). In this case, firm value increases in the spread $R - R_f$. The reason is that R is the effective riskless rate used for firm valuation according to equation (6.26), while R_f is the insurers' borrowing rate. Insurers earn a spread that reflects the "convenience yield" that households are willing to pay to insure idiosyncratic longevity risk. This spread is analogous to the liquidity premium that depositors are willing to pay in banking models.

The second source is the cost of regulatory frictions due to the risk-based capital constraint. By choosing a safer portfolio, insurers could reduce the cost of regulatory frictions. The third source is the underwriting profits that arise from market power, which are decreasing in the demand elasticity.

6.3.6 Insurers' Optimal Portfolio

Insurers choose a portfolio of risky assets to maximize their value (6.29). We assume that there is a continuum of atomistic insurers that do not account for price impact in choosing their portfolio. In particular, they take the other investors' portfolio choice as fixed and do not internalize the impact of their choice on the aggregate Lagrange multiplier λ. Because the insurance sector is concentrated in reality, the extension to strategic investors with price impact is a relevant direction for future research.

Substituting the cost of regulatory frictions (6.5) in equation (6.29), the first-order condition implies that

$$
\begin{aligned}
\mathbf{x}_I &= \frac{R - R_f + \lambda}{R_f(R + \lambda)} \exp(-\phi\boldsymbol{\beta})(\mathbb{E}[\mathbf{d}] - \gamma \mathrm{Var}(\mathbf{d})\mathbf{1}) \\
&= \frac{R - R_f + \lambda}{R_f(R + \lambda)} \exp(-\phi\boldsymbol{\beta})(\mathbb{E}[\mathbf{d}] - \gamma\sigma_F^2\boldsymbol{\beta}\boldsymbol{\beta}'\mathbf{1} - \gamma\sigma_\nu^2),
\end{aligned}
\tag{6.31}
$$

where the second equality follows from equation (6.3). The optimal portfolio trades off the gains from relaxing the leverage constraints of households and institutional investors through λ, the gains from providing longevity insurance to households through $R - R_f$, and the cost of regulatory frictions through $\exp(-\phi\boldsymbol{\beta})$.

For intuition, consider the special case when leverage constraints are not binding (i.e., $\lambda = 0$) and the markup exactly offsets the mortality credit on annuities (i.e., $R = R_L = R_f$). Then the optimal portfolio is $\mathbf{x}_I = \mathbf{0}$, which means that insurers hold only the riskless asset. Because risk-based capital regulation penalizes risky asset holdings, insurers choose the riskless asset to minimize the cost of regulatory frictions.

6.4 Empirical Implications

We explain how equation (6.31) is consistent with the two motivating facts in Section 6.1. First, insurers allocate a large share of their portfolio to corporate bonds with credit risk. Second, the credit risk of life insurers' bond portfolios has decreased relative to that of property and casualty insurers after the global financial crisis.

6.4.1 Demand for Low-Beta Assets

When $\lambda > 0$, insurers hold risky assets but tilt their portfolio toward low-beta assets. Differentiating the allocation to asset n with respect to its beta, we have

$$\frac{\partial x_I(n)}{\partial \beta(n)} = -\frac{R - R_f + \lambda}{R_f(R + \lambda)} \exp(-\phi\beta(n))$$

$$\times \left(\phi \mathbf{1}'_n(\mathbb{E}[\mathbf{d}] - \gamma \operatorname{Var}(\mathbf{d})\mathbf{1}) + \gamma\sigma_F^2(\beta(n) + \boldsymbol{\beta}'\mathbf{1})\right) < 0. \quad (6.32)$$

Thus, the optimal allocation to a risky asset decreases in its beta. This result holds even when capital regulation is not sensitive to risk (i.e., $\phi = 0$). When capital regulation is sensitive to risk, the demand for low-beta assets strengthens.

Insurers have significant leverage because of their liability structure, which they use to earn leveraged returns on low-beta assets. Leverage-constrained investors have high demand for the insurers' equity because holding low-beta assets indirectly through the insurance sector relaxes their leverage constraints. In equilibrium, insurers earn high expected returns on low-beta assets, reflecting their value in relaxing the leverage constraints of households and institutional investors. This central mechanism that depends on the insurers' access to cheap leverage could remain important because of demographic trends. The demand for annuities that provide longevity insurance and minimum return guarantees could continue to grow because of an aging population and the secular decline of pension plans.

6.4.2 Sensitivity to Risk-Based Capital

Ellul, Jotikasthira, and Lundblad (2011) find that insurers sell downgraded corporate bonds. This finding is consistent with equation (6.32) if we interpret a bond downgrade as an increase in its beta. Moreover, insurers with lower risk-based capital are more likely to sell downgraded corporate bonds. This finding corresponds to the second partial derivative:

$$\frac{\partial^2 x_I(n)}{\partial \beta(n) \partial \phi} = -\frac{R - R_f + \lambda}{R_f(R + \lambda)} \exp(-\phi \beta(n))[(1 - \phi \beta(n))$$

$$\times \mathbf{1}'_n (\mathbb{E}[\mathbf{d}] - \gamma \mathrm{Var}(\mathbf{d})\mathbf{1}) - \gamma \sigma_F^2 \beta(n)(\beta(n) + \boldsymbol{\beta}'\mathbf{1})]. \quad (6.33)$$

This expression is negative for $\beta(n) = 0$. More generally, it is negative for a low-beta asset because the quadratic equation inside the square brackets is positive for $\beta(n)$ sufficiently low. Thus, insurers with higher ϕ have lower risk-based capital, and they are more likely to sell downgraded corporate bonds. Ellul, Jotikasthira, and Lundblad (2011) find that when the insurance sector as a whole is relatively constrained, the selling pressure leads to an asset fire sale.[3]

Becker, Opp, and Saidi (2022) find that life insurers held on to downgraded non-agency MBSs after the global financial crisis, even though they sold downgraded bonds in the rest of their portfolio to reduce required capital. The reason is that state regulators eliminated risk-based capital regulation for non-agency MBSs by making required capital a function of expected loss instead of ratings. In the context of equation (6.33), life insurers effectively have a lower value of ϕ for non-agency MBSs than for the rest of their portfolio. When risk-based capital regulation is not sensitive to risk, insurers do not have an incentive to sell downgraded bonds.

Ge and Weisbach (2021) find that property and casualty insurers shift their portfolio toward safer corporate bonds after a severe weather event that causes operating losses. Operating losses could tighten a risk-based capital or value-at-risk constraint, which would be equivalent to an increase in ϕ. Thus, equation (6.33) could explain why insurers shift their portfolio toward safer assets in response to operating losses.

As we discuss in Section 2.1, variable annuities caused a significant shock to life insurers' balance sheets during the global financial crisis. Although they significantly reduced risk exposure on the liability side, as we discuss in Section 4.1, the evidence in Figure 6.4 on their portfolios does not show a significant reduction in credit risk. Ellul et al. (2022) also do not find a reduction

3. Ellul, Jotikasthira, and Lundblad (2011) and Becker and Ivashina (2015) emphasize discrete differences in selling pressure by NAIC designation, which we could model by making the risk weights an increasing step function of beta.

in credit risk, but they find that variable annuity insurers reduced equity risk by having a lower allocation to stocks and more short positions in stock futures.

6.4.3   Trend in Relative Credit Risk

As a consequence of the secular decline in interest rates, a growing literature discusses the incentives of institutional investors such as mutual funds, pension funds, and endowment funds as well as households to reach for yield (Choi and Kronlund, 2018; Lian, Ma, and Wang, 2019; Campbell and Sigalov, 2022). As other investors become more leverage constrained in a low interest rate environment, the model predicts that insurers increase their allocation to risky assets. According to equation (6.31), the insurers' allocation to risky assets increases in λ, which represents the tightness of other investors' leverage constraints. This force could partly explain why property and casualty insurers have increased credit risk.

For life insurers, there is an offsetting force that they were financially constrained during the global financial crisis and the subsequent low interest rate environment. Life insurers have had equity and interest risk mismatch as variable annuities have become their primary liability. As we discuss in Section 2.3.1, life insurers' stock returns are negatively exposed to long-term bond returns in the low interest rate environment. Moreover, variable annuity insurers that had low stock returns during the global financial crisis had low stock returns during the COVID-19 crisis, highlighting the persistent fragility of the life insurance sector. According to equation (6.31), the insurers' allocation to risky assets decreases in ϕ, which represents the tightness of the risk-based capital constraint.

As pension funds and sovereign wealth funds reach for yield in the low interest rate environment, property and casualty insurers have gained access to more debt financing through catastrophe bonds and insurance-linked securities. Hedge funds have invested in property and casualty insurers to access cheap leverage, as emphasized by the model. Similarly, private equity firms have invested in life insurers to increase leverage and reduce tax liabilities (Kirti and Sarin, 2020). This capital inflow into the insurance sector suggests that ϕ has decreased, especially for property and casualty insurers.

In summary, life insurers have become more financially constrained relative to property and casualty insurers after the global financial crisis. At the same time, other investors have become more leverage constrained in the low interest rate environment. The combination of these forces could explain why the credit risk of bond portfolios for life insurers has decreased relative to that for property and casualty insurers after the global financial crisis.

6.5   Potential Extensions

We have made simplifying assumptions to focus on why insurers are the largest institutional investors of corporate bonds. We conclude by discussing potential extensions of the model for future research.

6.5.1   Interest Risk Mismatch

In our two-period model, assets differ by beta but not by maturity. Thus, insurers choose credit risk but not interest rate risk. In reality, insurers affect not only credit risk but also interest rate risk by shifting their portfolio from Treasury to corporate bonds. Because Treasury bonds have a longer maturity distribution than corporate bonds, insurers may decrease the duration of their portfolio by shifting from Treasury to corporate bonds.

As we discuss in Section 2.3.1, insurers have a negative duration gap between their assets and their liabilities with minimum return guarantees. Insurers would increase the duration gap by shifting from Treasury bonds with longer maturities to corporate bonds with shorter maturities. Thus, insurers face a trade-off between earning a credit risk premium and reducing the duration gap. Although insurers could hedge interest rate risk through derivatives, the size of the hedging demand would be large relative to the size of the derivatives market. Consequently, insurers may have to accept interest risk mismatch to earn a credit risk premium on low-beta assets, which is the central force in the model.

Several papers show that interest rate risk is an important consideration in portfolio choice, especially when interest rates are low. In the low interest rate environment after the global financial crisis, US life insurers have increased the duration but not the credit risk of their portfolios (Ozdagli and Wang, 2019). Similarly, euro-area insurers have increased the duration but not the credit risk of their portfolios during the quantitative easing program that started in March 2015 (Koijen et al., 2021). Greenwood and Vissing-Jørgensen (2018) hypothesize that the liability hedging demand by insurers and pension funds could depress long-term government bond yields. Consistent with this hypothesis, they find a negative correlation between the slope of the government yield curve and the size of the insurance and private pension sectors across countries.

6.5.2   *Capital Structure*

In an economy with a low-beta anomaly, firms with low-beta assets have an incentive to increase leverage to take advantage of the anomaly (Baker and Wurgler, 2015; Baker, Hoeyer, and Wurgler, 2020). In the model, insurers hold low-beta assets and have significant leverage because of its liability structure. However, leverage is entirely determined by the demand for annuities because insurers cannot issue public debt or pay out dividends.

Depending on the strength of the low-beta anomaly, insurers may have an incentive to increase leverage by selling more policies, issuing public debt, or paying out dividends. Thus, capital structure choice is an interesting extension that could potentially explain the high level of leverage and its historical trend in Figure 1.5.

6.5.3   *Insurance Pricing*

We have assumed that annuities are not subject to risk-based capital regulation, which implies that the pricing of annuities (6.1) does not depend on the shadow cost of capital. In reality, risk-based capital depends not only on portfolio choice, but it also interacts with insurance pricing and capital structure choice. Depending on the strength of the low-beta anomaly, insurers may have an incentive to increase leverage by selling more policies at lower prices.

We have assumed that annuities are riskless because the insurers' dividends can be negative to ensure full payment of annuity claims. If we were to assume nonnegativity of dividends through limited liability, annuities would be defaultable. In that case, portfolio choice could interact with insurance pricing because demand could depend on the default probability.

6.5.4   *Agency Problems*

We have abstracted from agency problems that could affect portfolio choice and capital structure choice. For example, risk-shifting motives could arise from limited liability and the presence of state guaranty associations (Lee, Mayers, and Smith, 1997). The asset pricing literature has studied the impact of agency problems on other types of institutional investors such as mutual funds, hedge funds, and pension funds (Basak, Pavlova, and Shapiro, 2007; Huang, Sialm, and Zhang, 2011). The insights from this literature may be useful for studying insurers as well.

7

Research Topics and Policy Implications

7.1 Research Topics

We discuss five promising research topics based on the research presented in this book.

7.1.1 Insurance of New Risks

Insurers have been in the business of insuring traditional life, health, and accident risks for decades. They have decades of loss experience and policy-holder behavior to accurately estimate the loss distribution for the purposes of insurance underwriting. In contrast, new risks present opportunities and challenges for insurers. Three recent examples include climate risk (Giglio, Kelly, and Stroebel, 2021; Issler et al., 2021; Tomunen, 2021), cyber risk (Eisenbach, Kovner, and Lee, 2020; Florackis et al., 2020; Jamilov, Rey, and Tahoun, 2021), and global pandemics.

New risks present opportunities for insurers to open new markets and earn a higher return on capital. New risks also present challenges because the loss experience may be insufficient to accurately estimate the loss distribution with respect to both systematic and idiosyncratic risks. Policyholder behavior could also be difficult to predict for types of policies that allow policyholder discretion such as lapsation and surrender.

As we discuss in Chapter 4, insurers may increase prices or limit coverage when they face increased uncertainty. In extreme cases, insurers may not provide any insurance of a risk with an uncertain loss distribution. Expensive insurance or limited coverage could impact household and firm decisions. For example, firms may be slow to adopt a new technology because the cyber risk is too high.

In this context, the government may be able to help by collecting and distributing data necessary for estimating the loss distribution. For example, the government could keep a complete register of cyber attacks and associated losses and distribute aggregated or anonymized data that protect individual company privacy. The government could also act as a "reinsurer of last resort" for extreme tail risks that even large reinsurers are reluctant to take on.

7.1.2 Microfoundations of Insurance Demand

In Chapters 4 and 5, we modeled demand as a function of insurer and contract characteristics through the random coefficients logit model. We took this approach given the limited data on sales by insurer or contract. Better data could open up possibilities for a richer model of demand.

Life-cycle models predict that demand for annuities, life insurance, and health insurance depends on household characteristics such as age, family composition, income, and wealth. If insurers cannot or do not condition their pricing on some relevant household characteristics, demand could depend on these characteristics through adverse selection (Finkelstein and Poterba, 2004). Thus, modeling demand as a function of household characteristics would be natural if such data were available. Koijen, Van Nieuwerburgh, and Yogo (2016) find that about two-thirds of the demand for annuities, life insurance, and health insurance could be explained by household characteristics. An important question is what explains the remaining variation in insurance demand.

Beliefs about the loss distribution or trust of insurers could be an important aspect of insurance demand. Brown, Goda, and McGarry (2012) find that demand for long-term care insurance depends on beliefs about the likelihood of needing long-term care and on whether insurers could be trusted not to raise premiums or deny insurance claims. Gennaioli et al. (2022) propose that cultural and legal factors lead to variation in trust across countries, which explains the relative efficiency of homeowners insurance markets, particularly regarding insurance claims.

Financial advisors could also be an important part of insurance demand. Insurance markets are highly intermediated, and financial advisors and insurance agents play a central role. A growing literature highlights the importance of financial advisors in consumer financial markets (Mullainathan, Noth, and Schoar, 2012; Linnainmaa, Melzer, and Previtero, 2021) and insurance markets specifically (Bhattacharya, Illanes, and Padi, 2020; Egan, Ge, and Tang, 2022; Barbu, 2021). Incorporating financial advisors in the model of insurance demand in Chapters 4 and 5 could better explain the observed insurance choices and demand elasticities.

7.1.3 Regulatory Gaps

Chapters 3 and 5 highlight the importance of gaps in accounting standards and risk-based capital regulation for insurance pricing and reinsurance. Both academic and industry research that identifies regulatory gaps could inform policymakers and facilitate the efficient function of insurance markets and the stability of the insurance sector. In January 2017, state regulators adopted principle-based reserving for annuities and life insurance with mandatory compliance by January 2020. Principle-based reserving replaces the Standard Valuation Law that we discuss in Section 3.2, which caused the extraordinary pricing of annuities and life insurance during the global financial crisis. Principle-based reserving also replaces Regulation (A)XXX that we discuss in Section 1.4.3, which was the initial motive for shadow insurance. While the long-run implications are currently unknown, these regulatory changes could be positive developments.

Regulatory gaps could also affect portfolio choice, especially when insurers reach for yield in a low interest rate environment. As we discuss in Section 2.5, gaps in reporting requirements led to AIG's losses on securities lending during the global financial crisis. Becker and Ivashina (2015) find that life insurers tilt their portfolio toward corporate bonds with higher yields and risk (as measured by credit default swap spreads) within an NAIC designation. Becker, Opp, and Saidi (2022) find that life insurers held on to downgraded non-agency MBSs after the global financial crisis when state regulators eliminated risk-based capital requirements. These examples suggest that insurers increase investment risk when risk-based capital regulation is not sufficiently sensitive to risk.

7.1.4 Political Economy of Insurance Regulation

Recent work studies the incentives of state regulators and their impact on the insurance sector as part of a broader agenda on the political economy of financial regulation (Leverty and Grace, 2018; Liu and Liu, 2019; Tenekedjieva, 2021). Competition between states could leave more scope for regulatory capture and inconsistent regulation. For example, competition for insurance business between states and offshore domiciles led to the growth of shadow insurance that we discuss in Section 2.4. From the perspective of research design, differences in regulation across states are also useful for identification (e.g., Ellul et al., 2015).

Most of the work so far focuses on the United States, but large insurers operate globally and work with multiple regulators across countries. Differences in accounting standards, risk-based capital regulation, and tax treatments as well as boundaries in regulatory oversight are some of the important issues that arise between US and foreign regulators such as the European Insurance and Occupational Pensions Authority (EIOPA).

7.1.5   Optimal Insurance Regulation

Regulation affects all functions of the insurance sector, including insurance pricing, contract design, reinsurance, portfolio choice, and risk management. Regulation is not only important for our understanding of insurance markets, but it must also be properly designed to ensure the efficient function of insurance markets and the stability of the insurance sector. Therefore, optimal insurance regulation is an important topic of research.

Because life insurers have a different liability structure than banks, their risk-based capital regulation should also be different. Life insurer liabilities are less prone to runs, so short-term risk constraints designed to prevent bank runs may not be appropriate for life insurers. If asset prices are mean reverting (Campbell and Shiller, 1988), short-term risk constraints could force life insurers to liquidate long-term assets when their prices are low, leading to lower equity and more risk in the long run. Therefore, life insurers should be assessed by long-term risk measures that are different from the short-term risk measures for banks.

Research on this topic faces several modeling and empirical challenges. For example, long-term risk measurement is potentially sensitive to reasonable variation in modeling assumptions. We refer to Engle, Roussellet, and Siriwardane (2017) for an example in the context of the term structure of interest rates. Another challenge is that the maturity structure of life insurer liabilities is unknown, and the public financial statements are not sufficiently complete for accurate inference. Lack of data hinders the calculation of the market value and the duration of liabilities, which are important inputs into empirical work on risk measurement.

7.2   Policy Implications

We draw three policy implications of the research presented in this book.

7.2.1   Financial Disclosure

The risk profile of life insurers has become increasingly complex and opaque over the last two decades because of variable annuities, derivatives, and shadow insurance. Chapter 2 summarizes these sources of risk based on public financial statements. To better understand how these sources of risk could lead to overall risk mismatch, we suggest the following ways to improve financial disclosure.

1. Risk measures: Life insurers could report risk measures by line of business such as life insurance, fixed annuities, and variable annuities. In particular, they could report duration and convexity for interest rate risk, delta and gamma for equity risk, and vega for volatility risk. Such data would be useful for assessing overall risk mismatch. Interest rate risk is especially important in a low interest rate environment because of the negative duration gap between assets and liabilities, as we discuss in Section 2.3.1.

2. Derivatives: Life insurers could report the same risk measures for their derivative positions. Such data would be useful for assessing the effectiveness of their hedging programs.

3. Captive reinsurance: State regulators could release the financial statements of captives, following the lead of the Iowa Insurance Division (2014). Furthermore, restated financial statements, in which both assets and liabilities are reported under the statutory accounting principles, would be useful for assessing capital adequacy. The financial statements could also disclose the identity of the institutions that are backing the letters of credit.

4. International activity: Most of the research in this book is based on US data because financial statements at the same level of detail are not publicly available in Europe. Although transparency improved with Solvency II, European insurers could report public financial statements with sufficient detail regarding minimum return guarantees, derivatives, reinsurance, and securities lending to be able to assess overall risk mismatch at the international level.

7.2.2   Stress Tests

We suggest standardized stress tests at the level of operating companies, insurance groups, and state guaranty associations. Stress tests could focus on systematic financial risks such as interest rate risk, credit risk including a large-scale ratings migration, equity risk, and volatility risk. In addition, stress tests could consider changes in policyholder behavior such as a slowdown in lapsation and surrender rates in a low interest rate environment. Regulators could require insurers to hold more equity if the stress tests reveal fragility.

Stress tests could help identify not only activities that require more equity but also areas where the capital standards are overly conservative. For example, stress tests could have determined whether Regulation (A)XXX was overly conservative, and if so, they could have prevented the growth of shadow insurance. Well-designed stress tests could help regulators spot risk trends earlier. In hindsight, stress tests may have reduced the risks associated with variable annuities, shadow insurance, securities lending, and fire-sale dynamics in corporate bond markets. The results of stress tests could be made public, at least at the level of state guaranty associations, to ensure market discipline.

7.2.3   Regulatory Oversight

Although the NAIC coordinates insurance regulation across states, inconsistencies and gaps remain, and regulatory change is slow and incremental. Importantly, the NAIC does not have a financial stability mandate or enforcement authority. Therefore, we suggest expanding the role of the US Department of the Treasury's Federal Insurance Office in the following ways.

1. The Federal Insurance Office could be given a financial stability mandate.
2. The Director of the Federal Insurance Office could be made a voting member of the Financial Stability Oversight Council.
3. The Federal Insurance Office could collect and distribute data on risk measures by line of business and captive reinsurance. It could also provide analysis of risk mismatch at the level of operating companies, insurance groups, and state guaranty associations.
4. The Federal Insurance Office could design the standardized stress tests. Coordination with the Federal Reserve would ensure that banks and

insurers use the same stress scenarios (e.g., a low interest rate environment or an increase in credit risk).

The Federal Insurance Office needs additional resources to take up these important tasks. It would ideally have economists and actuaries to staff a research department and a financial stability department. It could collaborate with the Federal Reserve to learn best practices from banking regulation and make necessary adjustments to be appropriate for the insurance sector.

Data Appendix

A.1 Variables Based on the *Financial Accounts of the United States*

We define the following variables based on the *Financial Accounts of the United States* (Board of Governors of the Federal Reserve System, 2017).

- Life insurers.
  - Assets: FL544090005_Q.
  - Corporate and foreign bonds: LM543069105_Q + LM543063005_Q.
  - Government bonds: LM544022005_Q − LM543069105_Q − LM543063005_Q.
  - Equities: LM543064105_Q + LM543064205_Q.
  - Loans: FL544023005_Q.
  - Liabilities: FL544190005_Q − FL543194733_Q.
  - Life insurance: FL543140005_Q.
  - Annuities in the general account: FL543150005_Q.
  - Pension funds: FL593095005_Q.
  - Annuities in the separate account: LM543150085_Q.
- Property and casualty insurers.
  - Assets: FL514090005_Q.
  - Corporate and foreign bonds: LM513069103_Q + LM513063003_Q.
  - Government bonds: LM514022005_Q − LM513069103_Q − LM513063003_Q.
  - Equities: LM513064105_Q + LM513064203_Q.
  - Loans: FL513065503_Q.
  - Liabilities: FL514190005_Q − FL513194733_Q.

- Banks.
  - Assets: FL704090005_Q.
  - Liabilities: FL704190005_Q − FL763194735_Q − FL753194503_Q.
- Private defined contribution plans:
  - Liabilities: FL574090055_Q.
- Private defined benefit plans.
  - Liabilities: FL574190043_Q.
- Households.
  - Net worth: FL154090005_Q − FL154190005_Q.
- Corporate bonds: FL893163005_Q − FL313063763_Q − FL213063003_Q − LM263063005_Q.
  - Insurance: LM513063003_Q + LM543063005_Q.
  - Pension funds: LM573063005_Q + LM343063005_Q + LM223063045_Q.
  - Banks: FL763063005_Q + FL753063005_Q + FL743063005_Q + FL473063005_Q + LM613063003_Q + FL663063005_Q + FL733063003_Q + FL503063005_Q.
  - Mutual funds: FL633063003_Q + LM653063005_Q + LM553063003_Q + LM563063003_Q + FL643063005_Q.
  - Government-sponsored enterprises: FL403063005_Q.

A.2 Insurer Characteristics

We construct the following insurer characteristics based on the financial statements.

- Log assets: Logarithm of total admitted assets.
- Log liabilities: Logarithm of as reported total liabilities.
- Asset growth: Growth rate of total admitted assets.
- Leverage: The ratio of as reported total liabilities to as reported total assets.
- Net equity inflow: The ratio of capital and surplus paid in minus stockholder dividends to previous equity.

The A.M. Best Company constructs the following insurer characteristics as part of the rating process.

- A.M. Best rating: We convert the A.M. Best financial strength rating (coded from A++ to D) to a cardinal measure (coded from 175% to 0%) based on risk-based capital guidelines (A.M. Best Company, 2011, p. 24).
- Risk-based capital: A.M. Best capital adequacy ratio, which is the ratio of adjusted capital and surplus to required capital.
- Risk-based capital relative to guideline: A.M. Best capital adequacy ratio minus the guideline for the current rating (A.M. Best Company, 2011, p. 24).
- Current liquidity: A measure of balance sheet liquidity, defined as the ratio of current assets (i.e., unencumbered cash and unaffiliated investments) to total liabilities.
- Return on equity: A measure of profitability, defined as the ratio of net operating gain after taxes to the average capital and surplus over the current and prior year.

TABLE A.1. Publicly Traded US Life Insurers

Insurer	First observation	
AIG	January	1999
Allstate	January	1999
American National	January	1999
Ameriprise	November	2005
Assurant	March	2004
Brighthouse Financial	September	2017
CIGNA	January	1999
Farm Bureau Life	January	1999
Genworth	June	2004
Hartford	January	1999
Horace Mann Life	January	1999
Kansas City Life	January	1999
Lincoln	January	1999
Metropolitan Life	May	2000
Nationwide	January	1999
Phoenix Life	July	2001
Principal Financial Group	November	2001
Protective Life	January	1999
Prudential	January	2002
Symetra Life	February	2010
Voya	June	2013

This table reports the first observation for which monthly stock returns are available from January 1999 to December 2017.

- A.M. Best financial size category: A measure of company size (coded from 1 to 15) based on the adjusted policyholders' surplus for the insurance group.

A.3   Portfolio of US Life Insurers

We construct monthly returns on a value-weighted portfolio of publicly traded US variable annuity insurers, based on Table A.1.

Optimality Conditions for a Multiproduct Insurer

We derive a more general version of equations (4.14) and (4.17) for a multiproduct insurer that offers multiple contracts and chooses the fees and the rollup rates, accounting for demand elasticities across contracts. Let bold letters denote vectors corresponding to their scalar counterparts.

Generalizing equation (4.11), the insurer chooses a vector of fees $\mathbf{P}_t$ and rollup rates $\mathbf{r}_t$ to maximize firm value:

$$J_t = (\mathbf{P}_t - \mathbf{V}_{t,t})'\mathbf{Q}_t - C_t. \tag{B.1}$$

Generalizing equation (4.7), the law of motion for statutory capital is

$$K_t = R_{K,t}K_{t-1} + (\mathbf{P}_t - (1+\phi_t)\mathbf{V}_{t,t})'\mathbf{Q}_t, \tag{B.2}$$

where

$$R_{K,t} = \frac{A_{t-1}}{K_{t-1}}R_{A,t} - \frac{(1+\phi_t)L_{t-1}}{K_{t-1}}\frac{\mathbf{V}'_{t-1,t}\mathbf{Q}_{t-1}}{\mathbf{V}'_{t-1,t-1}\mathbf{Q}_{t-1}} \tag{B.3}$$

is the return on statutory capital.

The partial derivative of firm value with respect to the fee is

$$\frac{\partial J_t}{\partial \mathbf{P}_t} = \frac{\partial (\mathbf{P}_t - \mathbf{V}_{t,t})'\mathbf{Q}_t}{\partial \mathbf{P}_t} + c_t\frac{\partial K_t}{\partial \mathbf{P}_t}$$

$$= \mathbf{Q}_t + \frac{\partial \mathbf{Q}'_t}{\partial \mathbf{P}_t}(\mathbf{P}_t - \mathbf{V}_{t,t}) + c_t\left(\mathbf{Q}_t + \frac{\partial \mathbf{Q}'_t}{\partial \mathbf{P}_t}(\mathbf{P}_t - (1+\phi_t)\mathbf{V}_{t,t})\right)$$

$$= (1+c_t)\mathbf{Q}_t + \frac{\partial \mathbf{Q}'_t}{\partial \mathbf{P}_t}((1+c_t)(\mathbf{P}_t - \mathbf{V}_{t,t}) - c_t\phi_t\mathbf{V}_{t,t}). \tag{B.4}$$

The optimal fee satisfies

$$\frac{\partial J_t}{\partial \mathbf{P}_t} = \mathbf{0} \Leftrightarrow \mathbf{P}_t + \left(\frac{\partial \mathbf{Q}_t'}{\partial \mathbf{P}_t}\right)^{-1}\mathbf{Q}_t = \frac{1 + c_t(1+\phi_t)}{1+c_t}\mathbf{V}_{t,t}, \qquad (\text{B.5})$$

which generalizes equation (4.14).

The partial derivative of firm value with respect to the rollup rate is

$$\frac{\partial J_t}{\partial \mathbf{r}_t} = \frac{\partial (\mathbf{P}_t - \mathbf{V}_{t,t})'\mathbf{Q}_t}{\partial \mathbf{r}_t} + c_t\frac{\partial K_t}{\partial \mathbf{r}_t}$$

$$= -\frac{\partial \mathbf{V}_{t,t}'}{\partial \mathbf{r}_t}\mathbf{Q}_t + \frac{\partial \mathbf{Q}_t'}{\partial \mathbf{r}_t}(\mathbf{P}_t - \mathbf{V}_{t,t})$$

$$+ c_t\left(-(1+\phi_t)\frac{\partial \mathbf{V}_{t,t}'}{\partial \mathbf{r}_t}\mathbf{Q}_t + \frac{\partial \mathbf{Q}_t'}{\partial \mathbf{r}_t}(\mathbf{P}_t - (1+\phi_t)\mathbf{V}_{t,t})\right)$$

$$= -(1 + c_t(1+\phi_t))\frac{\partial \mathbf{V}_{t,t}'}{\partial \mathbf{r}_t}\mathbf{Q}_t + \frac{\partial \mathbf{Q}_t'}{\partial \mathbf{r}_t}((1+c_t)(\mathbf{P}_t - \mathbf{V}_{t,t}) - c_t\phi_t\mathbf{V}_{t,t})$$

$$= -(1 + c_t(1+\phi_t))\frac{\partial \mathbf{V}_{t,t}'}{\partial \mathbf{r}_t}\mathbf{Q}_t - (1+c_t)\frac{\partial \mathbf{Q}_t'}{\partial \mathbf{r}_t}\left(\frac{\partial \mathbf{Q}_t'}{\partial \mathbf{P}_t}\right)^{-1}\mathbf{Q}_t, \quad (\text{B.6})$$

where the last line follows from substituting equation (B.4). At an interior optimum, the rollup rate satisfies

$$\frac{\partial J_t}{\partial \mathbf{r}_t} = \mathbf{0} \Leftrightarrow -\frac{\partial \mathbf{Q}_t'}{\partial \mathbf{r}_t}\left(\frac{\partial \mathbf{Q}_t'}{\partial \mathbf{P}_t}\right)^{-1}\mathbf{Q}_t = \frac{1 + c_t(1+\phi_t)}{1+c_t}\frac{\partial \mathbf{V}_{t,t}'}{\partial \mathbf{r}_t}\mathbf{Q}_t. \qquad (\text{B.7})$$

Because $\partial \mathbf{V}_{t,t}'/\partial \mathbf{r}_t$ is a diagonal matrix, we can rewrite this equation as

$$-\text{diag}(\mathbf{Q}_t)^{-1}\frac{\partial \mathbf{Q}_t'}{\partial \mathbf{r}_t}\left(\frac{\partial \mathbf{Q}_t'}{\partial \mathbf{P}_t}\right)^{-1}\mathbf{Q}_t = \frac{1 + c_t(1+\phi_t)}{1+c_t}\frac{\partial \mathbf{V}_{t,t}'}{\partial \mathbf{r}_t}\mathbf{1}, \qquad (\text{B.8})$$

which generalizes equation (4.17).

The left sides of equations (B.5) and (B.8) correspond to the first terms inside the logarithm in equations (4.29) and (4.30), respectively. For the random coefficients logit model, we denote the vector of demand for all contracts that an insurer sells as

$$\mathbf{Q}_t = \int \mathbf{q}_t(\alpha_P)\, dF(\alpha_P). \qquad (\text{B.9})$$

The partial derivative of demand with respect to the vector of fees is

$$\frac{\partial \mathbf{Q}'_t}{\partial \mathbf{P}_t} = \int -\alpha_P (\mathrm{diag}(\mathbf{q}_t(\alpha_P)) - \mathbf{q}_t(\alpha_P)\mathbf{q}_t(\alpha_P)') \, dF(\alpha_P). \qquad (B.10)$$

The partial derivative of demand with respect to the vector of rollup rates is

$$\frac{\partial \mathbf{Q}'_t}{\partial \mathbf{r}_t} = \int \alpha_r (\mathrm{diag}(\mathbf{q}_t(\alpha_P)) - \mathbf{q}_t(\alpha_P)\mathbf{q}_t(\alpha_P)') \, dF(\alpha_P). \qquad (B.11)$$

Thus, the estimated model of variable annuity demand in Table 4.1 directly implies the left sides of equations (B.5) and (B.8).

BIBLIOGRAPHY

Acharya, Viral V., Lasse H. Pedersen, Thomas Philippon, and Matthew Richardson. 2017. "Measuring Systemic Risk." *Review of Financial Studies* 30 (1):2–47.

Acharya, Viral V., Thomas Philippon, and Matthew Richardson. 2017. "Measuring Systemic Risk for Insurance Companies." In *The Economics, Regulation, and Systemic Risk of Insurance Markets*, edited by Felix Hufeld, Ralph S. J. Koijen, and Christian Thimann, chap. 5. Oxford: Oxford University Press, 100–123.

Acharya, Viral V. and Matthew Richardson. 2014. "Is the Insurance Industry Systemically Risky?" In *Modernizing Insurance Regulation*, edited by John H. Biggs and Matthew P. Richardson, chap. 9. Hoboken, NJ: John Wiley & Sons, Inc., 151–179.

Acharya, Viral V., Philipp Schnabl, and Gustavo Suarez. 2013. "Securitization without Risk Transfer." *Journal of Financial Economics* 107 (3):515–536.

Adrian, Tobias and Adam B. Ashcraft. 2012. "Shadow Banking Regulation." *Annual Review of Financial Economics* 4:99–140.

Adrian, Tobias, Erkko Etula, and Tyler Muir. 2014. "Financial Intermediaries and the Cross-Section of Asset Returns." *Journal of Finance* 69 (6):2557–2596.

Adrian, Tobias and Hyun Song Shin. 2014. "Procyclical Leverage and Value-at-Risk." *Review of Financial Studies* 27 (2):373–403.

Allen, Franklin and Douglas Gale. 1997. "Financial Markets, Intermediaries, and Intertemporal Smoothing." *Journal of Political Economy* 105 (3):523–546.

A.M. Best Company. 1993–2012. *Best's Insurance Reports: Life/Health, United States and Canada*. Oldwick, NJ: A.M. Best Company.

———. 1999–2017. *Best's Statement File: Life/Health, United States*. Oldwick, NJ: A.M. Best Company.

———. 2003–2014. *Best's Schedule S: Life/Health, United States*. Oldwick, NJ: A.M. Best Company.

———. 2011. "Best's Credit Rating Methodology: Global Life and Non-Life Insurance Edition." *A.M. Best Methodology*.

———. 2013. "Rating Factors for Organizations Using Life Captive Reinsurers." *A.M. Best Special Report*.

Baker, Malcolm, Mathias F. Hoeyer, and Jeffrey Wurgler. 2020. "Leverage and the Beta Anomaly." *Journal of Financial and Quantitative Analysis* 55 (5):1491–1514.

Baker, Malcolm and Jeffrey Wurgler. 2015. "Do Strict Capital Requirements Raise the Cost of Capital? Bank Regulation, Capital Structure, and the Low-Risk Anomaly." *American Economic Review* 105 (5):315–320.

Ball, Laurence and N. Gregory Mankiw. 2007. "Intergenerational Risk Sharing in the Spirit of Arrow, Debreu, and Rawls, with Applications to Social Security Design." *Journal of Political Economy* 115 (4):523–547.

Barbu, Alexandru. 2021. "Ex-Post Loss Sharing in Consumer Financial Markets." Working paper, London Business School.

Basak, Suleyman, Anna Pavlova, and Alexander Shapiro. 2007. "Optimal Asset Allocation and Risk Shifting in Money Management." *Review of Financial Studies* 20 (5):1583–1621.

Bauer, Daniel, Alexander Kling, and Jochen Russ. 2008. "A Universal Pricing Framework for Guaranteed Minimum Benefits in Variable Annuities." *Astin Bulletin* 38 (2):621–651.

Becker, Bo and Victoria Ivashina. 2015. "Reaching for Yield in the Bond Market." *Journal of Finance* 70 (5):1863–1902.

Becker, Bo, Marcus M. Opp, and Farzad Saidi. 2022. "Regulatory Forbearance in the U.S. Insurance Industry: The Effects of Removing Capital Requirements for an Asset Class." *Review of Financial Studies* 35 (12): forthcoming.

Begenau, Juliane, Monika Piazzesi, and Martin Schneider. 2015. "Banks' Risk Exposures." Working paper 21334, National Bureau of Economic Research.

Berends, Kyal and Thomas B. King. 2015. "Derivatives and Collateral at U.S. Life Insurers." *Federal Reserve Bank of Chicago Economic Perspectives* 39 (1):21–37.

Berry, Steven, James Levinsohn, and Ariel Pakes. 1995. "Automobile Prices in Market Equilibrium." *Econometrica* 63 (4):841–890.

Berry-Stölzle, Thomas R., Gregory P. Nini, and Sabine Wende. 2014. "External Financing in the Life Insurance Industry: Evidence from the Financial Crisis." *Journal of Risk and Insurance* 81 (3):529–562.

Bhattacharya, Vivek, Gaston Illanes, and Manisha Padi. 2020. "Fiduciary Duty and the Market for Financial Advice." Working paper, Northwestern University.

Black, Fischer. 1972. "Capital Market Equilibrium with Restricted Borrowing." *Journal of Business* 45 (3):444–455.

Black, Fischer and Myron Scholes. 1973. "The Pricing of Options and Corporate Liabilities." *Journal of Political Economy* 81 (3):637–654.

Board of Governors of the Federal Reserve System. 2017. *Financial Accounts of the United States*. No. Z.1 in Federal Reserve Statistical Release. Washington, DC: Board of Governors of the Federal Reserve System.

Bretscher, Lorenzo, Lukas Schmid, Ishita Sen, and Varun Sharma. 2021. "Institutional Corporate Bond Demand." Working paper, London Business School.

Brown, Jeffrey R., Gopi Shah Goda, and Kathleen McGarry. 2012. "Long-Term Care Insurance Demand Limited by Beliefs about Needs, Concerns about Insurers, and Care Available from Family." *Health Affairs* 31 (6):1294–1302.

Brown, Jeffrey R. and James M. Poterba. 2006. "Household Ownership of Variable Annuities." In *Tax Policy and the Economy*, vol. 20, edited by James M. Poterba, chap. 5. Cambridge, MA: MIT Press, 163–191.

Brownlees, Christian and Robert F. Engle. 2017. "SRISK: A Conditional Capital Shortfall Measure of Systemic Risk." *Review of Financial Studies* 30 (1):48–79.

Brunnermeier, Markus K. and Lasse Heje Pedersen. 2009. "Market Liquidity and Funding Liquidity." *Review of Financial Studies* 22 (6):2201–2238.

Campbell, John Y. and Robert J. Shiller. 1988. "The Dividend-Price Ratio and Expectations of Future Dividends and Discount Factors." *Review of Financial Studies* 1 (3):195–228.

Campbell, John Y. and Roman Sigalov. 2022. "Portfolio Choice with Sustainable Spending: A Model of Reaching for Yield." *Journal of Financial Economics* 143 (1):188–206.

Captives and Special Purpose Vehicle Use Subgroup. 2013. "Captives and Special Purpose Vehicles." Working paper, National Association of Insurance Commissioners.

Célérier, Claire and Boris Vallée. 2017. "Catering to Investors through Security Design: Headline Rate and Complexity." *Quarterly Journal of Economics* 132 (3):1469–1508.

Chan, Yeung Lewis and Leonid Kogan. 2002. "Catching Up with the Joneses: Heterogeneous Preferences and the Dynamics of Asset Prices." *Journal of Political Economy* 110 (6):1255–1285.

Charupat, Narat, Mark J. Kamstra, and Moshe A. Milevsky. 2012. "The Annuity Duration Puzzle." Working paper, McMaster University.

Chodorow-Reich, Gabriel, Andra Ghent, and Valentin Haddad. 2021. "Asset Insulators." *Review of Financial Studies* 34 (3):1509–1539.

Choi, Jaewon and Mathias Kronlund. 2018. "Reaching for Yield in Corporate Bond Mutual Funds." *Review of Financial Studies* 31 (5):1930–1965.

Coimbra, Nuno and Hélène Rey. 2017. "Financial Cycles with Heterogeneous Intermediaries." Working paper 23245, National Bureau of Economic Research.

Cole, Cassandra R. and Kathleen A. McCullough. 2008. "Captive Domiciles: Trends and Recent Changes." *Journal of Insurance Regulation* 26 (4):61–90.

Compulife Software. 2002–2012. *Compulife Historical Data*. Harrodsburg, KY: Compulife Software.

Credit Suisse. 2012. "US Variable Annuities." *Credit Suisse Connections Series*.

Cummins, J. David, Richard D. Phillips, and Stephen D. Smith. 2001. "Derivatives and Corporate Risk Management: Participation and Volume Decisions in the Insurance Industry." *Journal of Risk and Insurance* 68 (1):51–92.

Cummins, J. David and Mary A. Weiss. 2014. "Systemic Risk and the U.S. Insurance Sector." *Journal of Risk and Insurance* 81 (3):489–528.

Cutler, David M. 1996. "Why Don't Markets Insure Long-Term Risk?" Working paper, Harvard University.

Damiani, Claudio, Naomi Bourne, and Martin Foo. 2015. "The HIH Claims Support Scheme." Working paper, Australian Department of the Treasury.

Dione, Goerges, editor. 2013. *Handbook of Insurance*. New York: Springer, second ed.

Dumas, Bernard. 1989. "Two-Person Dynamic Equilibrium in the Capital Market." *Review of Financial Studies* 2 (2):157–188.

Egan, Mark, Shan Ge, and Johnny Tang. 2022. "Conflicting Interests and the Effect of Fiduciary Duty—Evidence from Variable Annuities." *Review of Financial Studies*: forthcoming.

Einav, Liran and Amy Finkelstein. 2011. "Selection in Insurance Markets: Theory and Empirics in Pictures." *Journal of Economic Perspectives* 25 (1):115–138.

Einav, Liran, Amy Finkelstein, and Jonathan Levin. 2010. "Beyond Testing: Empirical Models of Insurance Markets." *Annual Review of Economics* 2 (1):311–336.

Eisenbach, Thomas M., Anna Kovner, and Michael Junho Lee. 2020. "Cyber Risk and the U.S. Financial System: A Pre-Mortem Analysis." Federal Reserve Bank of New York Staff Reports.

Ellul, Andrew, Chotibhak Jotikasthira, Anastasia Kartasheva, Christian T. Lundblad, and Wolf Wagner. 2022. "Insurers as Asset Managers and Systemic Risk." *Review of Financial Studies* 35 (12): forthcoming.

Ellul, Andrew, Chotibhak Jotikasthira, and Christian T. Lundblad. 2011. "Regulatory Pressure and Fire Sales in the Corporate Bond Market." *Journal of Financial Economics* 101 (3): 596–620.

Ellul, Andrew, Chotibhak Jotikasthira, Christian T. Lundblad, and Yihui Wang. 2015. "Is Historical Cost Accounting a Panacea? Market Stress, Incentive Distortions, and Gains Trading." *Journal of Finance* 70 (6):2489–2538.

Engle, Robert F., Guillaume Roussellet, and Emil Siriwardane. 2017. "Scenario Generation for Long Run Interest Rate Risk Assessment." *Journal of Econometrics* 201 (2):333–347.

Erhemjamts, Otgontsetseg and Richard D. Phillips. 2012. "Form Over Matter: Differences in the Incentives to Convert Using Full Versus Partial Demutualization in the U.S. Life Insurance Industry." *Journal of Risk and Insurance* 79 (2):305–334.

European Insurance and Occupational Pensions Authority. 2014. "EIOPA Insurance Stress Test 2014." Working paper 14-203, EIOPA.

European Systemic Risk Board. 2015. "Issues Note on Risks and Vulnerabilities in the EU Financial System." Working paper, European Systemic Risk Board.

Finkelstein, Amy and James Poterba. 2004. "Adverse Selection in Insurance Markets: Policyholder Evidence from the U.K. Annuity Market." *Journal of Political Economy* 112 (1):183–208.

Florackis, Chris, Christodoulos Louca, Roni Michaely, and Michael Weber. 2020. "Cybersecurity Risk." Working paper, University of Liverpool.

Foley-Fisher, Nathan, Borghan Narajabad, and Stéphane Verani. 2020. "Self-Fulfilling Runs: Evidence from the US Life Insurance Industry." *Journal of Political Economy* 128 (9):3520–3569.

Frazzini, Andrea and Lasse Heje Pedersen. 2014. "Betting Against Beta." *Journal of Financial Economics* 111 (1):1–25.

Friedman, Benjamin M. and Mark J. Warshawsky. 1990. "The Cost of Annuities: Implications for Saving Behavior and Bequests." *Quarterly Journal of Economics* 105 (1):135–154.

Froot, Kenneth A. 2001. "The Market for Catastrophe Risk: A Clinical Examination." *Journal of Financial Economics* 60 (2–3):529–571.

———. 2007. "Risk Management, Capital Budgeting, and Capital Structure Policy for Insurers and Reinsurers." *Journal of Risk and Insurance* 74 (2):273–299.

Froot, Kenneth A. and Paul G. J. O'Connell. 1999. "The Pricing of U.S. Catastrophe Reinsurance." In *The Financing of Catastrophe Risk*, edited by Kenneth A. Froot, chap. 5. Chicago, IL: University of Chicago Press, 195–232.

Gallanis, Peter G. 2009. "NOLHGA, the Life and Health Insurance Guaranty System, and the Financial Crisis of 2008–2009." Working paper, National Organization of Life and Health Insurance Guaranty Associations.

Ge, Shan. 2022. "How Do Financial Constraints Affect Product Pricing? Evidence from Weather and Life Insurance Premiums." *Journal of Finance* 77 (1):449–503.

Ge, Shan and Michael S. Weisbach. 2021. "The Role of Financial Conditions in Portfolio Choices: The Case of Insurers." *Journal of Financial Economics* 142 (2):803–830.

Gennaioli, Nicola, Rafael La Porta, Florencio Lopez-de-Silanes, and Andrei Shleifer. 2022. "Trust and Insurance Contracts." *Review of Financial Studies* 35 (12): forthcoming.

Giglio, Stefano, Bryan Kelly, and Johannes Stroebel. 2021. "Climate Finance." *Annual Review of Financial Economics* 13:15–36.

Greenwood, Robin and Annette Vissing-Jørgensen. 2018. "The Impact of Pensions and Insurance on Global Yield Curves." Working paper, Harvard University.

Gron, Anne. 1990. *Property-Casualty Insurance Cycles, Capacity Constraints, and Empirical Results.* Ph.D. thesis, MIT, Cambridge, MA.

———. 1994. "Evidence of Capacity Constraints in Insurance Markets." *Journal of Law and Economics* 37 (2):349–377.

Gron, Anne and Deborah J. Lucas. 1998. "External Financing and Insurance Cycles." In *The Economics of Property-Casualty Insurance,* edited by David F. Bradford, chap. 1. Chicago, IL: University of Chicago Press, 5–28.

Gürkaynak, Refet S., Brian Sack, and Jonathan H. Wright. 2007. "The U.S. Treasury Yield Curve: 1961 to the Present." *Journal of Monetary Economics* 54 (8):2291–2304.

Hanley, Kathleen Weiss and Stanislava Nikolova. 2021. "Rethinking the Use of Credit Ratings in Capital Regulations: Evidence from the Insurance Industry." *Review of Corporate Finance Studies* 10 (2):347–401.

Harrington, Scott E. 2009. "The Financial Crisis, Systemic Risk, and the Future of Insurance Regulation." *Journal of Risk and Insurance* 76 (4):785–819.

Hartley, Daniel, Anna Paulson, and Richard J. Rosen. 2017. "Measuring Interest Rate Risk in the Life Insurance Sector: The U.S. and the U.K." In *The Economics, Regulation, and Systemic Risk of Insurance Markets,* edited by Felix Hufeld, Ralph S. J. Koijen, and Christian Thimann, chap. 6. Oxford: Oxford University Press, 124–150.

He, Zhiguo, Bryan Kelly, and Asaf Manela. 2017. "Intermediary Asset Pricing: New Evidence from Many Asset Classes." *Journal of Financial Economics* 126 (1):1–35.

Hombert, Johan and Victor Lyonnet. 2022. "Can Risk Be Shared Across Investor Cohorts? Evidence from a Popular Savings Product." *Review of Financial Studies* 35 (12): forthcoming.

Horneff, Wolfram J., Raimond H. Maurer, Olivia S. Mitchell, and Michael Z. Stamos. 2009. "Asset Allocation and Location over the Life Cycle with Investment-Linked Survival-Contingent Payouts." *Journal of Banking and Finance* 33 (9):1688–1699.

———. 2010. "Variable Payout Annuities and Dynamic Portfolio Choice in Retirement." *Journal of Pension Economics and Finance* 9 (2):163–183.

Hortaçsu, Ali and Chad Syverson. 2004. "Product Differentiation, Search Costs, and Competition in the Mutual Fund Industry: A Case Study of S&P 500 Index Funds." *Quarterly Journal of Economics* 119 (2):403–456.

Huang, Jennifer, Clemens Sialm, and Hanjiang Zhang. 2011. "Risk Shifting and Mutual Fund Performance." *Review of Financial Studies* 24 (8):2575–2616.

Iowa Insurance Division. 2014. "Financial Statements—Single-State Life or Property." http://www.iid.state.ia.us/single_state_life_pc.

Issler, Paulo, Richard Stanton, Carles Vergara-Alert, and Nancy Wallace. 2021. "Housing and Mortgage Markets with Climate-Change Risk: Evidence from Wildfires in California." Working paper, University of California Berkeley.

Jamilov, Rustam, Hélène Rey, and Ahmed Tahoun. 2021. "The Anatomy of Cyber Risk." Working paper, London Business School.

Junus, Novian and Zohair Motiwalla. 2009. "A Discussion of Actuarial Guideline 43 for Variable Annuities." *Milliman Research Report.*

Kashyap, Anil K. 2002. "Sorting Out Japan's Financial Crisis." *Federal Reserve Bank of Chicago Economic Perspectives* 26 (4):42–55.

Kirti, Divya and Natasha Sarin. 2020. "What Private Equity Does Differently: Evidence from Life Insurance." Working paper, International Monetary Fund.

Knox, Benjamin and Jakob Ahm Sørensen. 2020. "Asset-Driven Insurance Pricing." Working paper, Copenhagen Business School.

Koijen, Ralph S. J., François Koulischer, Benoît Nguyen, and Motohiro Yogo. 2021. "Inspecting the Mechanism of Quantitative Easing in the Euro Area." *Journal of Financial Economics* 140 (1):1–20.

Koijen, Ralph S. J., Theo E. Nijman, and Bas J. M. Werker. 2011. "Optimal Annuity Risk Management." *Review of Finance* 15 (4):799–833.

Koijen, Ralph S. J., Stijn Van Nieuwerburgh, and Motohiro Yogo. 2016. "Health and Mortality Delta: Assessing the Welfare Cost of Household Insurance Choice." *Journal of Finance* 71 (2):957–1010.

Koijen, Ralph S. J. and Motohiro Yogo. 2013. "Shadow Insurance." Working paper 19568, National Bureau of Economic Research.

———. 2015. "The Cost of Financial Frictions for Life Insurers." *American Economic Review* 105 (1):445–475.

———. 2016. "Shadow Insurance." *Econometrica* 84 (3):1265–1287.

———. 2017. "Risk of Life Insurers: Recent Trends and Transmission Mechanisms." In *The Economics, Regulation, and Systemic Risk of Insurance Markets*, edited by Felix Hufeld, Ralph S. J. Koijen, and Christian Thimann, chap. 4. Oxford: Oxford University Press, 79–99.

———. 2019. "A Demand System Approach to Asset Pricing." *Journal of Political Economy* 127 (4):1475–1515.

———. 2022a. "The Fragility of Market Risk Insurance." *Journal of Finance* 77 (2):815–862.

———. 2022b. "Global Life Insurers during a Low Interest Rate Environment." *AEA Papers and Proceedings* 112:503–508.

———. 2023. "Understanding the Ownership Structure of Corporate Bonds." *American Economic Review: Insights* 5(1): forthcoming.

Lawsky, Benjamin M. 2013. "Shining a Light on Shadow Insurance: A Little-Known Loophole That Puts Insurance Policyholders and Taxpayers at Greater Risk." Working paper, New York State Department of Financial Services.

Lee, Soon-Jae, David Mayers, and Clifford W. Smith, Jr. 1997. "Guaranty Funds and Risk-Taking: Evidence from the Insurance Industry." *Journal of Financial Economics* 44 (1):3–24.

Leverty, J. Tyler and Martin F. Grace. 2018. "Do Elections Delay Regulatory Action?" *Journal of Financial Economics* 130 (2):409–427.

Lian, Chen, Yueran Ma, and Carmen Wang. 2019. "Low Interest Rates and Risk-Taking: Evidence from Individual Investment Decisions." *Review of Financial Studies* 32 (6):2107–2148.

Linnainmaa, Juhani, Brian T. Melzer, and Alessandro Previtero. 2021. "The Misguided Beliefs of Financial Advisors." *Journal of Finance* 76 (2):587–621.

Liu, Weiling and Jessica Liu. 2019. "The Effect of Political Frictions on Long Term Care Insurance." Working paper, Northeastern University.

Lombardi, Louis J. 2006. *Valuation of Life Insurance Liabilities*. Winsted, CT: ACTEX Publications, 4th ed.

Mayers, David and Clifford W. Smith, Jr. 1981. "Contractual Provisions, Organizational Structure, and Conflict Control in Insurance Markets." *Journal of Business* 54 (3): 407–434.

McDonald, Robert L. and Anna Paulson. 2015. "AIG in Hindsight." *Journal of Economic Perspectives* 29 (2):81–106.

Mergent. 2021. *Fixed Income Securities Database*. New York, NY: Mergent Inc.

Merrill, Craig B., Taylor D. Nadauld, René M. Stulz, and Shane M. Sherlund. 2021. "Were There Fire Sales in the RMBS Market?" *Journal of Monetary Economics* 122:17–37.

MetLife Investors USA Insurance Company. 2008. "MetLife Series VA Prospectus."

Milevsky, Moshe A. and Thomas S. Salisbury. 2006. "Financial Valuation of Guaranteed Minimum Withdrawal Benefits." *Insurance: Mathematics and Economics* 38 (1):21–38.

Moon, Hyungsik Roger and Frank Schorfheide. 2009. "Estimation with Overidentifying Inequality Moment Conditions." *Journal of Econometrics* 2 (153):136–154.

Morningstar. 2016a. *Morningstar Annuity Intelligence*. Chicago, IL: Morningstar, Inc.

———. 2016b. *Morningstar Direct*. Chicago, IL: Morningstar, Inc.

Mullainathan, Sendhil, Markus Noth, and Antoinette Schoar. 2012. "The Market for Financial Advice: An Audit Study." Working paper 17929, National Bureau of Economic Research.

Myers, Stewart C. and Nicholas S. Majluf. 1984. "Corporate Financing and Investment Decisions When Firms Have Information that Investors Do Not Have." *Journal of Financial Economics* 13 (2):187–221.

National Association of Insurance Commissioners. 1994–2019. *Annual Life InfoPro*. Kansas City, MO: National Association of Insurance Commissioners.

———. 2011a. "The Insurance Industry and Hedging with Derivative Instruments." *NAIC Capital Markets Special Report*.

———. 2011b. "Securities Lending in the Insurance Industry." *NAIC Capital Markets Special Report*.

Niehaus, Gregory R. 2016. "Managing Capital via Internal Capital Market Transactions: The Case of Life Insurers." *Journal of Risk and Insurance* 85 (1):69–106.

Ozdagli, Ali and Zixuan Wang. 2019. "Interest Rates and Insurance Company Investment Behavior." Working paper, Federal Reserve Bank of Dallas.

Paulson, Anna, Richard Rosen, Zain Mohey-Deen, and Robert McMenamin. 2012. "How Liquid Are U.S. Life Insurance Liabilities?" *Chicago Fed Letter* 302.

Peek, Joe and Eric S. Rosengren. 1997. "The International Transmission of Financial Shocks: The Case of Japan." *American Economic Review* 87 (4):495–505.

Peirce, Hester. 2014. "Securities Lending and the Untold Story in the Collapse of AIG." Working paper, George Mason University.

Roberts, Richard. 2012. "Did Anyone Learn Anything from the Equitable Life? Lessons and Learning from Financial Crises." Working paper, King's College London.

Robinson, Scott and Min Son. 2013. "The Captive Triangle: Where Life Insurers' Reserve and Capital Requirements Disappear." *Moody's Investors Service Report* 156495.

Rothschild, Michael and Joseph E. Stiglitz. 1976. "Equilibrium in Competitive Insurance Markets: An Essay on the Economics of Imperfect Information." *Quarterly Journal of Economics* 90 (4):630–649.

Sen, Ishita. 2022. "Regulatory Limits to Risk Management." *Review of Financial Studies* :forthcoming.

Sen, Ishita and David Humphry. 2020. "Capital Regulation and Product Market Outcomes." Working paper, Harvard University.

Shi, Yu. 2021. "The Nonfinancial Value of Financial Firms." Working paper, UCLA.

Siani, Kerry Y. 2022. "Raising Bond Capital in Segmented Markets." Working paper, Columbia University.

Small, Kenneth A. and Harvey S. Rosen. 1981. "Applied Welfare Economics with Discrete Choice Models." *Econometrica* 49 (1):105–130.

Stern, Hersh L. 1989–2011. *Annuity Shopper*. Englishtown, NJ: WebAnnuities Insurance Agency.

———. 2007–2009. *Comparative Annuity Reports*. Englishtown, NJ: WebAnnuities Insurance Agency.

Stern, Jeffrey, William Rosenblatt, Bernhardt Nadell, and Keith M. Andruschak. 2007. "Insurance Securitizations: Coping with Excess Reserve Requirements under Regulation XXX." *Journal of Taxation and Regulation of Financial Institutions* 20 (6):30–34.

Stock, James H. and Motohiro Yogo. 2005. "Testing for Weak Instruments in Linear IV Regression." In *Identification and Inference for Econometric Models: Essays in Honor of Thomas Rothenberg*, edited by Donald W. K. Andrews and James H. Stock, chap. 5. Cambridge: Cambridge University Press, 80–108.

Sun, Peter. 2009. "The VA Industry: An Analysis of Recent Activities." *Milliman Research Report*.

Sun, Peter, Ken Mungan, Joshua Corrigan, and Gary Finkelstein. 2009. "Performance of Insurance Company Hedging Programs during the Recent Capital Market Crisis." *Milliman Research Report*.

Tenekedjieva, Ana-Maria. 2021. "The Revolving Door and Insurance Solvency Regulation." Working paper, Federal Reserve Board of Governors.

Tomunen, Tuomas. 2021. "Failure to Share Natural Disaster Risk." Working paper, Boston College.

Yaari, Menahem E. 1965. "Uncertain Lifetime, Life Insurance, and the Theory of the Consumer." *Review of Economic Studies* 32 (2):137–150.

Yu, Yifan. 2021. "Hunt-for-Duration in Corporate Bond Market." Working paper, Princeton University.

INDEX

Page numbers in *italics* indicate figures and tables.

accounting standards, 1, 16, 19, 21–24, 49, 157–58

Actuarial Guideline 38, 22. *See also* Regulation (A)XXX

Actuarial Guideline 43, 24, 34, 86, 89, 98, 113

adverse selection, 17–18, 52, 156

Aegon: shadow insurance, 42; variable annuity liabilities, 31, *32, 95*

agency problems, 8, 42, 154

AIG: bailout, 20, 76, 78; counterparty risk, 49; equity drawdown, 38, *39, 40*; marginal cost of capital, 74–75; securities lending, 45–46, 47, 157; shadow insurance, 42; SRISK, 37, *37*; stock returns, *164*; variable annuity liabilities, *32, 95*

Allianz: default risk, *60*; marginal cost of capital, 74; recapitalization activity, 79; variable annuity liabilities, 31, *32, 95*

Allstate: bailout, 20, 76; default risk, *60*; equity drawdown, *39, 40*; marginal cost of capital, 75; recapitalization activity, 78; securities lending, 47; stock returns, *164*

A.M. Best Company: financial statements, 14–17; insurer characteristics in rating process, *163*; rating model, 115–17; regulatory uncertainty, 80

A.M. Best financial group, 42, *47, 48*

A.M. Best financial size category, 15, 115, *116*, 165

A.M. Best rating: data, 15, 164; insurance prices, 52, *53, 55, 56, 57*; insurance pricing model, 70–71, *72, 73*; life insurance market, 128–30, *131*; MetLife, 40, *41*; shadow insurance, 115–18, *116, 119*, 120, 129; shadow reinsurers, 16, 42, *43, 44*; variable annuity demand, 97, 100, *101*, 102; variable annuity supply, 106, 108, *109*

American Society of Actuaries. *See* mortality tables

annuities. *See* fixed annuities; life annuities; term annuities; variable annuities

annuity prices: during global financial crisis, 54–57, *55, 56, 58*; model of, 142, *144*; summary statistics, 52–54, *53. See also* fixed annuity prices; life annuity prices; term annuity prices; variable annuity fees

asset-backed securities, 45, *135*

asset prices, 48, 133–34, 146–49, 158

asset pricing model, 133, 141. *See also* Capital Asset Pricing Model (CAPM); intermediary asset pricing

assets. *See* financial assets; general account assets; low-beta assets; riskless asset; risky assets

Austria, 33

AXA: equity drawdown, 38; marginal cost of capital, 74; recapitalization activity, 79; variable annuity liabilities, 31, *32*, 94, *95* balance sheet dynamics, 25–26, 66, 88–90, 122–23

balance sheet shocks, 51, 56–57, 58, 69

banks: bailout, 76; derivatives, 15, 34; financial constraints, 21, 29; leverage, 7, 7; liabilities, 2, 2; letters of credit, 44; ownership of corporate bonds, 5, 6; regulation, 158, 160; risk transfer, 23; risk transmission through, 30, 47, 49–50; SRISK, 37; variables based on *Financial Accounts of the United States*, 163

Best's Insurance Reports, 14

Best's Statement File, 8, 9, 14, 19

bond portfolios, insurers', 133–40; credit risk of, *139*, 139–40, 150, 153; duration of, 30, 36, 137–38, *138*. *See also* corporate bond portfolio

Brighthouse Financial: equity drawdown, 38, *39*; shadow insurance, 41; SRISK, 37, *37*; stock returns, *164*

brokers, 52, 102, 127

Capital Asset Pricing Model (CAPM), 77, 134. *See also* asset pricing model

CAPM. *See* Capital Asset Pricing Model (CAPM)

capital structure, 141, 154

captive laws, 22–23, 40, 114, 117, 123

captive reinsurance, 16, 23–24, 50, 159–60

catastrophe bonds, 152

catastrophe insurance, 81

climate risk, 81, 155

Compulife Software, 17, 52, *131*

conditional tail expectation, 24, 98–99

consumer surplus, 103, *104*

contract design, 25, 81, 86, 158

convexity, interest rate risk, 30, 34, 159

corporate bond market: demand system asset pricing, 15; risk transmission through, 30, 47–50

corporate bond portfolio, 133, 135, *136*

corporate bonds: credit risk of, 9, 137, 143n2; institutional ownership of, 5, 6; sales of downgraded, 150–51; variables based on *Financial Accounts of the United States*, 163

cost function, 26–27, 90–91, 124–26

counterparty risk, 33, 49

COVID-19 crisis, 38, *39*, *40*, 152

credit default swaps, 46, 59, *60*

credit risk: of insurers' bond portfolios, *139*, 139–40, 150–53; of corporate bonds, 9, 133, 135, 137–38, 143n2; stress tests, 160–61; transmission to banks, 50

cyber risk, 81, 155

default risk, 4, 57–59, *60*, 139

deferred annuity liabilities, 57, *58*

defined benefit plans: liabilities, 2, 2–3, 3; variables based on *Financial Accounts of the United States*, 163

defined contribution plans: liabilities, 2, 2–3, 3; variables based on *Financial Accounts of the United States*, 163

Delaware Life, variable annuity liabilities, 31, *32*, 95

demand elasticity: insurance pricing model, 27–28, 67–71, 72, 142, 149; life insurance, 124–26, 128, 130; variable annuities, 82, 91–92, 96–97, 100–102, 111

Denmark, 33

derivatives: banks as counterparties, 49; financial disclosure, 159; hedging, 30, 33–34, 35, 153; Schedule DB, 14–15

differentiated product demand system: insurance policies, 25, 69; life insurance, 115, 122; variable annuities, 82, 94

discount rates, 60, 62, 64

duration, 30, 33–34, 36–37, 45, 137–38, 138, 153, 158–59

Equitable Life, United Kingdom, 32

equity drawdown, 38, 39, 40

European Insurance and Occupational Pensions Authority (EIOPA), 158

European insurers, 17, 22, 35, 159

Federal Insurance Office, 160–61

Federal Reserve, 160–61

Financial Accounts of the United States, 2, 3, 4, 5, 6, 7; variables based on, 162–63

financial advisors, 156–57

financial assets, 142–43

financial disclosure, 159

financial engineering, 1, 4

financial frictions: evidence for, 52, 57, 76–80, 140; identifying, 61; insurance pricing model, 1, 25, 26–28, 65–68; reinsurance, 124; variable annuity supply, 81–82, 90–91, 93–94, 102, 104, 110

financial institutions: leverage, 5, 7; liabilities, 2, 2; savings intermediated by, 127; SRISK, 37, 37; systemically important, 20

financial stability, 30, 37, 47, 98, 157–58, 160–61

Financial Stability Oversight Council, 20, 160

financial statements: accounting standards, 21–22; Best's Statement File, 19; captives, 23, 45; consolidated, 16; estimating life insurance sales, 127; financial disclosure, 158–59; General Interrogatories, 15; insurance data, 14–17; insurer characteristics constructed from, 163; international, 17; Schedule D, 15; Schedule DB, 15–16; Schedule S, 16

Fitch rating, 139

fixed annuities, insurance product, 10–11

fixed annuity liabilities, 30, 159

fixed annuity prices, 17–18, 29, 51–52

fragility, 38, 152, 160

France, 33

general account, 3, 4, 4, 5, 7, 9, 33–34, 88–89, 162

general account assets, 4–5, 6

General Interrogatories, financial statement, 14, 15, 19

generally accepted accounting principles (GAAP), 16, 22–24, 34, 43, 94, 127

Germany, 33

Genworth: bailout, 20, 76; default risk, 60; equity drawdown, 39, 40; marginal cost of capital, 74–75; recapitalization activity, 78; securities lending, 47; stock returns, 164; variable annuity liabilities, 32, 94, 95

global financial crisis: credit risk after, 137, 140, 150, 152–53; equity drawdown, 38, 40; financial frictions, 52, 76–77, 80, 90; insurance prices during, 29, 51, 54–58, 65, 68–69; leverage, 7; low interest rate environment after, 30, 35, 153; marginal cost of capital, 71; regulatory gaps, 157; sales of downgraded bonds, 49, 151; securities lending, 45–46; shadow insurance, 34, 43; systemic risk, 47; TARP, 20, 120–21; variable annuities, 24, 31, 81–84, 86, 93–94, 95, 97, 101–3, 110–11, 113

GLWB. See Guaranteed Lifetime Withdrawal Benefit (GLWB)

GMAB. See Guaranteed Minimum Accumulation Benefit (GMAB)

GMIB. See Guaranteed Minimum Income Benefit (GMIB)

GMWB. See Guaranteed Minimum Withdrawal Benefit (GMWB)

Guaranteed Lifetime Withdrawal Benefit (GLWB), 11–13, 12, 18–19, 88n1, 94, 95, 97, 100, 101, 106, 109, 110

Guaranteed Minimum Accumulation Benefit (GMAB), 13, 18–19, 34

Guaranteed Minimum Income Benefit (GMIB), 13, 18–19, 34

Guaranteed Minimum Withdrawal Benefit (GMWB), 13, 18–19, 34

Hartford: bailout, 20; equity drawdown, 39, 40; securities lending, 47; shadow

Hartford (*continued*)
  insurance, 42; stock returns, *164*;
  variable annuity liabilities, 31, *32*, 95
health insurance, 3, 156
Herfindahl index, 18n1
HIH Insurance Group, Australia, 49
holding company: default risk, 59, *60*;
  financial frictions, 52, 73, 76–77, 78–
  79, 80; financial statements, 16, 22,
  34; marginal cost of capital, 74–75, 76;
  reinsurance, 114, 121–22, 124–27
households: insurance demand, 155–
  56; portfolio choice, 133–34, 141–42,
  144–47, 149–50, 152; risk transmission
  through, 30, 47, 49; savings, 2–4, 3, 5,
  127; variable annuity demand, 102; variables based on *Financial Accounts of the
  United States*, 163; welfare, 103

informational frictions, 25, 81
ING Group: bailout, 76; marginal cost of
  capital, 75; recapitalization activity, *78*
institutional investors: agency problems,
  154; funding agreement-backed securities, 46; ownership of corporate bonds,
  5, 6, 15, 25, 48, 153; portfolio choice,
  133–34, 141–42, 145–47, 149–50; reach
  for yield, 152
insurance agents, 17, 156
insurance data: financial statements, 14–17;
  insurance prices, 17–19. *See also* financial
  statements
insurance demand. *See* life insurance
  demand; variable annuity demand
Insurance Holding Company System
  Regulatory Act, 77, 124
insurance markets: instrumental variable,
  117; intermediation in, 156; model of,
  25, 65, 81, 86–87, 140, 148; model of
  life insurance, 127–32, *131*; regulation,
  157–58; traditional theories of, 25
insurance prices. *See* fixed annuities; life
  insurance premiums; property and
  casualty insurance prices

insurance pricing model: baseline model,
  25–29; estimating, 69–76, *74–75*; extension to contract design, 81, 86; extension
  to multiple policies, 51–52, 65–69;
  extension to reinsurance, 114, 121–27
insurance products, 1, 8–14, 49; fixed annuities, 10–11; life insurance, 10; variable
  annuities, 11–14
insurance regulation: life insurance, 40,
  114; policy, 158, 160; political economy
  of, 157–58
insurance sector: asset pricing with, 141–
  50; financial frictions in, 140, 151;
  overview of, 1–9; portfolio choice, 133,
  136, 137; regulation, 20, 158, 161; risks
  in, 30, 38, 47, 98, 132, 152, 157
insurers. *See* life insurers; property and
  casualty insurers
interest risk mismatch, 30, 33–37, 138, 152,
  153
intermediary asset pricing, 134, 141
Iowa Insurance Division, 45, 159

Jackson National: variable annuity liabilities, 31, *32*, 95. *See also* Manulife
  Financial
John Hancock: equity drawdown, 38;
  marginal cost of capital, 74; shadow
  insurance, 42; variable annuity liabilities,
  32, 95

letters of credit, 23, 41, 44, 50, 159
leverage: capital structure choice, 154;
  financial institutions, 5–7, 7; insurance
  prices, 57, *58*; insurance pricing model,
  70–71, 72, 73, 74–75, 76; insurer characteristics, 14, 163; life insurance market,
  128, 130–32, *131*; life insurers, 1, 8,
  30, 32; risk-based capital, 21; shadow
  insurance, 44, 114, *116*, 118; SRISK,
  37
leverage constraint: institutional investors,
  133–34, 141–42, 145–46, 148–50, 152;
  insurance pricing model, 65, 67–69

liabilities: financial institutions, 2, 2–4; life
insurers, 4, 4, 5, 8, 8, 9; insurance and
pension, 3. *See also* deferred annuity liabilities; fixed annuity liabilities; variable
annuity liabilities
life annuities: conversion from variable
annuities, 13; insurance product, 11;
mortality risk, 27; statutory reserve
regulation, 62–64, 63
life annuity prices: data, 17–18; during
global financial crisis, 51, 55–56, 56, 58;
summary statistics, 52, 53, 54
life-cycle model, 96, 156
life insurance: accounting standards,
22; composition of liabilities, 3–4, 4,
5; insurance product, 10; statutory
reserve regulation, 62, 63, 64–65. *See
also* term life insurance; universal life
insurance
life insurance demand, 127–28
life insurance market, 52, 115, 117, 127–32,
131
life insurance premiums. *See* term life insurance premiums; universal life insurance
premiums
life insurers: bond portfolios, 134–40, 135,
136; credit risk of bond portfolios, 139,
139–40; duration of bond portfolios,
137–38, 138; equity portfolio of, 165;
general account assets, 6; leverage, 5, 7,
7; liabilities, 2, 2–3, 3, 4, 4, 5, 8, 8, 9; variables based on *Financial Accounts of the
United States*, 162
Lincoln Financial: bailout, 20, 76, 78;
equity drawdown, 38, 39, 40; marginal
cost of capital, 74–75; shadow insurance, 42; SRISK, 37, 37; stock returns,
164; variable annuity liabilities, 32,
95
liquidity premium, 141, 149
liquidity risk, 44–46, 50
long-term care insurance, 81, 156
low-beta assets, 133–34, 137, 141–42, 148,
150–51, 153–54

low interest rate environment, 30, 32,
35–36, 86, 113, 140, 152–53, 157,
159–61

Manulife Financial: equity drawdown, 38;
marginal cost of capital, 74; recapitalization activity, 76, 79; securities lending,
47
marginal cost of capital: definition, 27–28,
67, 91, 124–25; estimating, 52, 70–73,
72, 73, 74–75, 76, 110, 122; insurance
pricing model, 68–69, 81; reinsurance,
125
market completeness, 81, 86
market portfolio, 133, 136, 137
McCarran Ferguson Act of 1945, 19
MetLife: default risk, 60; marginal cost
of capital, 74–75; recapitalization
activity, 73, 76–77, 79; securities
lending, 47; shadow insurance, 38,
40–41, 41, 42; SRISK, 37, 37; systemically important financial institution,
20
MetLife Series VA, 11, 12
Metropolitan Life: equity drawdown, 38,
39, 40; marginal cost of capital, 75;
shadow insurance, 41; stock returns,
164; variable annuities, 31, 32, 95. *See
also* MetLife
minimum return guarantee, 1, 4, 11, 13–15,
24, 31–36, 38, 57, 81–84, 84, 85, 86–89,
93, 97, 100–103, 105–6, 110, 111, 113,
138, 150, 153, 159
Model Regulation 830, 22. *See also*
Regulation XXX
Moody's: composite yield on corporate
bonds, 61, 64; yield on Aaa corporate
bonds, 70
Moody's Investors Service, 44
Mood's rating, 139
moral hazard, 145
Morningstar, 18n1, 18–19
mortality tables: annuity, 18, 62–63; life
insurance, 17, 64

mortgage-backed securities (MBSs), 45, *135*, 141, 143n2; non-agency, 9, 151, 157; residential, 49

mutual companies, 8, *8*, *9*, 33, 106

mutual funds: in asset pricing model, 141, 145, 154; outside asset, 97–98, 127; ownership of corporate bonds, 5, *6*; reach for yield, 152; sales, 82, *83*; underlying variable annuities, 4, 11–12, 15, 24, 31, 83, 86–88, 93, 105; underlying variable life insurance, 10

NAIC. *See* National Association of Insurance Commissioners (NAIC)

NAIC designation, 135, *136*, 137, 140, 143, 151n3, 157

Nash equilibrium, 27, 67, 91, 124, 128

National Association of Insurance Commissioners (NAIC), 14, 16, 19, 22, 160

Netherlands, 33

ownership structure: insurance companies, 7–9; life insurers' liabilities by, 8, *8*, *9*

Phoenix Companies: bailout, 76; marginal cost of capital, 74; recapitalization activity, *78*; stock returns, *164*

political economy, 157

portfolio choice: effect of regulation on, 157–58; households, 96, 144–46; institutional investors, 145–46; insurers, 25, 37, 133–34, 137, 139, 142, 147–50, 153–54; life insurers, 23, 48; puzzle, 140–41

private equity firms, 8, 152

product differentiation, 25, 96, 122, 127

property and casualty insurance prices, 28

property and casualty insurers: bond portfolios, 134–35, *135*, *136*, 137; credit risk of bond portfolios, *139*, 139–40; duration of bond portfolios, 137, *138*, *138*; general account assets, *6*; leverage, 5, 7, *7*; liabilities, 2, 2–3, *3*; variables based

on *Financial Accounts of the United States*, 162

Protective Life: bailout, 76; marginal cost of capital, *74–75*; recapitalization activity, 76, *78*; stock returns, *164*

Prudential Financial: bailout, 20, 76; equity drawdown, *39*, *40*; marginal cost of capital, *74*; recapitalization activity, 76, *79*; securities lending, *47*; SRISK, 37, *37*; stock returns, *164*; variable annuity liabilities, *32*, 95

reach for yield, 152, 157

Regulation (A)XXX, 22, 43, 123, 157, 160

Regulation XXX, 22, 117, 127

regulatory gaps, 46, 157

regulatory oversight, 158, 160–61

reinsurance: model of, 121–27; summary statistics, *43*, 43–44, *44*; within MetLife, 40–41, *41*. *See also* shadow insurance

reinsurance share of variable annuities, 15, 94, *95*, 98–99, *101*, 106, 108, *109*, 129

reserve to actuarial value, 61–62, *63*, 64–65, 70–71, 92, 123

reserve valuation: insurance pricing model, 28–29, 52, 60–64, *62*; life insurance, 22; variable annuities, 15, *31*, 31–32, *32*, 93–94, *95*, 98–99, *101*, 106, 108, *109*

retail market, 25, 97, 114–15, 121, 131–32

risk-based capital: definition, 20–22; financial frictions, 67; financial statements, 15; life insurance market, 128, 130–32, *131*; portfolio choice, 48–49, 133, 150–52, 154, *164*; relative to guideline, 57, *58*, 70–71, *72*; shadow insurance, 43, 115, *116*, 117–18, *119*, 120, 122, 126–27; variable annuities, 24, 86, 93

risk-based capital constraint, 21, 34, 48, 81, 86, 94, 133, 140–42, 149, 152

risk-based capital regulation, 20–21, 26, 48–49, 58, 66, 123, 140, 143, 150–51, 154, 157–58 risk constraint, economic, 21, 27, 81, 86, 90, 94

risk measures: adjusted for shadow insurance, 114–15, 117, *119*; financial disclosure, 158–60

risk mismatch: balance sheet, 1, 4, 7, 21, 44, 88–89; credit, 133, 135; equity, 30, 33; financial disclosure, 159; interest rate, 30, 33–37, 138, 152–53

riskless asset, 133, 141–42, 144–45, 149–50

risky assets, 58–59, 133, 141–46, 149–50, 152

rollup rate, *12*, 12–13, 18–19, 24, 81–82, 84, *85*, 86–91, 94, 96–98, 100, *101*, 102, *109*, 166–68; optimal, 92–93, 104–8, *105*, 110–11, *112*, 113

S&P 500 index: drawdown, 38, *39*; funds, 54, 102

S&P rating, *139*

Schedule D, financial statement, 15

Schedule DB, financial statement, 15–16

Schedule S, financial statement, 16

Securities Holding Statistics, 17

securities lending, 30, 45–46, *47, 48*, 49, 157, 159–60

separate account, 4, *4*, 5, *9*, 37, 88, 162

shadow cost of capital, 82, 91–93, 97, 103–8, *105*, 110–13, *111, 112*, 125, 128, 154

shadow insurance: financial frictions, 124, 128n2, 128–29; life insurance market, 129–32, *131*; model of, 25, 127; motive for, 22, 34, 99, 157; relation with ratings, 115–17, *116*; risk of, 30, 49, 115–21, *119, 121*; summary statistics, 38, *42*, 42–45, *43, 44*, 114, 158, 160; within MetLife, 38–42, *41, 42*

shadow reinsurers, 16, 42, *42, 43*, 44, *44*, 114, 118, 128n2

SNL Financial, 14

South Carolina: captive laws, 22–23; reinsurance within MetLife, *41*

SRISK, 37, *37*

Standard Valuation Law, 60–61, *63*, 64, 70

state guaranty associations, 1, 19–20, 33, 57, 120, 124, 132, 142–43, 154, 160

state regulators, 20, 61, 77, 151, 157, 159

statutory accounting: corporate bonds, 49; financial statements, 14, 16, 21; hedging, 33–34; insurance pricing model, 25; life insurance, 22, 127; reinsurance, 41, 43, 45, *45*, 159; variable annuities, 24, 94

statutory capital, 26–29, 61, 65–68, 71, 73, *73*, 89–92, 122–26, 166

statutory reserve regulation: insurance pricing model, 51–52, 59–65; life annuities, 62–64; life insurance, 64–65; term annuities, 61–62

stock companies, 42, 106, 117; liabilities, 8, *8, 9*

stress tests, 160

Sweden, 33

tail risk, 5, 28, 140, 156

TARP. *See* Troubled Asset Relief Program (TARP)

tax: advantage of insurance policies, 2, 18, 142n1; advantage of variable annuities, 11, 14, 83, 98–99, 103; benefits of reinsurance, 23, 122; deductibility of guaranty association assessments, 20, 120; insurance regulation, 158; private equity firms, 152

taxpayers, 20, 120, 132

term annuities: insurance product, 10–11; statutory reserve regulation, 61–62, *63*, 64

term annuity prices: data, 18; during global financial crisis, 51, 54–55, *55*, 58, 59, *60*; insurance pricing model, 72; summary statistics, 52, *53*

term life insurance: instrumental variable, 116–17, *116*; insurance product, 10; statutory reserve regulation, 41 term life insurance premiums: data, 17, *131*; insurance pricing model, 69

Troubled Asset Relief Program (TARP), 20, 76, *78–79*, 120

United Kingdom, 32, 35

universal life insurance: insurance product, 10; statutory reserve regulation, 22, 41, 63, 65; insurance pricing model, 69

universal life insurance premiums: data, 17; during global financial crisis, 51, 56, 57; summary statistics, *53*, 54

US agency bonds, *6*, 135, *135*, 137, *138*, 139, *139*

US Treasury bonds: in insurers' portfolios, *6*, 59, 133, 135, *135*, 137–40, *138*, *139*, 153; replicating insurance liabilities, 9, 27; returns on, 35–37, *36*

US Treasury yields: computing actuarial value, 10, 17–18, *53*, *55*, 56, *57*, *62*, 63; computing reserves and required capital, 24, 61, *62*, 65; estimating expected loss, 120; estimating marginal cost of capital, 70

variable annuities: accounting standards, 24; consumer surplus, 103, *104*; insurance product, 11–14, *12*; risk exposure, 31–33, *36*

variable annuity demand: estimating, 94–103, *101*, 107, 129, 168; model of, 82, 87, 96–98

variable annuity fees, 11, *12*, 13–14, 18–19, 24, 69, 81–84, *85*, 86–89, 93–94, 96–103, *101*, 105–8; optimal, 90–92, 103, 110–11, *111*, 166–68

variable annuity liabilities, 15, 24, 31, *31*, 32, 38, 48, 51, 94

variable annuity market: modeling, 86–88, 94; summary statistics, 31, *31*, 81–86

variable annuity supply: estimating, 103–13, *109*; evidence for financial frictions, 82, 93–94, *95*; model of, 86–94, 97–98

variable life insurance, 10

Vermont: captive laws, 23; reinsurance within MetLife, 41, *41*

Voya: equity drawdown, *39*; shadow insurance, *42*; stock returns, *164*; variable annuity liabilities, 31, 32, *95*

WebAnnuities Insurance Agency, 17, 52

CPSIA information can be obtained
at www.ICGtesting.com
Printed in the USA
JSHW010233280423
40623JS00001B/1/J

9 780691 193267